To my pers[onal]
expert — hope [to]
help you in your quest of
more knowledge!

Happy 30 th Birthday

Giny

The Wines of Germany

Bernkastel and the Mosel from the Doktor vineyard.

THE WINES
OF
GERMANY

FRANK SCHOONMAKER'S CLASSIC

Completely Revised Edition

by

PETER M. F. SICHEL

Illustrated with Maps, Labels and Photographs

HASTINGS HOUSE · PUBLISHERS

New York 10016

FOR CRISTINA

Library of Congress Cataloging in Publication Data

Sichel, Peter M   F
    The wines of Germany.

    Previous ed. by F. Schoonmaker.
    Bibliography: p.
    Includes index.
    1. Wine and wine making—Germany, West.
I. Schoonmaker, Frank, 1905– Wines of Germany.
II. Title.
TP559.G3S3   1980   641.2'22'0943   80-10542
ISBN 0-8038-8100-2

Published simultaneously in Canada by
Saunders of Toronto, Ltd., Don Mills, Ontario
Printed in the United States of America

CONTENTS

PICTURE CREDITS:

Vignettes: courtesy of "the Christian Brothers Collection."
Dustjacket photograph courtesy of the Deutsche Wein-Information.
Maps specially created by John L. Hadden.

Page 20: courtesy Graf E. Matuschka Greiffenclau. Page 36: courtesy Graf von Schönborn-Wiesentheit. Pages 2, 24, 30, 34, 59, 69, 83, 110, 120, 169, 191 and 193: courtesy Deutsche Wein-Information. Page 77: courtesy Reichsgraf von Kesselstatt. Page 99: Foto Hirschenhein, Hochheim. Page 113: courtesy Graf E. Matuschka Greiffenclau. Page 141: courtesy Winzergenossenschaft Rheinfront Nierstein. Page 163: courtesy Dr. Bürklin-Wolf. Page 183: courtesy Zentralkellerei Badischer Winzergenossenschaften. Page 187: H & G. Stuttgart.

PREFACE TO THE
REVISED EDITION

FRANK SCHOONMAKER WROTE "The Wines of Germany" in 1956. He revised it twice, in 1966 and in 1969, each time limiting his revisions to corrections and updatings of the original text. It has now been out of print for 5 years and has become a collector's item, especially as nothing has replaced it in the English wine literature.

Frank was a man of enormous erudition who had acquired his knowledge of German Wines first as a writer and then as a wine selector and importer.

His book was based on 21 fairly extended trips throughout the German wine country in the course of 24 years. With a scholar's mind and a writer's ability to synthesize he produced a gem. A short book both practical and elegant, it gave all the information that is necessary to guide one through the complexities of German wines.

However, the book was written a long time ago and in order to bring the reader up-to-date, I must omit certain old paragraphs and add many new ones as a personal contribution to this classic.

It is my intention in this rather extensive revision, to preserve as much of Frank's style and original text as possible for I know of no other writer who has communicated his taste and his knowledge as clearly and as distinctly.

The last twenty-two years have seen monumental changes. Many of Frank's German friends are no longer alive and have been replaced by their sons. The Mosel Valley has become warmer ever since the river became an important waterway. Whole vineyards have been uprooted and hillsides levelled under an ambitious governmental program for more efficient viticulture. The program is called *"Flurbereinigung"* literally meaning "rectification of the fields."

In the last fourteen years there has been a 34% increase in planted vineyards in Germany and a 17% reduction of families and Estates that own them. The average holdings have gone from 1.37 acres to 2.2 acres, an enormous consolidation.

7

The Müller-Thurgau has replaced the Silvaner as the dominant grape variety. Clonal research has improved old grape varieties and introduced new ones contributing to larger crops with riper grapes. Though harvest fluctuations continue, in the ten years prior to the first publication of this book the average yearly crop was 57 million gallons. The average crop now is 203 million gallons. Even more remarkable is the increase of the average yield from 420 gallons to 1,022 gallons per acre.

New cellar techniques combined with new grape varieties have immeasurably improved the average German wine, and have contributed to a larger share of the crop being outstanding.

The greatest change, however, has been brought about by a new German Wine Law which was enacted in 1969 and became effective with the 1971 vintage. It has since been revised several times in order to conform with the European Economic Community Wine Regulations. The law reduced the number of existing individual vineyards from over 20,000 to a mere 2,600 and established some 130 general vineyard sites and 31 viticultural districts. It also set strict norms for quality gradations and for information that can be shown on the label of a German wine. It eliminated whole categories of designations, which had formed the basis of quality evaluation in the last hundred years, particularly on the Mosel.

There have been other significant changes. The last twenty-five years have seen German wine exports climb from 575 thousand to well over 25 million gallons, 11% of the 1977 crop. Finer wines are bottled in larger sizes, (the *Beerenauslese* in Magnum has become a sales gimmick) and wine auctions have been largely supplanted by wine fairs and markets.

All this has been integrated into this edition.

I hope that this volume will give the basic information the interested buyer of German wines needs in a way in which he can easily use it. Ultimately the only truth is in tasting. This book can but serve as encouragement.

ACKNOWLEDGMENTS

by Peter Sichel

I AM INDEBTED TO MANY for counsel and help in this revision of Frank Schoonmaker's book, though I must state at once that some of the advice was contradictory, so that all statements must perforce be mine.

The hospitality I enjoyed during my field research, the advice and knowledge which was shared was in all cases extraordinary.

Frank was, as I am, a wine merchant/shipper. A wine shipper selects wines from different regions and from various growers and sells them with his endorsement, in Frank's case as "Frank Schoonmaker Selection." He also, as in my case, buys raw wine, stabilizes and finishes it, blends and bottles it and finally sells it under his own name.

Essential to the business of the wine merchant is the wine broker as the honest middleman between the countless growers and himself. Over the years a wine shipper develops very close ties with his brokers. He depends on them for samples of hundreds of lots of wines from almost as many growers, for advice and counsel, and for that rare thing: purchase contracts that are considered fair by both the grower and the shipper. After all one cannot live without the other, and good business relationships depend on both parties feeling that a fair deal has been made.

In due course the relationship between a wine shipper and his broker becomes very similar to the one we should all have with our doctor and our lawyer. Eventually this relationship extends to some of the growers who consistently seem to provide the wines that please the wine merchant most.

So Frank had his ties with Otto and Günther Dünweg, brokers on the Mosel and Josef Becker in the Rheingau. He also had close ties with various growers. Some of those I revisited, though by and large I consulted my own brokers, friends and acquaintances. Although I would have found Frank's friends as informative, it was just more convenient and efficient to deal with people I knew well.

The book, however, gave me the opportunity to make new ac-

9

quaintances based on Frank's past experiences and this I will always count as the great contribution that this book has made to my life.

I would like to express my gratitude to:

Artur Meier, Director of H. Sichel Mainz, who more than anyone else was instrumental in educating me during the last twenty years about German wines, taking me to all the major regions and guiding my palate and my judgement through its formative and mature stage. He was of immense help to me on this book, and I dare say I will continue to depend on his advice as long as we are both around.

My other colleagues at H. Sichel, my cousins, Walter and Dennis Williams, who taught me how to taste and select; Riquet Hess, who with the help of Ludwig Oppenheim, ran down the thousand questions I had and contributed advice and counsel, as well as Vera Bossmann, Frau Hohlfeld and Frau Fuchs who types countless letters in order to clarify the smallest detail and followed up on the correspondence.

Josef Kettern Jr. of Piesport without whose help the chapter on the Mosel-Saar-Ruwer would never have been written. Ken Onisch of Chateau and Estate Wine Company who shared his opinions and experiences of the Mosel-Saar-Ruwer and gave most valuable advice.

Werner Tyrell of the Karthäuserhof, Andreas von Schubert of Maximin Grünhaus, Fritz and Hans Joachim Zilliken of Forstsmeister Geltz Erben, Gert Nussbaum, administrator of Reichsgraf von Kesselstatt, Dieter Ebert of Schloss Saarstein, Bert Simon of Weingut Herrenberg, Friedrich Ludwig of the Verwaltung of Bischöflicher Weingüter, all spent long hours with me and explained many things that were invaluable for my Mosel-Saar-Ruwer Chapter.

Karl Heinz Lauerburg and his charming wife and sons who have guided me for the last twenty years on the marvels of wines from Bernkastel, sharing more extraordinary bottles and knowledge than I could ever repay.

Egon Müller of the Scharzhof and Manfred Prüm of J. J. Prüm who shared their philosophies and gave me most instructive tastings without which I would not have comprehended the enormous changes of the wine law of 1971. If nothing else, the research of this book brought me in touch with these two extraordinary artists of the vine, men who have perfected one of the most difficult arts.

Dr. Hans Ambrosi of the Staatsweingut and Dr. Helmut Becker of Geisenheim who shared their immense knowledge with me, the former on the Rheingau, the latter on his specialty: the cultivation and improvement of grape varieties.

Georg Kirsch for running down endless details on the Rheingau and Dr. Franz Michel for kindly reading the draft on the Rheingau and giving me valuable advice.

Edgar Schätzler for helping me on my research on Rheinhessen, Hermann Schmitt and Franz Karl Schmitt for guiding me over the years to more fully understand the diversity of the wines from Nierstein and Friedrich Bohn and Dr. Otto Curlle for reading the draft of the Rheinhessen chapter and giving me some valuable advice and guidance which resulted in major revisions.

Egon Anheuser who over the years has proven to be a staunch friend and counsel and who was kind enough to read the draft of the chapter on the Nahe and give me valuable advice.

Ludwig von Bassermann Jordan and his charming wife who spent many days researching my endless questions on the Rheinpfalz and kindly read the draft on that area giving me invaluable advice in addition to the hospitality which included many superb meals with even better wines. Friedrich Seyler, who patiently helped me with my other questions on the Rheinpfalz, questions that never seemed to end.

Carl E. Ott, Josef Bullinger and Jochen Freihold who all three gave me valuable advice on Franconia. Direktor Strub and his staff at the Central Cooperative in Breisach in Baden who shared their information on the region with me and Klaus Blankenhorn of Schliengen in Baden who contributed valuable additional insight. And finally Wilhelm Wasum who gave me evenhanded advice on the Mittelrhein.

Alexis Bespaloff spent a week with me in Germany, sharing some of my interviews on the Mosel-Saar-Ruwer and Rheingau and helped me in many useful ways.

This revision would not have been possible without my daughter Alexandra who helped with some of the painstaking research and finally without the enormous help and counsel of my wife Stella. She kept me to the grindstone many times when temptation pulled me elsewhere, gave me constructive advice on every facet of the book and more importantly served as my editor on every chapter and page. Without her the book would never have been finished, it would have been less readable and we would not have had as many pleasant evenings at home working in harmony on a common task.

ACKNOWLEDGMENTS

by Frank Schoonmaker

I SHOULD INDEED COUNT myself ungrateful if I did not say, at the very outset of this little book, that whatever virtues it may possess are in large part due to the counsel and assistance of a number of old friends. When I first began to take something more than a layman's interest in German wines, twenty-odd years ago, I had the great good fortune to fall at once into the hands of the best possible guides, and I am glad to say that when I returned to Germany in 1946, after three years' service in what we used to call the ''European Theater of Operations,'' I found my respect and regard for these particular German friends in no way tarnished or diminished.

Two of the best of them have not lived to see these lines in print, and are citizens today of a country where spring frosts and hailstorms and bad vintages are unknown. In the field of Moselle wines, Otto Dünweg, of Neumagen, was an expert of unique integrity and competence: not reading English with facility, he was kind enough to arrange for two separate translations into German of my chapter on the Moselle, and correct them in his own hand before his death last August. Dr. Wilhelm Bewerunge, of Bonn and Berlin and more recently of Oppenheim, died in November 1954, before I could submit even part of the manuscript for his revisions and suggestions; I am glad to be able to pay him a small tribute by reproducing some of the excellent photographs of vineyards which he himself took with his own camera.

I am also glad to acknowledge a special debt to Josef Becker, of Niederwalluf, unequalled in his knowledge of the Rheingau and a friend of more than twenty years' standing, and to Frau Becker.

However, I should perhaps do an unintended disservice to these friends, as well as to others whom I list below, if I did not say clearly once and for all that the opinions and comparative ratings of districts

12

and towns and vineyards, and vintages, even, were not theirs, but wholly and entirely my own. They are based on twenty-one fairly extended trips through the German wine country in the past twenty-four years in the course of which I tasted (it seems impossible) over seventeen thousand different German wines, of which I have kept a writtent record of more than half.

This said, I should like to express my gratitude to:

Dr. Albert Bürklin-Wolf, one of the great vineyard owners of the Pfalz and President of the *Verband Deutscher Naturwein-Versteigerer,* the association of German estate-bottlers, who was good enough to read and check my chapter on the Palatinate.

Richard Graf Matuschka-Greiffenklau, owner of Schloss Vollrads, and President of the German Wine Producers' Association, who helpfuly supplied much important data on the Rheingau.

Herman Franz Schmitt, proprietor of the celebrated Franz Karl Schmitt domain in Nierstein, past President of the Wine Producers' Association of Hessen, whose assistance was particularly valuable in assembling the material for my section on the wines of Hessia.

Dr. Rudolf Gareis, former director of the State Domain in the Rheingau, now retired and living in Eltville, a fountainhead of information and anecdote on the subject of his beloved Rheingau.

Dr. Jost and Dr. Decker, able present directors of the State Domains in the Rheingau and Moselle respectively.

Dr. Krämer and Weinguts-Oberamtmann Karl Nägler of Würzburg who were both most generous with their help and advice on the subject of Frankenwein, and Steinwein.

Dr. Melsheimer, the leading vineyard owner of Traben-Trarbach on the Moselle.

Dr. von Bassermann-Jordan, dean of German wine-producers, whose books on the history of German viticulture are monuments of thoroughness and scholarship.

Raban Graf Adlemann of Kleinbottwar in Württemberg, and Dr. Villforth of the important State vineyard school at Weinsberg, near Heilbronn, who kindly furnished much information concerning the vineyards of Württemberg, which I knew hardly at all.

Freiherr von Neveu of Durbach, in Baden, who was equally helpful in connection with my all-too-brief study of the vineyards and wines of his native province.

The publisher and the editors of *GOURMET* for permission to reprint certain chapters which appeared, in partial and abbreviated form, in its pages.

Lastly, I should be reluctant to conclude this brief acknowledgment without a word or two of thanks to a great many friends for their hospitality and kindness: Paul and Tatiana Metternich, Herr Labonte, their general manager, and Allinger, who presides over the cellars at Schloss Johannisberg; Jakob Graf Eltz of Eltville, Dr. Weil and Freiherr von Ritter zu Groenesteyn of Kiedrich, the Müller family of the Scharzhof on the Saar and the Rautenstrauch family of Eitelsbach on the Ruwer, the many members of the Prüm clan at Wehlen, young Herr Koch of Wiltingen, Gunther Dünweg of Neumagen, the worthy son of an old friend, and more others than I could possibly here list. They have all helped make the weeks and sometimes months that I have spent in their vineyard country both happy and memorable, which is only fitting, for they all belong to that timeless fraternity of good wine, which has united people of good will in all centuries and in all countries.

—Frank Schoonmaker

Palamós, Spain. April, 1956.

The Wines of Germany

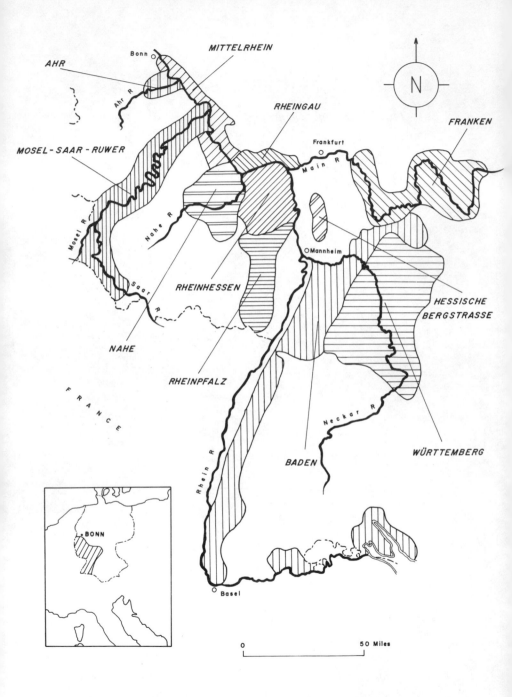

AHR

MITTELRHEIN

Bonn

Ahr R

MOSEL - SAAR - RUWER

RHEINGAU

Frankfurt

Main R

FRANKEN

Mosel R

Nahe R

Saar R

RHEINHESSEN

NAHE

RHEINPFALZ

Mannheim

HESSISCHE
BERGSTRASSE

F R A N C E

Neckar R

WÜRTTEMBERG

Rhein R

BADEN

BONN

Basel

N

0   50 Miles

I

GERMAN WINES

The Land. The Vine.
The Vineyards. The Vintage.
The Cellar. The Bottle

AN invisible line, a frontier much more enduring[1] than any national boundary or iron curtain, runs across Western Europe, traced by the sun. It starts north of Nantes on the Atlantic coast of France, parallels the Loire as far as Orleans and continues east to Auxerre, cuts abruptly north to Chateau-Thierry and the Marne hillsides, runs on east to Luxembourg and thence northeast to the Rhine; beyond the Rhine it turns sharply south to Würzburg, Stuttgart and the Black Forest. This line is not, although it sounds like it, a tourist's itinerary—it is the northern limit of the vine.

Beyond this line grapes will not ripen in an average year; along this line, close to it but south of it, are produced the lightest, the most delicate, the most fragrant, the loveliest white wines of the world.

The Mosel and Rhine wines are the undisputed queens among

---

[1] This "northern limit of the vine" may be less permanent than it appears. Three hundred years ago the wines of Nantes, northwest of Paris, were among the most famous of France. Wines used to be made in the province of Picardy, due north of Paris, and almost within the memory of man were produced, on a commercial scale, on the slopes of Montmartre, in Paris itself. None of these vineyards exists today although Montmartre has preserved, as a sort of symbol and something of a joke, a tiny plot of Franco-American hybrids. The wine is scarcely one of the principal attractions of Paris.

these "border vintages," fine, pale, cold-country wines, so light in alcohol that many of them could not legally be classified as wine if they were produced in California. The vineyards from which they come are as far north as northern Newfoundland, almost at the latitude of Winnipeg. There is already snow in the Hunsrück and the Eifel and the Black Forest by the time the grapes are ripe on the lower hillsides in late October; and there is still danger of frost when the first timid leaves appear and the days of the "Ice Saints" come round in early May.

These *Eis-Heiligen,* or Ice Saints, in the German calendar are four: May 12, St. Pancratius; May 13, St. Servatius; May 14, St. Bonifacius; and May 15, die *Kalte Sophie,* or cold St. Sophia. According to tradition, the vines are safe from freezing once these days are past, but a sudden cold snap during the Ice Saints' days has ruined any number of otherwise excellent vintage years. You will see smudge pots out in many German vineyards by May 10, ready to be lighted on short notice if the Ice Saints live up to their reputation, and although they are listed as saints in the calendar, Cold Sophia and her friends are regarded as hardly fit subjects for canonization by the average wine grower.

A hundred days of full sunshine are needed between May and October, the Germans say, to produce good wine, and a hundred and twenty to produce great wine. They get their hundred about every other year, and their hundred and twenty about twice in a decade.

Germany is not, therefore, a wine-producing country in the same sense as Italy and France and Spain. Grapes are grown and wines are made commercially only on a few southern slopes in certain favored valleys. Actually the Bordeaux district of France, with its Graves, Sauternes and Clarets, produces a greater variety of wines than all the vineyards of Germany put together, and the annual production of a single French *département,* the Herault, is three times that of all Germany. Yet Germany, despite the fact that her wines are limited, in quantity and also in range, ranks, in the special field of fine wines, almost on a par with France.

Leaving out of consideration the German red wines (few of which could be described as fine by the most charitable of judges) it can be said that *all* German wines, from the most inconsequential Gutedels and Kleinbergers of Southern Baden and the Neckar Valley to the noblest and most aristocratic Rieslings of the Rhine, have a decided and unmistakable family resemblance. German vintners, in other words, do only one thing—but they do that one thing supremely well. German wines have, beyond· any question, a higher average of excellence than the wines of any country in the world.

THE LAND

"Rhineland," says the old German proverb, is "wine-land," and certainly, as far as Germany is concerned, this is gospel. Every German wine of the slightest consequence, from the *Drachenblut*, that rather anemic "Dragon's Blood" which the slopes of *Drachenfels*, near Bonn, yield in the north, to the pleasant little *Seeweine* produced on the shores of Lake Constance in the south, is, in the last analysis, a Rhine wine, or at least a wine produced in the Rhine basin. Not only the Rhine Valley itself, but the valleys of almost all its tributaries, have their wines. Thus the picturesque and charming little valley of the Ahr, which joins the Rhine some twenty miles south of Bonn, has acquired a special and largely local fame for its red wines, which can be most agreeable on a restaurant terrace in summer. The Mosel of course needs no introduction; its waters meet those of the Rhine at Koblenz—the name Koblenz, incidentally, comes directly from the Latin and means confluence. A little farther south, there is the Nahe: along its precipitous and rocky banks is produced a whole collection of wines which are little known outside Germany but which are often admirable. The Main, which gives its name to Mainz (or Mayence) winds down out of the Franconian highlands, by way of Würzburg and Frankfurt; the vineyards of Hochheim, although classified as belonging to the Rheingau, actually overlook the Main, not far from its junction with the Rhine; and along the upper Main are the hills which produce the *Frankenweine* which come to us in the characteristic *Bocksbeutel*. Lastly there is the Neckar, Heidelberg's river, which between Heilbronn and Stuttgart is flanked with vines.

And in addition, of course, in all their unending numbers, there are the wines of the Rhine Valley itself.

Most of this vineyard country, oddly enough, has a trace or a whiff or a what-you-will of Southern Europe in its make-up. The villages are typically and charmingly German, with half-timber houses and high gables, old, painted wrought-iron signs over the tavern doors, ruined castles on a good many of the hills, and window-boxes full of flowers along every main street of every important town. And yet this feeling of the South persists—you will see fig trees and al-

A ripe cluster of Riesling grapes in the Rheingau.

mond trees and apricot trees in the sheltered gardens, and life seems a good deal less rigid and less stern than it is in Prussia. Constantly, and almost everywhere, you will find something reminiscent of Northern Italy or Southern France or Spain, and even now, after eighteen hundred years, something that will make you remember that most of this Rhine country, this vineyard country, was once part of the Roman Empire, influenced by Latin customs and subject to Roman law.

There are the remains of Roman buildings or the relics of Roman life almost everywhere: bronze pruning knives, eighteen centuries old but very like those used today, in a museum; the great dark indestructible mass of the Porta Nigra in Trier; a carved stone signpost across the river from Piesport; a ruined amphitheater; a wine amphora in a private collection; even the Latin names of towns—Cologne, from *Colonia Agrippina,* Mainz, from *Moguntiacum,* Trier, or Trèves, from *Augusta Trevirorum.*

But even more than all these, there is, in the life of this wine country, something ancient and good, a feeling of an old civilization, of well-tilled and well-loved soil.

THE VINE

The Rhine Valley is one of the few, rare districts in Europe where the vine grows wild—as if Nature had set out to prove that the Rhineland had been destined from the beginning to be a "wineland." This wild vine, however, is of course not the conventional *vitis vinifera,* the "wine-bearer" of almost all European vineyards—it is *vitis silvestris,* much like the familiar *vitis labrusca,* the wild grape of our New England woods. German geologists have even found the clear print of grape leaves in fossils of the tertiary period; these seem to belong to an unknown species which has been christened *vitis teutonica,* and is presumably the earliest German vine. We can safely assume that it was a less good wine grape than the Riesling.

For the *RIESLING,* in Germany, is king. To it, and to it alone, the wines of the Mosel and Saar and Ruwer owe the floweriness of their bouquet and their extraordinary delicacy of flavor. Its tight little bunches of yellow-green grapes, which become deep golden as they ripen, are responsible for practically all the great wines of the Rheingau and the Nahe, and for all the best of those of Rheinhessen and the Pfalz. This may, incidentally, be as good a time as any to point out once more that the name is pronounced *Reece-ling,* not *Rye-sling.*

Even transplanted to other countries, the Riesling preserves a good deal of its astonishing quality and breed. In California it is known as the "white Riesling," or "Johannisberg Riesling," and from it come some of the best wines produced in the country around San Francisco Bay. It is called the "Johannisberg" (presumably after Schloss Johannisberg) in Switzerland, and along the upper reaches of the Rhone Valley, east of Lake Geneva, it yields wines not unworthy of their great name. It is grown to a certain extent in the vineyards of Soave, which is perhaps the best of Italian white wines, and in Alsace, of course, overlooking its native Rhine, it is completely at home. There are even unlikely stories to the effect that one or two of the better Graves, in the Bordeaux Country, owe their finesse to a proportion of Rieslings planted among the Semillons and Sauvignons which predominate in their vineyards.

Despite this ability to survive and prosper in other countries, the Riesling is at its best in Germany, as no one who has ever tasted a great Scharzhofberger, or a great Marcobrunner, or a Forster Kirchenstück, can for a moment doubt. This, of course, is partly a matter of climate (the Riesling needs warm weather and can subsist with a minimum of moisture), partly a matter of soil (the Riesling is not fussy about the soil and does well in unfertile and stony ground), and partly a matter of the loving care with which the vine is cultivated and with which the grapes are picked and sorted and pressed. Such loving care the Germans give to the Riesling, full measure and running over. And what the Riesling gives in return is beyond praise.

The Riesling accounts for slightly more than 23% of the White Grape varieties grown in Germany. Vastly more German wine is made from other, more productive, less distinguished grapes than from the Riesling itself. Most of these have the virtue of a higher yield per acre, plus an ability to ripen quicker, an eternal problem in a Northern vineyard area. The two other main grape varieties are Müller-Thurgau, today the most prevalent white variety grown in Germany and accounting for fully 31% of total white grape planting, and the Silvaner, which accounts for 17%. The Müller-Thurgau carries the name of the scientist who created it in 1882 from crossing two clones of Riesling, and it was first planted commercially in 1913. It produces on an average at least a third more per acre than the Riesling and ripens early. Its wines are light and fruity with a slight Muscat taste and with less acidity than the Riesling. It requires better soil and more rain than the Riesling, but is less fussy about sun and heat. When limited in its production it can produce wines of elegance and charm, reminiscent of the Riesling. The Grüner (Green) Silvaner was the dominant grape variety only ten years ago, and is still the second variety after Müller-Thurgau in the Nahe, Rheinhessen, the Rheinpfalz and Franconia. It ripens some fifteen days before the Riesling and produces a full, though somewhat neutral wine. It is the most copious producer after the Müller-Thurgau. Ideal as a blending wine, it also makes an admirable everyday wine, quite drinkable when only a few months old. Like the Riesling, which it in no way resembles, the Silvaner has a confusing multiplicity of names. In the Rheingau, where it is little grown, it is called the *Österreicher*, which would seem to indicate that it originated in Austria. In the Pfalz it goes by the name of the Franken, or "Franconian." Around Würzburg, in Franconia, the Steinwein country, it is sometimes even called the "Franken Riesling"—but this name is almost in the nature of a joke, like Welsh Rabbit or Scotch Woodcock. However, in the United States, the Silvaner has had the effrontery to call itself simply "Riesling," instead of "Franken Riesling," and this absurd misnomer has received, alas! official sanction, so that in order to get a true Riesling wine from California, the consumer now has to ask for "Johannisberg Riesling." It would be hard to find a more illegitimate appropriation of a great name. It is also rather amusing to note that Swiss usage is the exact opposite of American in this connection: a Swiss wine labeled "Johannisberg" may be made from either Silvaner or Riesling; one labeled "Riesling" may be made only from the true Riesling grape.

Germany would not produce the quality or quantity of wine it does, if it did not benefit from the most advanced scientific research. It is the only country where clonal selection is used both for the rootstock and the grafted scion and has resulted in greater vine productivity, disease resistance and development of new crossings.

There is a permanent scientific effort to develop grape varieties that combine the elegance and taste of the Riesling without its long maturing period. Other varieties are developed for blending wines in order to enable an unripe Riesling grape to still produce an elegant and fine wine when nature has not permitted it to mature fully. Some of these varieties may indeed become prevalent thirty or forty years from now, just as the Müller-Thurgau achieved this distinction only recently. It is a fascinating game of man against nature, requiring patience and ingenuity. German statistics show 38 accepted grape varieties, classifying any additional ones under a statistical "all others"

The scientific pruning cut.

category, one of which may well contain the Riesling of tomorrow. The principal permitted types besides the Müller-Thurgau, Riesling and Silvaner are:

Bacchus. Wines similar to Müller-Thurgau with more pronounced Muscat taste. (Even earlier ripening than Müller-Thurgau, prolific producer.)

Elbling. The original Mosel grape variety, now only grown on the lower Mosel. Prolific producer, wines usually used for Sparkling Wine.

Faber. Early ripening, wines with traditional elegance, slightly Muscat taste, higher in acidity than the Müller-Thurgau, though less prolific.

Gutedel. Called the Fendant in Switzerland and the Chasselas in France. Productive. Mostly planted in Baden where it yields wines of secondary quality and not much flavor.

Kerner. Productive. Lively wines with body and a slight Muscat taste. Ripens earlier than Riesling, good acidity.

Morio-Muskat. Prolific, early ripening, wine with pronounced Muscat taste, principally used as blending grape for Silvaner.

Ruländer. (Pinot Gris) Produces full bodied, juicy wines in Baden, Rheinpfalz and Württemberg, as indeed it does in Alsace.

Scheurebe. Small producer but ripens earlier than the Riesling with Riesling type wines, good body, ideal as blending wine for Rielsing.

Traminer or Gewürztraminer. Excellent. Late ripening, shy bearer. Celebrated in Alsace, produces a few unusual and highly aromatic wines in the Rheinpfalz. Incidentally Gewürztraminer means "spicy" Traminer.

Spätburgunder (Pinot Noir). One of the greatest of all red wine grapes.

THE VINEYARDS

The vineyards of Germany are very ancient. Many of them, certainly those of the Moselle and of Hessia and the Pfalz, date back to the dawn of the Christian era, a century or so after Caesar's conquest of Gaul. At the beginning, their expansion was limited by very severe laws forbidding the planting of the vine in Roman colonies—perhaps the first but certainly far from the last protectionist legislation in the field of wine. These laws were finally abrogated in the third century A.D. by the Emperor Probus, who is today regarded as the father of German viticulture, although whether he ever tasted a glass of German wine is at least doubtful.

In any case, a hundred years later, the Latin writer Ausonius, who gave his name to Chateau Ausone, in France, published a famous descriptive poem about the *Mosella* and its wines, and many of the Roman relics that have been unearthed date from approximately the same period.

There exist dozens of stories and legends about these historic vineyards, but it is a little difficult to say how many of them are worthy of credence. Thus it is told that Charlemagne, from the great palace which he built at Ingelheim on the Rhine near Mainz, perceived that there was one slope across the river, in what is now called the Rheingau, on which the snow melted earlier than elsewhere; he ordered that it be planted with vines, and this is now the steep vineyard of Schloss Johannisberg.

As everywhere in Europe, the early history of the vineyards is closely bound up with the history of the Church and of the monastic orders, particularly the Cistercians and the Benedictines. A surprisingly high proportion of the great German vineyards was created by monks and was at one time ecclesiastical property despite the fact that most of these holdings have long since been secularized, it is still possible to buy a wine (and a very good wine, too) produced and bottled by the Cathedral of Trier.

Through the ages more than 20,000 individual vineyard names were registered in their communities, and at least a quarter of them became famous among the wine drinking public in Germany. The new German Wine Law decreed that no single vineyard should be less than 12.5 acres in size and that its soil and climate should be homogeneous enough so that wines grown in any part of the vineyard would be similar in quality and taste.

It also allowed the grouping of several vineyards under one vineyard name, provided again that there are enough similarities in the conditions of climate and soil to make similar wines. These "general vineyard sites" or "*Grosslagen,*" as they are called in German, are indistinguishable from the individual vineyard names. In addition to this Germany was divided into eleven wine growing regions, and each region, except for Ahr and Rheingau, was subdivided into two or more subregions, called *Bereiche*. The designation *Bereich* appears on the label, preceding the main geographic location within the Bereich, such as Bereich Nierstein. With the exception of about a dozen internationally known names (such as Schloss Vollrads and Steinberger) all vineyards are coupled with the name of the geographic community. Under the present law it is possible to use any one of the communities within a *Grosslage* as the community name appearing on the lable in conjunction with the name of the *Grosslage*. Obviously the most prestigious community within the *Grosslage* is invariably used. The common market wine authority is challenging this and it is not certain if this liberal practice will survive. The vineyards were democratically selected by each community through a commission of growers, brokers and members of the Wine Trade. Obviously the more famous designations were enlarged to include those with less famous names, thus inflating the size of formerly small and renowned vineyards. To aid the consumer, each chapter dealing with a specific wine growing district will identify the *"Grosslagen"* and *"Bereiche"* of that district. There are a total of 11 Regions, 31 *Bereiche* (sub regions), 130 *Grosslagen* (general vineyard sites) and about 2,600 *Einzellagen* (individual vineyard sites).

An outline map of Western Germany, showing only the rivers, is surprisingly like a wine map of the country. There are differences, of course. The Rhine north of Bonn runs through flat land unsuited to vines. But German vineyards, as a whole, are river vineyards and hillside vineyards; in this northern latitude the grape requires a maximum of sun, which only a hillside vineyard, facing south, can provide, and most such slopes are along river valleys. The majority of German vineyards, for the same reason, are steep, and have to be created, cultivated and maintained by hand labor.[2] Each individual vine, on the Mosel, has its stake, taller than a man; along the Rheingau and in Rheinhessen and the Pfalz, the vines are strung on wires and tailored until they look like hedges in a formal garden.

An inconceivable amount of care goes into the selection of the vines themselves. Along the Mosel you will see colored rings, quite often, painted on the vine stakes; these, like ribbons at a dog show, are the marks of a champion, a particularly sturdy or particularly productive vine, and it is from these that cuttings are taken for propagation.

Like practically all the wine-producing vines of France, those of Germany are for the most part grafted, and on "American" roots. In the latter half of the last century, an insect pest invaded Europe from the United States, probably carried on some native American grape cuttings brought over for experimental purposes. The name of the pest is *phylloxera vastatrix;* it is a tiny louse which lives on the roots of vines; in the Eastern United States, the roots of the hardy native vine are tough enough to survive. In Europe (as in California where the vineyards are planted with European varieties) its arrival was a major catastrophe. It devastated and destroyed three-quarters of the famous vineyards of the world in less than fifty years. The remedy was found

---

[2] There is an old wine-growers' proverb that tells us, *"Wo ein Pflug kann gahn, soll kein Rebstock stahn!"*, or "Where a plow can go, there no vine should grow."

at last—to bring over to Europe, and from the Eastern States into California, the wild, native American vine, or a hybrid descended from it, and to graft on this resistant stock the Rieslings, the Silvaners, etc., which, unlike the wild American vine, produce grapes for fine wine.

Although Germany produces a far higher proportion of fine wine, as compared with cheap and ordinary wine, than any other major country, there is plenty of the latter. Certainly not over a fifth of Germany's wine could be considered fit for export, even if a foreign market existed for it, and even if the thirsty Rhinelanders did not drink it themselves. The superior vineyards, with which this book is principally concerned, are surprisingly limited in extent; the biggest of them is tiny in terms of an American farm: including the best as well as the worst, there are less than 7,145 acres under vines in the whole Rheingau, and the internationally famous Steinberg, for example, consists of 80 acres of sloping and priceless ground. Here are a few statistics which will perhaps make the picture even clearer.

As of 1977 there existed in all of Western Germany 225,785 acres of producing vineyard; at the same time there were 101,225 vineyard owners; the average holding therefore, consisted of 2.23 acres of vines, and an acre, in an average year yields one thousand gallons, or roughly five thousand bottles of wine.

The Rheinpfalz, or Palatinate, is the largest wine-growing district of Germany with some 51,805 acres under vines, and an average annual production of 59,450,000 gallons. Apart from growers' cooperatives, 42 vineyard-owners with total holdings of only 1,054 acres have formed an association of quality wine producers and ended up by producing half or more than half of all the fine wines of the Rheinpfalz. Perhaps the most famous of these estates is that of Dr. Bassermann-Jordan, whose name, like his charming, old-fashioned label, is known to wine lovers in every country on earth. This estate consists of 99 acres of vines—divided into 24 separate holdings in as many different vineyard plots, each one legally delimited, and having its own traditional and well established name.

Similarly, one of the greatest vineyard properties of the Mosel is that of the Catholic Seminary, the *Bischöfliches Priesterseminar,* of Trier. This consists of roughly 70 acres of vines, divided into nine different holdings in seven different parishes or townships, and the total production amounts to some 200 casks, or *Fuders,* of wine a year. When it is kept in mind that each one of these casks will be marketed under the precise name of the township and the vineyard plot from which it comes, it is obvious that we are not dealing with something produced in industrial quantities.

The major vineyard districts of Germany, their acreage under vines and their approximate average production are as follows:

Mosel-Saar-Ruwer. Some 29,542 acres, of which less than one third produce wines of superior quality. Average yield about twenty five million gallons.

Rheingau. Some 7,310 acres, perhaps two-thirds of which could be called good. Average yield about 5,725,000 gallons.

Rheinhessen. 54,550 acres, of which only about 8,000 are in the eight townships which produce wines of top quality. Average yield fifty million gallons.

Nahe. Some 10,942 acres, perhaps a quarter of them above average. Average yield 9,500,000 gallons.

Rheinpfalz. Some 51,870 acres, not over one fifth of which produce superior wine. Average yield about 62,500,000 gallons.

Franken. Some 8,500 acres, less than 10% superior. Average yield 6,250,000 gallons

Baden. Some 33,395 acres, about 10% producing superior wines. Average yield 34,900,000 gallons.

Württemberg. Some 18,993 acres. Average yield 17,875,000 gallons.

THE VINTAGE

The vintage, or harvest, in Germany rarely begins before mid-October, and in certain extraordinary years it continues through November, long after the wine has been pressed out and fermented and safely stored away in its cellar in other countries. The truth is, of course, that most grapes would simply not ripen at all in the pale, cool autumn sunshine of the Moselle and Rhine. Yet it is this same process of long maturation under a sun that never bakes the grapes which gives German wines their incredible elegance and flavor. A whole family of new grape varieties have been developed by German scientists that

Measuring the sugar content of the grape juice.

mature early, the Müller-Thurgau being the most famous and most successful one. Unfortunately the Riesling takes a long time to mature, yet its hardiness and incredible fragrant fruit has made it the best of the fine grape varieties the Germans grow. The Silvaner matures earlier than the Riesling, but later than the Müller-Thurgau, which is why it is supplanted by the latter.

This question of ripeness is an exceedingly important one: in the field of German wine, it is the key to everything—to vintage charts and vineyard ratings, to nomenclature, and even price. The most expensive wines are those made from grapes that are not only ripe, but over-ripe; the cheapest from grapes so green and sour that sugar has to be added to their juice in order to produce something that can pass for wine. The "great" vintage years are those in which a high proportion of grapes achieve full maturity, just as the "great" vineyards are those favored slopes on which grapes ripen more often and more completely than on neighboring hillsides.

German wines are the only wines in the world which are classified not only by geographic origin and by vineyard, but also by degree of ripeness at the time of picking. Prior to the New German Wine Law the vintners, and particularly the Estates, had many gradations describing ripeness based not as much on the existing regulations as on the growers dedication to diversity. All that has been done away with, and today there are strict regulations as to the degree of grape sugar a wine must have at time of picking to be allowed to be sold as

wine altogether, or to be entitled to one of the other designations identifying quality and type. In addition there are strict regulations forcing
the grower not only to report each lot as it is picked, but also to submit
the wine to an official panel for approval before releasing it for sale.
Before 1971 the wine law was so complex and diverse that it was almost impossible to set a guideline as to the different designations.
Now it is so specific that the consumer can have no doubt that the
wine he buys is legally entitled to its name of origin and designation of
quality.

There are set minimum sugar requirements for every region,
grape variety and quality designation. The Riesling has the lowest
requirements since it is the last to ripen and the most ambrosial of all
grape varieties. It is what the Germans call *extraktreich* (full of es-
sence).

Before we go into the different gradations which describe the
degree of ripeness it is just as well to point out that frequently the
finest vineyards of France and Germany produce grapes that need the
addition of sugar before fermentation. Without that addition the wine
made from such unripe grapes would be too low in alcohol to keep;
would lack balance and would not be agreeable. Though this was
never an issue with French wines it has been a hotly discussed controversy in the perfectionist German wine world. Perhaps because the
Germans have always talked about sugaring the wine or enriching it,
whereas the French have more diplomatically called it *Chaptalisation*
after Napoleon's Minister of Agriculture who promulgated the first
regulations for this practice. The sugar is added not to the wine but to
the grape juice before fermentation in quantities strictly regulated by
law, and it is all converted into alcohol during fermentation. The purpose of this is not to make the wine sweet but to give it the necessary
minimum alcohol that will make it drinkable and will preserve it.
Twenty years ago no self-respecting German Estate owner would have
put his label on a bottle of sugared wine. Now everyone, including the
prestigious Schloss Johannisberg and the Steinberg sell wines that
have been "enriched." One of the reasons, obviously, is improved
cellar techniques that not only enrich but also deacidify the must of
partially ripe grapes. It is interesting that in an average year the wine
so treated is usually more palatable than the Kabinett wine from the
same vineyard. Conversely, however, in great years the enriched
wines are usually less good than the ones that had enough of their own
sugar to start with.

Here are the gradations of quality. There are three large categories: *Tafelwein, Qualitätswein* and *Qualitätswein mit Prädikat.*
Tafelwein. This is the lowest designation given to a wine grown in Germany in one of four regions especially named for Tafelwein and made only from permitted grape varieties that contain the very minimun of natural grape sugar. These are the daily wines of the German *Weinstuben* and are usually consumed within twelve months of the harvest. (German Tafelwein that has been blended with table wines from countries of the European Economic Community bear the inscription *"Wein aus mehreren Mitgliedstaaten der EG"* or "EEC Table Wine.")

By far the largest quantity of German Wine made is *Qualitätswein Bestimmter Anbaugebiete,* usually called *Qualitätswein b.A.* This literally means Quality Wine of designated areas of origin. They are grown in designated areas from permitted grape varieties with enough natural sugar to give the wine the style, elegance and taste of their grapes and regions of origin, yet still needing some enrichment in order to gain full balance and maturity. They must be granted approval both through official chemical analysis and by a governmental tasting panel. The tasting panel not only judges the wine for soundness, but also for conformity of taste with the designation on its label.

The finest German wines go under the collective name of Qualitätswein mit Prädikat, which literally means Quality Wine with "Special Distinction." These wines are never sugared and are entitled to "special distinctions" or attributes in ascending order of quality: *Kabinett:* a wine made from ripe grapes, usually light, elegant and in average years lighter than the *Qualïtswein b.A.* from the same vineyard and year. Such wines make up the bulk of the crop from better than average vineyards in better than average years. But there are other and higher rungs on the ladder.

For at this point, beyond what might be called the normal ripening brought about by sunshine and warmth, there is another factor that enters the equation. This is the so called "Noble Mold" (technically *botrytis cinerea*). The Germans call it *Edelfäule* and the French *la pourriture noble.* Long before the discovery of penicillin, German and French vintners, like the makers of Roquefort and Camembert cheese, had learned that some molds are not only harmless but extraordinarily beneficial and useful—without *botrytis,* neither the great Sauternes of France nor the great Mosels and Rhines of Germany would be what they are.

The Noble Mold comes late in the season, and it exists only in a few vineyard districts, generally in those where September and October are months of warm days and cool nights with heavy dew and a good deal of fog. It appears first as a grey down, hardly more than a shadow, on the ripening grapes; gradually, through its action, the grapes tend to become shrunken and their skins almost transparent—the water in their juice evaporates while their sweetness and flavor become more and more concentrated. At the end, even whole bunches are covered with the gossamer of the mold: shriveled, discolored, to the unpracticed eye they look anything but appetizing or attractive, but from such grapes are made the rarest and the most expensive of all white wines.

All sorts of stories are told, both in Germany and in France, about the discovery of the effects of *botrytis,* for this was almost certainly accidental.

Many years ago, they say, when most of the great Rheingau vineyards were still Church property and their cultivation carried on by monks, the Bishop of the nearby town of Fulda was required, every year, to give his official consent before the grape harvest could begin. One particular fall (and as to the year the chroniclers are a little vague)[3] a messenger was dispatched as usual to Fulda when the grapes were ripe. On his way he was set upon by robbers and failed to return. After an anxious fortnight had gone by, and the grapes were becoming over-ripe, a second messenger set out for Fulda. He too disappeared. Finally, as his beloved grapes became more and more grey and apparently withered, the despairing Abbot sent a third courier, who at last brought the Bishop's authorization. Although convinced that his crop was a total failure, the Abbot decided to salvage what he could, and sent his pickers into the vines. To his astonishment, and that of everyone in the Rheingau, the wine was the best that had ever been made.

We know a great deal more about the Noble Mold[4] today than the Bishop of Fulda and his Abbot, but we are a long way from knowing everything about it. We have learned what conditions are favorable to its appearance and its development, and something of how it works

---

[3] There is some evidence that would lead us to believe that this happened in 1783. It was certainly in the latter half of the 18th century.

[4] The Noble Mold also exists in the U.S. A small amount of exceedingly fine wine is made almost regularly from noble rotted White Riesling grapes in the Northern Counties of California and in the Finger Lake District of New York State.

Recreation of the arrival of the courier from the Bishop of Fulda in front of Schloss Johannisberg.

its miracles on the ripening grapes, but of where it comes from and why, we are as ignorant as ever.

In good years, grapes that are harvested late have of course a higher proportion of bunches that have been touched by the Noble Mold than grapes harvested early, and of course, quite apart from the Mold, they are sweeter and riper. Vineyard owners who are willing and able to afford the risk will therefore often delay picking for a period of days and even weeks after the vintage has officially begun— a date which varies from year to year and is set by a local committee of producers and experts. Again they may harvest part of the crop at the normal time, and send their pickers through the vines not once but even three or four or five times. Granted good weather, wines from the later picking are entitled to the *"Prädikat Spätlese"* which literally means late harvest. They are of markedly superior quality, softer, finer, and a little less dry, and they command, as indeed they should, a higher price.

In an effort to achieve something even better, the German vintners have devised a whole series of special techniques and stratagems which they employ at vintage time. Almost every one of these involves a vast amount of additional and highly specialized work, and most of them entail as well a considerable sacrifice in the total quantity of wine produced.

Practically all of the better growers, for example, deliberately produce, in a given vineyard and a given year, three or four or even more quite different and wholly dissimilar wines. One of these will be a wine made quite simply from grapes that are normally ripe and called *Kabinett*. One will be a *Spätlese*, from grapes that have been allowed to hang on the vines to get the benefit of an additional fortnight or month of autumn sunshine, and one, at least, will be a wine entitled to the *"Prädikat" "Auslese,"* which literally means selective harvest.

This *Auslese*, which is a wine a good deal sweeter and a great deal more expensive than what might be called the run-of-the-mill, is made entirely from bunches that have been selected, as they were picked, as being either especially ripe or touched more than the average by the Noble Mold. Obviously, a grower who uses all such grapes in the making of *Auslese* wines sacrifices thereby the general quality of his crop; the ideal is to strike a fair and good balance, a few casks of *Auslese* for the connoisseurs' great occasions, and perhaps ten times as many casks of good and sound wine for general sale.

But there are even further refinements. The greatest and most expensive German wines of all, and they are both astonishingly great and fabulously expensive, are almost in the nature of dessert wines. Like the famous Sauternes, like Chateau d'Yquem, for example, they are far too sweet to be drunk straight through a meal; one glass of them, in general, is enough, but even one glass is an experience.

These are the *Beerenauslesen* and *Trockenbeerenauslesen—Auslese*, as before, meaning a selection, and *Beeren* meaning berries or individual grapes, and *trocken*, of course, meaning dry or dried. These quite incredible names are wholly descriptive and wholly accurate, for such wines are indeed made out of grapes that have been picked one by one, with the aid of a tiny scissors or a needle, grapes completely covered with the Noble Mold or grapes that have almost turned to raisins on the vine. During the *Lese*, or grape harvest, these are carefully placed in special little pannikins, clipped to the shallow wooden buckets into which the pickers put their grapes. They are pressed separately and fermented separately, and although the best wines so made sometimes bring prices of $100.00 or more per bottle,

Selection of "nobly rotted" grapes for Trockenbeerenauslese.

their production is not infrequently quite as much a matter of pride as it is of profit. These extraordinary golden nectars are made, quite literally, drop by drop.

There is a designation used in addition to the above on "Prädikatswein," which is *Eiswein* (ice wine). This designation is used for wine made from grapes that have been picked and pressed frozen. Since the ice in the grapes is water, and since that ice is removed prior to fermentation, the wine has an extraordinary concentration of both acidity and sweetness. *Eiswein* can only be made from fully ripened or overripe grapes and the designation is usually used in conjunction with *Spätlese* or *Auslese*. Since their production depends upon a freak condition—fully ripened grapes caught by a sudden sharp frost—these wines are rare and usually more expensive than *Beerenauslese*. A recent regulation has added yet one more possible designation to the German Wine Lable, the word *"Trocken"* and *"Halbtrocken."* Most German wines have a degree of sweetness and the top priced ones are very sweet. This sweetness, particularly in *Qualitäts—Kabinett* and *Spätlese* wines, is acquired from the treatment given the wines immediately after fermentation or shortly before bottling. In other words the wine maker has complete control, within legal limits, of how sweet his wines will be. Recently and as the demand for drier wines increased it became important for the consumer to be able to identify the drier German wine, which is the reason for the new designation of *Trocken* meaning really dry and *Halb Trocken,* semi dry wines.

As in all wine-producing countries, the vintage season in Germany, particularly if the quality is good, is a time of general gaiety and rejoicing. There are festivals in the vineyard towns, and more than once in the soft October dusk, I have seen loaded carts coming back from the vines, the pickers singing as they followed, and the oxen themselves garlanded with grape leaves. In this atmosphere of bounty and gratitude and good cheer it is all too easy to forget the devotion and skill and endless labor which have made the harvest possible, and the risks and complexities of the harvest itself. Every cart that rolls so happily and so easily toward press and cellar is really in the nature of a little victory, won against heavy odds in a long battle in the most difficult wine-producing country in the world.

THE CELLAR

From a purely technical point of view, German cellars on the whole are better equipped than those of any other wine-producing country. There are a great many large producers, and most of the small ones (generally referred to as *Winzer,* or wine-growers, as distinguished from *Weingutsbesitzer,* or vineyard-proprietors) have banded themselves together into co-operatives. The State has done its part through the creation of viticultural stations and excellent technical schools, and German industry has contributed all sorts of remarkable inventions in the way of presses, filters and special fermenting tanks, insecticides for the vines and methods of clarification, which even France would do well to copy.

Even since the last War, great changes have taken place in German wine-making methods. Some of these have surprised and perhaps shocked the old-fashioned, but certainly their general effect is all to the good (the consumer's good). The principal trend, like that in France and in America, is all in the direction of younger wines, wines that can be consumed in all the fruit and freshness of their youth, after eighteen months or two years rather than after five or ten. Naturally such wines are on the whole less expensive; it is possible that they will never achieve quite those extraordinary peaks of excellence which made the fame of the 1893's and the 1911's, the 1920's and the

1921's (although having tasted all of these, and more recently the 1949's and 1959's, I am inclined to doubt it). Almost certainly they will be short lived. But the difference, I am convinced, is a net gain.

Cellar methods differ to a certain minor degree from one German district to another, but much less than they did fifty years ago. In general the grapes come direct from the vineyard to the press-house, although sometimes, if the distance is too great, they are stemmed and crushed into a cask on a cart along the roadside. When they reach the *Kelterhaus,* they are pressed as soon as possible in hydraulic presses[5] and the resulting *Most,* or Must is set to ferment.

The barrels, or casks, in which this fermentation takes place, and in which the wine is stored for aging after fermentation, vary quite surprisingly from one district to another in Germany. On the Mosel, the traditional and universal cask is the *Fuder,* of roughly 1,000 liters capacity; in terms of bottles, it is generally estimated at 1,333 bottles, or 111 cases, give or take a few bottles, and it is in terms of *Fuders* that almost all Mosel wines are sold by the producers.

In the Rheingau, and in Rheinhessen the unit is the *Halbstück* (literally the half-piece—although in France a piece is a barrel, generally one of just over 50 gallons). A *Halbstück* is a cask of 600 liters—it gives approximately 800 bottles or about 66 cases.

Still another standard of measurement is used in the Palatinate or Rheinpfalz. Here, just as in Alsace to the south, the casks are usually considerably larger, often oval rather than round, and in size they range anywhere from about 600 liters (roughly 150 gallons) to six or seven times that size. The wines are sold, before bottling, in units of 1,000 liters, a rather arbitrary standardization made necessary by the widely varying size of the barrels. These 1,000-liter lots are often referred to as *Fuders* even when the wines in question are stored in much larger or much smaller casks.

Many of the large and small Estates continue to ferment and ma-

---

[5] A sensational new press, the Willmes Presse, developed since the War, is rapidly replacing the standard hydraulic press in most of the better German cellars. It consists of an elastic, plastic sleeve, inside a stainless steel cylinder, mounted horizontally on a metal frame which, in turn, is on rollers. When the sleeve is inflated (just as the inner tube of a tire is inflated) and the cylinder slowly revolved, outward pressure is exerted on the grapes, and the juice passes through hundreds of narrow slits in the cylinder's surface, into a stainless steel trough mounted directly below it. Being on rollers, the press can be moved around the press-house as easily as a piece of furniture.

ture their wine in wooden casks and it is hard to tell whether they do it for reasons of economy or quality. Certainly fermentation can be better controlled in stainless steel though finer wines may indeed mature better if they spend some time in wood. As stainless steel is increasingly replacing the *Fuder* and *Doppelstück* casks in German cellars, the control of fermentation has become easier and the wines have become fresher and better. At least one prominent Rheingau grower has told me that he would have converted to stainless steel long ago if he could find room in his ancient cellar. He would obviously keep some wooden casks for romance and publicity but certainly not for efficiency and quality.

Needless to say, good German cellars are cool—I have seen the thermometer reading 54 degrees in a cellar in Bernkastel in mid-August when it was well over 90 degrees in the vines, fifty feet from the cellar door. In less cool cellars, German wines could not conceivably preserve the freshness, the pale green-gold color, the lightness and fruitiness which make their charm. Nor would they preserve these qualities if they were not scrupulously cared for. In a cellar used for the maturing of fine wine, perfect cleanliness is as necessary as in a hospital. The casks have to be kept brim full, and are checked at least once a week. The wine, at certain stages in its development has to be "racked"—siphoned off from one cask to another, leaving the sediment or "lees" behind. Then at the proper time it has to be clarified, or "fined."

This is a process almost as old as wine-making itself. Just as farmers used to drop eggshells into the coffeepot "to make the grounds settle," so there are certain products which, stirred into a cask of wine, will form an invisible, tenuous network in the wine, and settle carrying the sediment to the bottom and leaving the wine brilliant and clear. Whites of eggs, for example, have been used for this purpose for centuries, especially for red wines, and the Germans have developed other very special clarifying agents which are of more interest to the wine chemist than to the consumer. These do their work extremely well, for sediment, in a German wine, is almost unknown, and a bottle with even a trace of cloudiness ranks as an extraordinary exception.

There is, however, a sediment that plagues the German winemaker. In good years the finer wines, particularly the *"Prädikatsweine"* can throw a deposit of tartaric crystals. The concentration of tartrate in the wine forms crystals during the aging process, which look not unlike glass splinteres in the bottom of the bottle. In Germany they are regarded as signs of distinction; it is harder to convince the foreign consumer. The only way to eliminate this is to store the wine in below freezing temperature before bottling. This is possible, though costly, for large lots, but impractical for small ones. One can also decant the wine and filter it, which is not only expensive, but also invariably results in a loss of quality.

During the months following fermentation, particularly once they have "fallen bright" and been racked for the first time, light white wines like those of the Moselle and Rhine change and develop quickly: they lose the characteristic yeastiness of unfinished wine, they begin to acquire bouquet, their initial "greenness" disappears. Naturally the "little" wines that are destined to be short-lived pass through the diverse stages of their evolution more rapidly than their fuller-bodied and finer contemporaries. But for one and all there comes a day, perhaps after only seven or eight months, perhaps after eighteen, when the cellar-master tastes them again and pronounces them *abfüll-fertig*—ready for the bottle. Long before this graduation day, the unworthy will have been eliminated: the poorly balanced will have been shipped away to some blending cellar, the small and unpromising to be served by the carafe or glass in the local *Weinstuben;* only those considered fit to receive the diploma, in the form of a branded cork, an estate label and an honored name, are still in the cellar on their bottling day.

THE BOTTLE

Germany has given us two basic patterns in the way of wine bottles— one, of course, is the familiar, slender, long-necked *Schlegelflasche,* the traditional bottle of the Moselle and Rhine; the other is the amusing *Bocksbeutel,* the round-bellied flagon used for the *Steinweine,* the wines of Franconia, and occasionally for certain of those of Baden. Both are attractive, and both have been used for supposedly similar but often quite dissimilar wines, in countries all the way from Italy and Spain to Chile and California.

Let us confine ourselves, for the moment, to the standard bottle; it contains one fifth of a gallon (roughly .75 liters), it is green on the Moselle, brown in the Rheingau, Rheinhessen and the Pfalz (though, oddly enough, green in Alsace). A few cheap wines are shipped in litre-bottles (just under a quart) of the same form. German bottles are often filled very full, sometimes so that there is hardly a perceptible bubble of air next to the cork, and it is decidedly risky to store them in a warm place, since the natural expansion of the wine will, under such conditions, sometimes push up the cork.

The corks come mostly from Spain and Portugal. They are generally shorter than those used in France (the wines being sooner ready and on the whole shorter-lived), and most of them are branded with the name and sometimes with the coat-of-arms of the producer. As a matter of fact, you will rarely see an unbranded cork in a superior bottle of German wine.

Even when the wine is *abfüllfertig,* or ready for the bottle, it invariably requires a little final processing, usually in the form of filtration. The Germans are past masters in the field, and the great Seitz factory in Bad Kreuznach on the Nahe, has made astonishing contributions to this rather exact science.

German wines being low in alcohol and usually containing some residual sugar are the hardest to bottle safely. Fortunately the scientists at Seitz have invented a process that assures the stability of these delicate wines. It is called sterile bottling, a pumping of the wine through an exceedingly fine filter, which not only removes all traces of sediment, but also all yeast cells which might conceivably cause a later, secondary fermentation as well as clouding. The bottles and corks are sterilized in addition. This filtration is but one of the many systems that have been developed in Germany in order to assure the clearest must and the most brilliant wine, all valiant efforts that have contributed to an early bottling, usually in the spring following the harvest that captures all the youth, elegance and charm of these, the lightest white wines in the world.

It is such wines that Germany is able to send us today, and they are in every sense the result of the best possible combination of a respect for tradition and a willingness to accept all that modern science has achieved in the past fifty years. They are not the product of primitive farms and they are not the product of factories—they are wines made with care, with intelligence and with love.

NOMENCLATURE

*German Wine Labels
and What They Mean*

O the uninitiated layman, the label on a really distinguished bottle of German wine (or on one that pretends to be) appears at first sight about as intelligible as so much Sanskrit. In most cases, it is quite attractive, with a landscape or an old coat-of-arms in color (which may or may not be the coat-of-arms of the producer). Next comes a vintage year (probably a good one, possibly a poor one) followed by a series of three or four fairly long German words, all of them unfamiliar, and finally the name of some institution or individual corporation which may be anything from a count to a cathedral, from a peasant wine-producer to a large commercial wholesaler of wines and spirits. After one or two encounters with this sort of problem, most people fall back on something called Liebfraumilch or Mosel-blümchen, and no wonder.

To do so, however, is to miss entirely the wines that have made the international fame and glory of German vineyards, and these are certainly among the greatest white wines in the world. As a matter of fact, German wine labels are not as complicated as they look—they are very like what youngsters used to call "pig Latin" . . . you have to learn a trick or two, and the rest is easy. Once you can read them, they turn out to be the most accurate and informative wine labels in existence, for they give you the background and tell you the life story of what you are about to drink in terms which are a model of directness and precision.

Almost all of the fine wines of Germany (like almost all of the fine wines of France) bear names that are geographical in origin—the name of the village from which they come, or that of a particularly famous vine-covered hillside, or that of a castle which overlooks the vineyard.

German wine labels tell a complete and an honest story—they may or may not be attractive, but they are at least unfailingly informative. This is what they tell you, or are supposed to tell you:

To begin with they tell you the category of the quality of the wine. There are three such categories, as we discussed on page 32. *Tafelwein, Qualitätswein b.A.* or *Qualitätswein mit Prädikat*. The latter also gives the "Special attribute" but oddly enough this attribute usually appears tagged onto the more specific geographical name of origin of the wine and its grape variety if the latter is given (e.g. Piesporter Goldtröpfchen Riesling Auslese). The quality designation must be printed on every label or the wine can not be sold legally.

If a wine is a *Qualitätswein* or a *Qualitätswein mit Prädikat* it must bear an A.P. Number. A.P. stands for *Amtliche Prüfungsnummer,* meaning official approval number. Each fine wine must be approved by a governmental board before it can bear its name. Each lot of wine that is bottled must be analysed officially and submitted to a regional tasting office. It is tasted blind by a panel which then either gives it an official number, entitling it to its name of origin and quality category or turn it down. The tasting panel is there to insure that even after all the legal requirements are met, the wine does not fall short on taste. For it is very important that it actually has the typical taste of the geographical region, grape variety, vintage and quality that are claimed by its label. If the tasting authority does not approve the wine, it can either give it a lower designation—say approve a *Spätlese* for a requested *Auslese*—or turn it down altogether. If turned down, the applicant has the right to have it tasted by a different panel, and if turned down again to request a more experienced review panel. If it is turned down a third time, the applicant has either the option of going to court or blending the wine (the professionals call it "drowning") into a better lot. I can bear witness to the fact that wines are turned down and down graded. The system works well and thereby makes for better selection, treatment, bottling and care than if the book were the only stricture as in so many other countries. Each wine is tasted by an authority in the region of origin, rather than the region where it is bottled, assuring it of a tasting by experts of the particular type which is being submitted. The busiest approving authority is the one in Alzey where several tasting panels handle 30,000 individual lots a year.

Once a wine is approved it is given an A.P. number (official approval) which must be shown on each and every label of the lot. Two countersample bottles of the approved wine are kept for two years to enable the authority to recheck the wine should there be a consumer complaint. The A.P. number tells its own story, e.g.

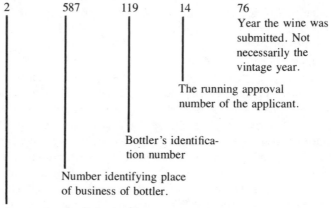

| 2 | 587 | 119 | 14 | 76 |

Year the wine was submitted. Not necessarily the vintage year.

The running approval number of the applicant.

Bottler's identification number

Number identifying place of business of bottler.

Approval authority's number.

The next thing the label tells you is the geographical origin of the wine. This usually appears on the top. In order to avoid confusion in the mind of the consumer, the regions for Tafelwein are different from the ones used for *Qualitätswein* and *Qualitätswein mit Prädikat*. There are four Tafelwein regions with four subregions: *"Rhein und Mosel"* (with subregions Rhein and Mosel) *"Main," "Neckar"* and *"Oberrhein"* (with subregions *Römertor* and *Burgengau*). There are eleven *Qualitätswein/Qualitätswein mit Prädikat* regions; *Ahr, Hessische Bergstrasse, Mittelrhein, Nahe, Rheingau, Rheinhessen, Rheinpfalz, Mosel-Saar-Ruwer, Franken, Württemberg* and *Baden*.

Next the label tells you even more specifically where the wine comes from. Generally speaking, this is a village, and the name of the village is the name of the wine. Just as a man from New York or London is a New Yorker or a Londoner, so a wine from Rüdesheim is a Rüdesheimer, a wine from Nierstein is a Niersteiner and a wine from

Piesport is a Piesporter. A few great castles and a few extraordinary vineyards are more famous and more important than the townships in which they lie, and these give the vineyard name, rather than the township name, to the wines they produce. Thus we have Schloss Johannisberger (from Schloss Johannisberg), Steinberger (from the Steinberg vineyard, near Hattenheim), Scharzhofberger (from the Scharzhofberg, near Wiltingen, on the Saar), and so on. But these are exceptions, and the basic rule holds true.

On the finer wines, the name of the village is followed by the name of the individual vineyard which unfortunately is indistinguishable from the name of the collective vineyard. The uninitiated therefore will find it difficult to differentiate between Hattenheimer Deutelsberg and Hattenheimer Nussbrunnen on a label. The former is the *"Grosslage,"* (collective vineyard site) covering 17 vineyards in Erbach and Hattenheim of a total area of 1,132.5 acres. The latter is one of the finest individual vineyards in Hattenheim of 27.5 acres. Nussbrunnen is one of the 17 vineyards in the Deutelsberg collective name. Obviously the finer wine would be sold under the vineyard name Nussbrunnen. There is every reason that wines should be sold under one collective name if they are grown in a region where similar climatic and soil conditions prevail. My only problem is that it would be helpful to the consumer if the word *Grosslage* appeared behind the name, or at least the letters *GL.*

Though each wine has the right to an individual vineyard designation it is often impractical even for the best Estates to market some of their wines under such a designation. Either their holdings in a particular vineyard are too small to make the use of the name of the vineyard desirable, or the name of the Grosslage is better known, and therefore easier to market. This is particularly true in the Mosel-Saar-Ruwer and the Rheingau, where certain *Grosslagen* have gained a considerable following and reputation. Obviously an Estate with a reputation for quality has no problems marketing wines under a *Grosslage* name. It is no coincidence that some of these *Grosslagen* names were formerly well known and respected individual vineyard names. I will try to identify those *Grosslagen* names which are likely to be used with more discretion than others. Every vineyard site is exactly delineated in the land-registry office of its area, and since *Grosslagen* are a collection of individual vineyard sites, their exact area is similarly delineated. I will identify under each region the *Grosslagen* belonging to that region and where available the acres and villages it covers.

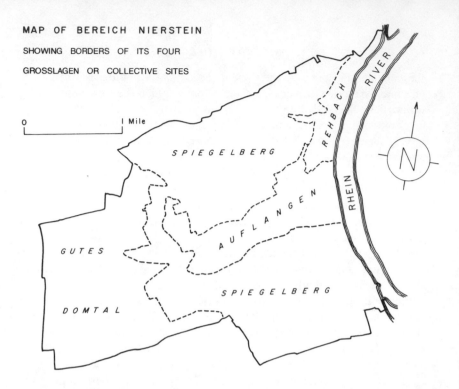

MAP OF BEREICH NIERSTEIN

SHOWING BORDERS OF ITS FOUR

GROSSLAGEN OR COLLECTIVE SITES

0 ⊢ I Mile

SPIEGELBERG

REHBACH

RHEIN

RIVER

AUFLANGEN

GUTES

SPIEGELBERG

DOMTAL

N

Bereich Nierstein with its four Grosslagen and Auflangen, one of the Grosslagen, with its six individual vineyards.

MAP OF GROSSLAGE AUFLANGEN

SHOWING BORDERS OT ITS SIX

EINZELLAGEN OR INDIVIDUAL VINEYARDS

0 ⊢ I/2 Mile

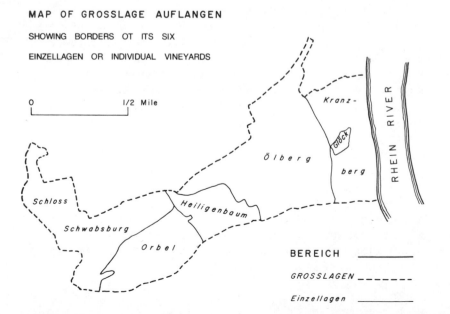

Kranz-

Glöck

Ölberg

berg

RHEIN RIVER

Schloss

Heiligenbaum

Schwabsburg

Orbel

BEREICH ——————

GROSSLAGEN – – – – –

Einzellagen ——————

The names of the individual vineyards, or *Lagen* as the Germans call them, are usually very old, and sometimes both picturesque and descriptive. There are roughly 2,600 of them, and in many of them are combined some fairly common word, and some purely local designation. Thus one runs across, over and over again, vineyard names that end or start with *Berg* (hill), *Baum* (tree), *Burg* or *Schloss* (castle), *Bach* (stream), *Brunnen* (fountain or spring), *Dom* (cathedral), *Kirche* (church), *Kloster* (monastery or convent), *Hof* (court or manor-house), *Garten or Gärtchen* (garden, or little garden), *Kreuz* (crucifix), *Mauer* (wall), *Pfad* or *Weg* (path or road), *Stein* (stone), *Turm* (tower), *Kopf* or *Kupp* (hilltop or summit), *Sonne* (sun or sunny), *Lay* (slate rock), *Fels* (cliff), *Stück* (piece of land), *Morgen* (rough equivalent of an acre), *Feld* or *Acker* (field), *Abt* (abbot), *Graf* (count), *Bischof* (bishop), *Herren* (lords), etc. Keeping in mind that *alt* or *alten* means old, and *neu*, new, that *unter* means below, that *nieder* means lower and *ober*, upper, that *lange* is long and *hohe* is high, that *schwarz* is black, *weiss*, white, *rot*, red, and *gold*, gold, it is possible to make sense out of at least a majority of German vineyard names. Here are a dozen examples:

Geisenheimer Fuchsberg	—from the "Fox Hill" vineyard of Geisenheim
Piesporter Grafenberg	—from the "Count's Hill" in Piesport.
Deidesheimer Hohenmorgen	—from the "High Acres" of Deidesheim.
Forster Kirchenstück	—from the "Church Section" of Forst.
Deidesheimer Paradiesgarten	—from the "Garden of Paradise" in Deidesheim.
Erbacher Honigberg	—from the "Hill of Honey" in Erbach.
Neumagener Rosengärtchen	—from the "Little Rose Garden" in Neumagen.
Rüdesheimer Berg Rottland	—from the "Hill that was made arable" in Rüdesheim
Ürziger Schwarzlay	—from the "Black Slate" vineyard in Ürzig
Zeltinger Schlossberg	—from the "Castle Hill" of Zeltingen.

| Eltviller Sonnenberg | —from the "Sunny Hill" of Elt-ville. |
| Graacher Himmelreich | —from the "Kingdom of Heaven" in Graach. |

Besides the name of the individual vineyard (*Lage*) or collective vineyard (*Grosslage*), a wine can also bear the name of a subregion or viticultural district called *"Bereich."* All of the regions, except two, have two or more *Bereiche*. The word *Bereich* precedes that of the most important community in the *Bereich* that gives the *Bereich* its name, such as *Bereich* Nierstein, *Bereich* Johannisberg etc. Two names that appear frequently on German wine labels, are Liebfraumilch, or Liebfrauenmilch and Moselblümchen. The latter is a designation for a blend of Mosel wines which only appears on *Tafelwein*. Liebfraumilch, however, is a name that has appeared for well over 150 years on German wines, particularly those that are exported, giving the exporter the ability to sell large quantities of wine of similar taste under one label which often is also accompanied by a brand name such as Blue Nun, Hanns Christof, Glockenspiel, and Madonna. Liebfraumilch is invariably a *Qualitätswein*, but never a *Qualitätswein mit Prädikat*. At present it can be made from authorized grape varieties grown in the Rheingau, Nahe, Rheinhessen and the Rheinpfalz. Within the next few months, however, a Liebfraumilch region will be established very likely limited to a smaller and better defined area.

German labels also tell you, in a majority of cases, in what year the wine was made. All good German wines carry a vintage, and it is fairly safe to bet that any wine that does not is ashamed of the year of its birth. But it is important to remember that all but the very best German wines mature early—only the true elite among the 1971s are still improving and the lesser wines, even of that incomparable vintage, are growing old.

The next thing that can (but not necessarily) appear on the label is the grape variety from which the wine is made. In the past it was generally accepted that wines from the Mosel-Saar-Ruwer and the Rheingau were automatically made from the Riesling grape. Though this is still largely true of the Rheingau, it is not true anymore of the Mosel-Saar-Ruwer. More and more wine therefore from the different regions bears the name of a grape variety such as Riesling, on finer traditional wines, or Gewürztraminer, Scheurebe, Silvaner etc. when a clear indication of the taste of the wine is needed. The grape variety (and this can be two, but not more than two such as Riesling/Silvaner) usually appears after the name of the wine and before the *"Prädikat"*, if the wine has one. A good example is Johannisberger Erntebringer Riesling Auslese. If the grape variety appears on the label, the wine must be made of at least 85% from that grape variety and must taste of it. The official tasting panel obviously checks the honesty of the grower/bottler on this. If two grape varieties appear on the label the wine must have been solely made from these two grape varieties at a more or less equal proportion. In other words no Riesling/Silvaner consisting of 5% Riesling and 95% Silvaner. The label can also give an indication of the degree of dryness or sweetness of the wine by the words *"Trocken,"* *"Halbtrocken,"* *"Lieblich"* and *"Süss."* Obviously there are exact norms for each designation.

Finally, the German label tells you the alcoholic strength of the wine, expressed in percentage by volume, the contents of the bottle expressed in liters and the name of the shipper. There are three broad designations that are important on this subject. A wine that was grown, harvested, fermented, aged, and bottled by an Estate bears the designation *"Erzeugerabfüllung"* *(producer's bottling) or the legend* *"Aus dem Eigenem Lesegut"* (from our own harvest) followed by the name of the Estate. A wine that is bottled by a bottler or shipper entirely from an Estate produced wine can bear the designation: *"Aus dem Lesegut von———"* (name of the Estate). This means literally "from the harvest of———." Lastly, the bottler's and shipper's name appears with his address (the village or city where his business is located) on the label. The German wine law has clearly defined what *must* appear on the label and also what *can*. The more prevalent label information is provided as a glossary at the end of this chapter.

The Germans, like so many other winegrowers, submit their wines to competitive tastings in order to get prizes and thereby enhance the reputation of their wines and cellars. You can therefore find on German wine bottles a whole slew of different ribbons usually showing the particular bottle as part of a lot which either won a *Grosser Preis* (big prize), a *Silberner* (silver) *Goldener* (golden) *Preis* (prize), or a *Kammerpreismünze* (prize medal given by official Agricultural organization).

Each state has its own award giving panel and there is one for the whole Federal Republic that goes under the abbreviation DLG. In ad-

dition to this, there is a stamp of quality (*Deutsches Weinsiegel*) given
by a tasting panel that has somewhat stricter guidelines than the A.P.
panel. It appears in three colors: Red for wines in general, yellow for
dry wines (with the imprint *Trocken*) and green for the half dry wines
(with the imprint *Halb-Troken*). Though the red seal of quality rarely
appears on exported wines (an earlier Export Seal having failed completely), it is likely that the *Trocken* and *Halb-Trocken* seal will find
its way into the export wine market.

Because the grapes are selectively picked, it is not unusual for a
given vineyard in a given year to produce a whole family of different
wines, some of them worth ten times as much per bottle as others.
Each label will give specific information about the maturity of the
grapes from which the wine was made. For example the following
wines were made in 1975 in the Rüdesheimer Schlossberg vineyard:

Rüdesheimer Schlossberg (Qualitätswein) A wine which was enriched
and is fairly dry.
Rüdesheimer Schlossberg Kabinett (a fairly dry and elegant wine,
made from normally ripe grapes. Lighter than the Qualitätswein).
Rüdesheimer Schlossberg Spätlese (somewhat finer, a little less dry,
worth perhaps 30% to 50% more than the first, and 20% to 40%
more than the second).
Rüdesheimer Schlossberg Auslese (much fuller bodied, somewhat
sweet, made from especially selected grapes during the
harvest, worth at least twice as much as the Rüdesheimer
Schlossberg Kabinett.)
*Rüdesheimer Schlossberg Beerenauslese, or Trockenbeerenauslese or
Eiswein* (the latter in combination with *Spätlese, Auslese* or even
Beerenauslese). These are great rarities, produced in extremely
limited quantities, essentially dessert wines, very sweet and very
expensive.

Before the new German wine law the different estates used many
gradations within each *"Prädikat." Fein* and *Feinste Spätlese* or *Auslese* was not uncommon, *Bestes Fass* (best cask) was inevitable in a
good year, and in addition each cask had its own number and its own
following, alas small, since a cask on the Mosel, where this practice
was most widely in use, contains but 1,333 bottles. All this is no

longer legal, but it is hard to break a habit. Some of the Mosel growers have adopted a series of gold capsules of different lengths imitating an old tradition of Schloss Vollrads and Schloss Johannisberger. These famous Rheingau Estates have always had a complex system of capsules in almost all colors of the rainbow in order to confound their customers on the different qualities they sell. It obviously defies memorizing, particularly as it changed after 1971 and no doubt will again, since this large proliferation of qualities is hardly suitable to the present day marketplace. It is a hangover from a more leisurely era where only the titled and rich drank such wine.

It seems hardly necessary to add that over a period of years or decades or even centuries certain estates and certain families have acquired a reputation for the excellence of their wines which they have laboriously earned and scrupulously kept intact, and which they fully merit. The names of these members of what might be called the elite have been listed in the following chapters in connection with the villages where their vineyards lie. Their labels are known to every lover of German wines, and their names are regarded with deference and affection by all those, in whatever country, who respect craftsmanship and honesty and fine wine.

Terms frequently used on German wine labels, other than the name of the wine, the vintage and the grape variety:

Abfüller	Bottler
Abgefüllt durch	Bottled by
Abgefüllt für	Bottled for
A.P.	Approval number for QbA and QmP wines
Aus eigenem Lesegut	Estate bottled
Auslese	Selectively harvested. A wine made from selected grapes, richer, sweeter, more expensive than others of the same year and vineyard.
Badisch Rotgold	Designation for Rosé wine from Baden.

Beerenauslese	Literally and actually means that the ripest grapes have been set aside, grape by grape, at vintage time, and a separate wine (this) made from them. A sweet and very expensive wine.
Burg	Castle
Domäne	Domain, or vineyard property or properties.
"e"	Appears after the liter, milliliter or centiliter content of the bottle, means Europe.
Eiswein	Wine made from grapes caught by a sudden sharp frost. Must be used with another designation such as *Spätlese* or *Auslese* on *Qualitätswein mit Prädikat*.
Erben	Heirs
Erzeugerabfüllung	Estate bottling
Freiherr	Baron
Fürst	Prince
Gebrüder	Brothers. *Gebrüder* Schmitt means Schmitt brothers.
Geerntet durch	Harvested by
Geschwister	Brothers and sisters. *Geschwister* (or Geschw.) Berres means Brothers and Sisters of the Berres family.
Graf	Count
Halbtrocken	Half dry
Kabinett	The lowest designation on *Qualitätswein mit Prädikat*.
Keller	Cellar

Kellerei	Cellars or winery
Lieblich	Used for slightly sweet wines.
Pfarrgut	Vineyard forming part of the endowment of the local clergy.
Rentamt	Revenue Office
Rotwein	Red wine
Qualitätswein b.A.	Quality wine of designated areas of origin.
Qualitätswein mit Prädikat	Quality wine of designated area of origin with predicate. (Predicate such as *Spätlese*, must always be carried on label.)
Schloss	Castle, palace
Schillerwein	Designation used for Rosé wine
Spätlese	Late-picking. A superior wine made from grapes picked late in the season.
Stiftung	A charitable foundation, and its endowment.
Süss	Sweet
Tafelwein	Table wine
Trocken	Dry
Trockenbeerenauslese	A step above *Beerenauslese*. The individually picked grapes have been so ripe and sweet as to be practically dry (*"trocken"*) or raisined. Such grapes give infinitesimal quantities of very sweet, wholly remarkable, and fabulously expensive wine.
Verwaltung (Gutsverwaltung)	Administration, or central office
Weinbau	Winegrowing, viniculture

Weinhändler	Wine merchant or shipper
Weingut	Vineyard property, or domain. Its use on a label is not a guarantee of estate-bottling
Weingutsbesitzer	The owner of the vineyard property.
Weinkellerei	Wine-cellar, winery
Weissherbst	A name given to a white wine made from a red grape. Usually it is slightly pink, the color of a partridge's eye.
Winzer	Grape grower
Winzergenossenschaft	A cooperative association of grape-growers that have set up a winery and cellar and who sometimes do their own bottling.
Winzerverein	A producers' cooperative, generally made up of smaller growers than the members of a *Winzergenossenschaft*.

3

MOSEL-
SAAR-
RUWER

AS far as their wines, as well as their waters, are concerned, the Mosel and its little tributaries, the Saar and the Ruwer, make up a single basin or *Gebiet*. It is true that a person (and not necessarily an expert) who tastes them comparatively can usually detect in the wines of the Saar a finesse and elegance together with fresh apple acidity which is their special charm, and which the Mosels as a whole do not possess. Similarly the Ruwers are fresh, with a little more spice and fruit and a little fuller than the Saars. The Mosels have a substance which is both broader and softer than that of the tributaries; yet all three share a taste altogether different from wines made anywhere else.

At their best the wines of that whole region have a honeyed fragrance like a bunch of spring flowers, a lightness and fruity acidity that makes them unique. It is common to find a slight effervescence in most of them, a remainder of carbon dioxide that was left in the wine after fermentation, a fleeting prickle on the tongue that enhances their lightness and charm. They are the lightest of the great wines of the world, hardly ever exceeding ten percent of alcohol by volume.

The Mosel-Saar-Ruwer is Germany's fourth largest wine region, about thirty-two thousand acres. In bumper years, it can produce as

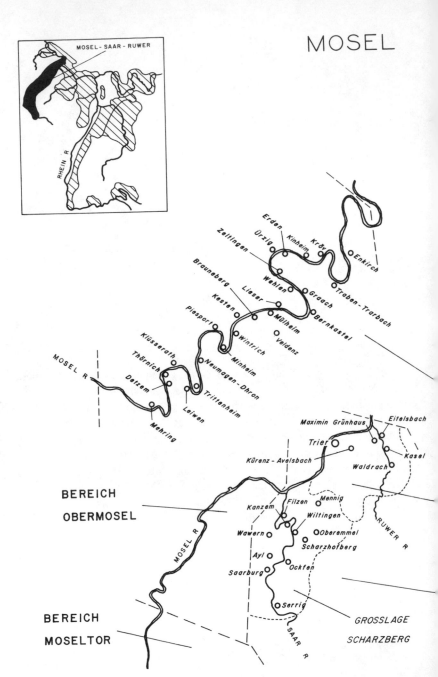

MOSEL

MOSEL - SAAR - RUWER

RHEIN R

Erden
Zeltingen
Ürzig Kinheim Krōv
Enkirch

Brauneberg
Wehlen
Lieser Graach Traben-Trarbach
Kesten
Bernkastel
Piesport Mülheim
Wintrich
Klüsserath Veldenz
Thörnich Minheim
Detzem Neumagen-Dhron
Leiwen Trittenheim

MOSEL R

Mehring

Maximin Grünhaus Eitelsbach
Trier
Kürenz - Avelsbach Kasel
Waldrach

BEREICH

OBERMOSEL
Mennig
Kanzem Filzen
Wiltingen
Wawern Oberemmel
Ayl Scharzhofberg
Saarburg Ockfen

MOSEL R

RUWER R

Serrig

BEREICH
GROSSLAGE
MOSELTOR
SCHARZBERG

SAAR R

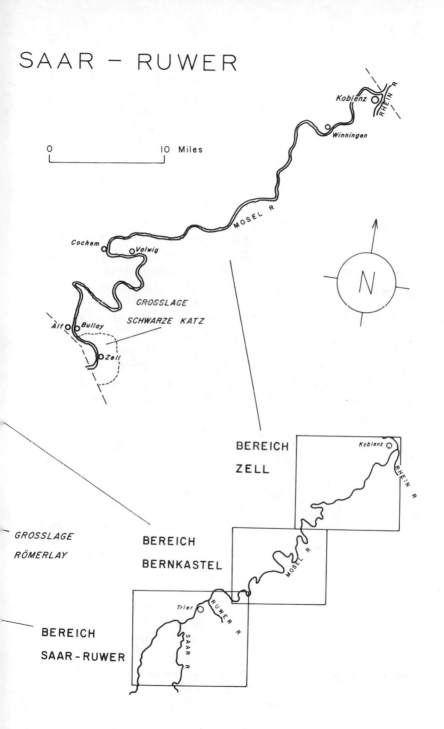

SAAR – RUWER

0   10 Miles

Koblenz
RHEIN R
Winningen

MOSEL R

Cochem
Valwig

GROSSLAGE
SCHWARZE KATZ

Alf   Bullay

Zell

N

BEREICH
ZELL

Koblenz
RHEIN R

GROSSLAGE
RÖMERLAY

BEREICH
BERNKASTEL

MOSEL R

Trier
RUWER R

BEREICH
SAAR-RUWER

SAAR R

much as thirty six million gallons (enough wine to fill sixteen million cases of twelve bottles each). But as this is the most northern wine area in the world, in bad years it can also produce half this amount or, worse still, the grapes can be so unripe that the farmers will be forced to sell their wines to the German sparkling wine industry which in turn will make something quite delicious from the acid grapes that were not blessed with enough sunshine and could not produce the great wines they do when they ripen.

The Mosel-Saar-Ruwer has changed tremendously in the last twenty five years. When this book was originally written most of the wines were made entirely from the Riseling grape: Mosel-Saar-Ruwer wines were Riesling wines to such an extent that the grape variety never appeared on the label; it was an accepted fact that only Riesling went into their making. This is still true of the best of them, but the great popularity of the region, the enormous demand for its wines, and the uncertainty of its climate which will allow the Riesling to ripen only three or four years out of ten has changed all that. The stark facts are that only 64% of the planted grapes are Riesling, 20% being Müller-Thurgau, 9% Elbling (an old German variety) and the rest newer varieties such as Kerner, Bacchus, Optima and Ortega. All the other varietals will guarantee, even in the worst of years, ripe grapes that will make decent wines and will not force the vintner to sell his crops to the *Sekt* makers. Also, as they yield more than the Riesling per acre, one can safely assume that half the crop of the region is no longer made from Riesling grapes. The climate and slate soil, however, are so dominant that even the non-Riesling wines have some of the characteristic charm and taste of this region. Nevertheless there is no doubt that the best of the wines are still made from Riesling, either entirely or in such a high degree that the negligible percentage of other juice will not mar the elegance and breed of this noble grape.

The region has changed in many other ways as well. The sleepy valley with the picture postcard villages scattered among fields of wheat and sugar beet with the vineyards planted only on the steeply terraced black-blue slate hillsides, has now become one uninterrupted vineyard where the Müller-Thurgau produces large quantities of pleasant but by no means great wine. The Mosel has been made navigable by thirteen locks built along its meandering way. It is 153 miles long from its entrance into Germany at Perl until it joins the Rhine at Koblenz; yet it is only a little over 87 miles as the crow flies.

The canalization of the river, which has facilitated the transpor-

A Roman relic found in Neumagen on the Mosel.

tation by barge from the heartland of Western Europe—the Saar and Lorraine—to the industrial region of the Ruhr and the ocean going steamers in the Dutch and Belgium ports, has not changed the charm of the valley, but in its subtle way it has changed its climate. It has added about one degree centigrade to the average yearly temperature, particularly during the ripening season, so that in bad years the area produces better wines, and in great years fuller wines than it did twenty-five years ago.

Here as elsewhere in Germany there has also been a steady consolidation of vineyard properties. As recently as 1969 the average individual holdings of some 17,435 growers were 1.4 acres. By 1977 there were only 9,163 growers left with 32,180 acres of vineyards, an average of 3.5 acres to a grower.

The Mosel-Saar-Ruwer is singular in one other respect. Whereas most if not all of the European vineyards are planted today with American roots on which European vines have been grafted, the Mosel still has about 40% original European vines. The plant louse, phylloxera, first appeared here in 1912 and has not ravaged the vineyards as it did in most other European areas.

As in Greece and parts of Portugal, the soil seems to protect the vines from this scourge. To what extent the original European vines contribute to the quality of the wines is hard to say. There are as many proponents claiming that quality stems from them, as there are opponents claiming that allegiance to the original vines contributes to the unevenness of production.

Unlike the other large wine-producing areas of Germany, the cooperative movement is comparatively small here. It only handles 15% of the total production. 25% is marketed directly by large and small growers, and the remaining 60% by large and extremely modern bottlers.

The old established growers of the Mosel-Saar-Ruwer used to make a fetish of never selling any wines that had been sugared. They formed the backbone of what is now called the *"Verband Deutscher Prädikatsweingüter"* or "Association of German Prädikat Wine Estates." The word *"Prädikat"* clearly indicated that the Estates did not sell any sugared wines.

Formerly the only way to make a palatable wine in bad years was to not only add sugar but also to add water to the must in order to reduce the excessive acidity. Had the small farmer-growers not done this, they could not have survived as wine growers. The large wine growers, however, preferred to only sell their best, obtained the higher price for their best, and sold off their unripe wines to the Sparkling wine industry.

With modern technology today both the farmers and the prestigious Estates are able to make wines in lesser years without the addition of water, and many a wine so made, even though sugared, is better than the small *Kabinett* wines made formerly or even today. There is a logical reason for this. The sugar that is added to the must lacking in natural sugar is completely converted into alcohol, giving the wine balance and substance. A *Kabinett* wine that is made at the lowest permissible level of natural grape sugar often lacks this balance.

Since 1971 all the major Estates sell Estate Bottled wines to which sugar has been added prior to fermentation, i.e., *Qualitätswein*, usually under their prestigious labels; although some use secondary Estate labels or make some other differentiation in their labeling for such wine. (In this way they have become as pragmatic as the prestigious Estate owners in Bordeaux and Burgundy.)

The Mosel-Saar-Ruwer is also the last area in Germany where the yearly auctions of the famous organization called: *"Grosser Ring der Prädikatswein-Versteigerer"* create the same excitement as the auctions of the Hospice de Beaune. Such auctions set the price of the finer wines of a crop, or the price of former outstanding crops in today's market. Though only about 10% of the total production of the participating estates is submitted to these auctions, they nevertheless exert an important influence in the market for fine wines.

Mosel-Saar-Ruwers are marketed either as shipper's or as Estate bottled wines under the legends *"Erzeugerabfüllung"* or *"Aus eigenem Lesegut"* (both terms mean Estate Bottling) followed by the name of the grower. In rare cases where a grower cannot bottle his own product it may even be bottled by a shipper again with the *"Aus dem Lesegut von . . ."* followed by the name of the grower on the label.

With the exception of Liebfraumilch, there are more regional wines exported from the Mosel than from any other region of Germany. Regional Qualitätsweine such as Piesporter Michelsberg, Bereich Bernkastel, Zeller Schwarze Katz or Moselblümchen (little flower of the Mosel) have to no small extent made the reputation of the region.

Modern bottlers do not only select well made wines and blend them, but also bottle them young, and preserve their freshness and charm. In former days these wines were often marred by the unpleasant taste of sulphur. Today it is rare to find a wine so flawed. In many ways the Mosels are the German white counterparts of Beaujolais. Fragrant and fruity, light and slightly effervescent, their greatest charm is youth. They should be drunk within two years of their bottling, which means three years from the date on the label since the vintage is usually in October or November. They are bottled by late spring, May or June, in order to capture and preserve a bit of the carbon dioxide left in the wine which contributes so much to its freshness. *Spätleses* and *Ausleses* particularly from good and great vintages last longer, and often only reach their peak after three or four years. *Qualitätswein* and *Kabinett,* however, are race horses and as such youth is their greatest charm.

There is no doubt that the regional wines of the Mosel-Saar-Ruwer with names such as Bereich Bernkastel, Piesporter Michelsberg, Zeller Schwarze Katz and the like are better today than when this book was first written. Formerly, a whole 25% of a wine with a regional label could be from another region, usually the Südliche Weinstrasse of the Rheinpfalz. This obviously contributed little to the style and regional character of the blended wine and it fortunately stopped with the 1971 Wine Law.

On the Mosel-Saar-Ruwer, as elsewhere in the German Wine Regions there are some thirty "great" producers of established reputation. The names of the members of this aristocracy are mentioned in the following pages, in connection with the villages in which they have their holdings. But a list of them is interesting just the same, for it constitutes a special index of the small, complicated world of the Mosel-Saar-Ruwer.

Though all these producers have earned their reputation over many years, if not generations, some are indisputably more outstanding than others. One vineyard site may be more blessed by the sun, another grower-bottler more adept at controlling a fermentation and bottling at the exact right time. Whatever the reason, some of the justly "great" growers are even greater than others. Egon Müller and J. J. Prüm are good examples of that last bit of elegance and style that can be squeezed out of the grape in this region. When buying great wines, it is finally only quality that should count. In the complex system of the Mosel-Saar-Ruwer there are wines from reputable growers with the same name, designation and year, and yet one will be better than the other, though probably all of them good. It is this quality that has ultimately caused some half a dozen growers to price their wines higher than their neighbors.

Here is a list of the "great" growers, a list which will be supplemented by smaller dependable growers in the detailed descriptions of the main communities. No list can ever be complete and if I have neglected one or the other grower it is by oversight and not by intention:

Verwaltung der Staatlichen Weinbaudomänen (Property of the State of Rheinland-Pfalz). Very large holdings (225 acres) not all of them first class, around Trier and in the Saar valley—Avelsbach, Ockfen and Serrig.

Verwaltung der Bischöflichen Weingüter, a central cellar and administration which runs three important estates that belong to the Catholic Church as well as four small vineyards that belong to a monastery and three churches along the Mosel-Saar-Ruwer; a total of 256 acres of vines. The wines are sold under the old labels of the individual Estates, of which the main three are:

1. *Hohe Domkirche* (Cathedral of Trier). The sole owner of the Avelsbacher Altenberg, and holdings in the Scharzhofberger and the Wiltinger Rosenberg.
2. *Bischöfliches Priesterseminar* (Catholic Seminary). Major holdings in Erden, Ürzig, Dhron, Trittenheim, Kasel, Canzem, Wiltingen, and Ayl.
3. *Bischöfliches Konvikt* (heavily endowed Catholic refectory for students) with good vineyards in Piesport, Eitelsbach, Kasel, Avelsbach, Ayl and the sole owner of the Ayler Herrenberger.

Vereinigte Hospitien (charitable foundation established by Napoleon and maintaining a home for the aged and a hospital). Important holdings in Serrig, Piesport, Zeltingen, Scharzhofberger, Kanzem and Trier.

Stiftung Staatliches Friedrich Wilhelm Gymnasium (a school; one of its students was Karl Marx). Vineyards in Ockfen, Trittenheim, Neumagen Dhron, Graach, Zeltingen, Bernkastel and some lesser well known townships. 115 acres of vines.

Reichsgraf von Kesselstatt, a major Estate with first class vineyards in Kasel on the Ruwer; Oberemmel, Wiltingen, Niedermennigen and Scharzhofberger on the Saar and Piesport, Graach and Wehlen on the Mosel. Sole owner of the Josephshof in Graach, the largest property on the Mittelmosel. Almost 150 acres of vines.

Stephanus Freiherr von Schorlemer-Lieser. The von Schorlemer family were formerly the largest landowners on the Mosel. Most of the Estates have changed hands, this being the only one remaining in the family, with holdings in Wintrich, Brauneberg, Piesport and Lieser. 42.5 acres of vines. Large Landowners on the Saar and Ruwer:

Egon Müller-Scharzhof. Owner of the largest and best site in the Scharzhofberger as well as other vineyards in Wiltingen. 21 acres of vines. Egon Müller distinguishes his outstanding Prädikat wines with a Golden Capsule; thereby offering for instance a regular Scharzhofberger Auslese and one with a Gold Capsule which might be 50% more expensive and 50% better. He also owns the Estate of Le Gallais in Kanzem.

Apollinar Joseph Koch. Holdings in the Scharzhofberger and first class vineyards in Wiltingen. 34 acres of vines.

Von Hövel, Eberhard von Kunow. Sole owner of the Oberemmeler Hütte, as well as vineyards in the Scharzhofberger, and other sites in Oberemmel. 30 acres of vines.

Dr. Fischer. Foremost producer in Ockfen, with 17½ acres in the Ockfener Bockstein. Vineyards in Saarburg and sole owner of the Wawerner Herrenberger. 50 acres of vines.

Adolf Rheinart Erben. Vineyards in Ockfen, Wiltingen and Ayl. 37 acres of vines.

Staatsminister a.D. Otto Van Volxem. Vineyards in Oberemmel, Wiltingen and the Scharzhofberger. 15 acres of vines.

Weingut Herrenberg, Bert Simon. First class estate, most vineyards on the Saar and only a few on the Ruwer. Sole owner of Serriger Herrenberg, Serriger Würtzberg and Staadter Maximiner Prälat. Also leases an Estate called Fritz Patheiger with vineyards in Niedermennig, Eitelsbach and Mertesdorf. 65 acres of vines.

Schloss Saarstein, Dieter Ebert. Sole owner of Serriger, Schloss Saarsteiner and vineyards in Wiltingen and Saarbrug. 21 acres of vines.

Forstmeister Geltz Erben. Vineyards in Ockfen and Saarburg. 22 acres of vines.

Von Schubert. Major producer on the Ruwer; sole owner of the Maximin Grunhäuser Bruderberg, Abtsberg and Herrenberg vineyards. 80 acres of vines.

Eitelsbacher Karthäuserhof. Major producer in Eitelsbach and sole owner of the Karthauserhofberger Kronenberg, Sang and Burgberg. The present owner Werner Tyrell is the President of the German growers association. 45 acres of vines.

Thiergarten Georg Fritz von Nell. Major owner in Trier, Ayl and Wiltingen. Sole owner of the Trierer Benediktinerberg and the Trierer Kurfürstenhofberg. 100 acres of vines.

Wwe. Dr. H. Thanisch. One of the owners of the Bernkasteler Doktor vineyards and first class sites in Bernkastel, Graach, Wehlen, Brauneberg and Lieser. 34 acres of vines.

Deinhard. The largest owner of the original Bernkasteler Doktor and other vineyard properties in Bernkastel and Graach. 27 acres of vines.

Joh. Jos. Prüm. Major producer in Wehlen with first class sites in Graach, Bernkastel and Zeltingen. Owns the best segment of the Wehlener Sonnenuhr and is justly famous for its wines. 34 acres of vines.

There are a large number of Estates under the names *Prüm* or *Zach. Bergweiler-Prüm Erben,* all related to the original Prüm. They are of some importance in their area and will be discussed under the communities in which they have vineyards. The most important ones are *Zach. Bergweiler-Prüm Erben Weingut Dr. Pauly-Bergweiler* and *Dr. Zach Bergweiler* in Wehlen, *Hermann Thaprich* in Bernkastel, *Dr. Melsheimer,* Traben Trarbach.

The Mosel-Saar-Ruwer is divided into five Bereiche and 20 Grosslagen. Its 192 wine producing villages have a total of 525 individual vineyards. Here are the five Bereiche:

1. Bereich Zell, also called Untermosel. It covers the river from Zell of Schwarze Katz fame to the outskirts of Koblenz, where the Mosel joins the Rhine.

2. Bereich Bernkastel, also called Mittelmosel. This stretch, from Kenn to Briedel, contains the renowned vineyard towns that have made the Mosel famous; towns such as Erden, Ürzig, Zeltingen, Wehlen, Graach, Bernkastel, Brauneberg and finally Piesport.

3. Bereich Saar-Ruwer. It includes all the vineyards on the Saar and Ruwer as well as the ones around Trier that are part of the Grosslage Römerlay, Grosslage of the Ruwer.

4. Bereich Obermosel. It is largely planted in Elbling, a grape variety that has existed on the Mosel since the Roman times. The robust variety produces large amounts of neutral wine with high acidity most of which is used for making Sekt.

5. Bereich Moseltor (which literally means gate of the Mosel). A small Bereich that should have been incorporated into the Obermosel,

since they both produce wines largely from the Elbling though, here as on the Obermosel, there is also some Müller-Thurgau.

With very few exceptions this chapter will deal only with the Mittelmosel and the Saar-Ruwer, the two Bereiche that have given the valley its world reputation. Before we start with the Mittelmosel it is just as well to talk about the river and its people. The little vineyard towns of the Saar and the Ruwer and the Mittelmosel are strung along their respective rivers like a string of beads. The high, green vine-covered slopes which have made their fame are divided into several plots or Lagen, each one with its special name, often shared by five or six or even more producers. In most cases there is no visible line, certainly no wall or natural boundary, which separates one Lage from another, but the growers know very well where one begins and the other ends, and the lines on the whole are scrupulously respected. All of the really outstanding vineyards have been listed in the following pages, under the heading of the village to which they belong.

It would be hard to write anything in the way of a paragraph or two which would do justice to the Mosel's unique beauty and its charm. The Mosel's best publicity agents are those that travel, in bottle, the world over, and perhaps the highest compliment is to say that the country is as lovely as its wines.

TIIE MITTELMOSEL—BEREICH BERNKASTEL

Though the term Mittelmosel or central Mosel has existed as long as its fine wines, it was not clearly defined until 1971 when the great re-classification of the German vineyards decided exactly which villages and vineyards should belong to that stretch of the river which under the name Mittelmosel has always enjoyed the reputation of producing the best wines.

The present definition covers the Mosel from Kenn to Briedel, both villages rather unknown for their wines. Frank Schoonmaker originally put the Mittelmosel into a shorter stretch of the river, between Mehring and Enkirch leaving out the villages on either end that have not particularly contributed to the reputation of the area. He included all the great villages and it is as well to follow his thoughts on the matter:

This little book does not pretend to be a geography. It is a book about wine, and with a bow of apology to geologists and other learned folk, I have preferred to define the Mittelmosel in terms of its vine-yards and its wine. Wine, after all, is the Valley's life and its liveli-hood; with one or two wholly minor exceptions, all of the really great wines produced on the banks of the Mosel come from its central sec-tion. Arbitrarily, then, for us, the Mittelmosel is the Mosel's district of great wines, it being understood that the equally great wines of the tributary Saar and Ruwer are to be considered separately and apart.

The Mittelmosel thus begins about ten Roman miles northeast of Trier—I say "Roman miles" since perhaps the best starting point is Mehring, and Mehring is just next door to the little village of Detzem, which takes its name from what was once the tenth milestone (*ad decimum lapidem*) on the old Roman road from Trier to Mainz. It ends at Enkirch, the last of some thirty villages which produce outstanding wine, a dozen or more out of the thirty being internationally famous. It is certainly one of the most interesting, as it is one of the most spec-tacularly beautiful, of all the wine-producing districts of the world.

Mehring is only about fifteen miles from Enkirch as the crow flies. And yet by road or by railway or by shallow-draft river steamer the two are almost forty miles apart. There is no short-cut and no easy way round. No reluctant country schoolboy ever took so devious a route on his way to school as the Mosel on its way to join the Rhine at Coblenz, and perforce the road and the railway follow the river, since the steep valley walls are often six hundred to a thousand feet high. The river winds in loops and hairpin turns—its general direction is northeast, but the water is often running due southwest, or northwest or southeast, for that matter. About half of the slopes—never more—are covered with vineyards. All of these face more or less south—west-south-west to east-south-east being the extreme limits. They are extraordinarily steep, so steep that until recently very few of them could be worked by horse, let alone by tractor. Every corner and every shelf, be it under a cliff or on top of a cliff, that faces south or can be made to face south by skillful grading, has its quota of vines.

The reason is very simple. At this northern latitude grapes will only ripen with a more-or-less southern exposure, and they will only produce fine wine if they face practically due south, and are protected from the cold winds that blow, as late as May and as early as Septem-ber, off the cold uplands of the Hunsrück and the Eifel. ("The grape-vine," says a German proverb, "is a child of the sun; it loves the hills and hates the wind." *"Die Rebe ist ein Sonnenkind, sie liebt den Berg und hasst den Wind,"*)

Planting vines in a typical Mosel vineyard.

The soil, on the whole, is almost as forbidding as the climate. The hills are mostly slate, and slate for roofing can often be mined in the vineyards themselves. Virtually nothing will grow on this soil except the vine, and among vines only the Riesling does well—hardy, shy-bearing, late-bearing, hard to cultivate. Fortunately, it is one of the two best white wine grapes in the world, the Chardonnay or Pinot Chardonnay of Burgundy and Champagne being the other.

The labor is hand labor and there is no end to it. Every vine has its stake, an eight-foot sturdy support of peeled pine, and there are generally well over three thousand to the acre, all carried up from the road at the foot of the vineyard on the backs of men, like the manure which the vines must have in order to live, and the chips of slate, spread under the vines to hold the sun's warmth in autumn. These are annually washed down by the winter's rains, and annually replaced in the spring. At the vintage season, the grapes are brought down to the road in the same fashion, in great cone-shaped hods, but all year long the traffic is in the other and more difficult direction—tanks of copper sulphate spray (which gives an extraordinary almost sea-green color to the vine leaves in late summer), stakes, slatechips, new vines for replanting, cord to tie the vines.

A good deal of this enormous yearly load goes up four or five hundred feet, by paths so steep that they are often quite literally stairways. With perhaps the single exception of the vineyards of the Vaudois, on the northern shore of Lake Geneva east of Lausanne, there are surely no wines on earth which require such an unconscionable amount of human labor per ton of grapes, or per bottle of wine.

Today the great rearrangement of nature (*Flurbereinigung*) has improved the backbreaking labor conditions and has simplified the cultivation of the vine. Roadways were cut into the hillsides to provide access to the peaks of the vineyards by tractor and an ingenious system of pulleys was invented to facilitate mechanical plowing between the rows of vines. The roads also allow the tourist some breathtaking views of the river and the never-ending vineyards, views that were formerly reserved for the hardy climber with a very sure footing.

You will go a long way before you find happier people, or people who take a greater pride in what they do, than those who cultivate their vines and make their pale, delicate, wonderful wine along the Mittelmosel. There are vintage festivals in almost every village in the fall; the villages are clean and the cellars immaculate, and the *Winzer* are a long, long way from being sorry for themselves. Like most people having to do with wine, they are extremely hospitable, and few things seem to give them greater pleasure than a compliment paid to their wine by a discriminating stranger.

The countryside, along the whole length of the river, is remarkably beautiful, and its air is one of quiet and pervading peace. Nothing on the Mittelmosel ever seems quite as important as the quality of the current year's vintage and perhaps, in the long run, nothing is.

By car, the trip from Detzem to Enkirch, which can be made in anywhere from an hour to a week, is one of the most memorable in Germany. Certainly few wine-producing countries have the same combination of picturesqueness and color and great wine.

All the vineyards of the Mittelmosel are in the Bereich Bernkastel so that when you see that name on a label you can assume that it is a blend of wines from the Mittelmosel. It is usually a shipper's own blend of Mittelmosel wine prepared for his customers and it is likely to have a certain consistency.

Here starting upriver are the main wine-producing villages with their vineyards, *Grosslagen,* growers and a rating from one to three stars (*) for the villages with the best wines.

GROSSLAGE PROBSTBERG

Mehring (1000 acres of vineyards). It can hardly be classified as part of the Mittelmosel. Its thin, short lived wines have nothing in common with the great aristocrats of Piesport, Bernkastel and Wehlen. The *Friedrich Wilhelm Gymnasium* is the leading producer and the Zellerberg is regarded as the best vineyard.

GROSSLAGE ST. MICHAEL

Detzem (450 acres of vineyards). More of a milestone than anything else. The best wines are only fair.

Thörnisch (575 acres of vineyards). Produces nothing of consequence except in the very greatest years. *Thörnischer Ritsch* and *Thörnischer Enggass* are its best known vineyards and wines. *Adams, Ludes* and *Botzet-Zisch* are dependable producers.

Klüsserath (875 acres of vineyards). The wines of Klüsserath are rarely exported as they enjoy a certain popularity in Germany. The main grower is the Friedrich Wilhelm Gymnasium. There are only two vineyards; the better known *Klüsserather Brüderschaft* and the *Klüsserather Königsberg.*

Leiwen (1,125 acres of vineyards). Wines from Leiwen in a great year can be quite extraordinary. The best vineyard, the *Leiwener Laurentiuslay,* is shared with neighboring Köwerich.

GROSSLAGE MICHELSBERG

The area from Sehlem to Minheim is all in the Grosslage Michelsberg. It includes the famous wine producing towns of Piesport, Neumagen, Dhron, and Trittenheim. It also includes less known villages called Sehlem, Hetzerath, Rivenich and Minheim who are more likely to market their wines under the prestigious name of *Piesporter Micheslberg* than under their own.

** *Trittenheim* (750 acres of vineyards). Caught in a hairpin loop of the river, its vineyards crowned with a picturesque little chapel dedicated to St. Lawrence (the Laurentiusberg), Trittenheim is the first major stone in the necklace of the Mittelmosel. Its extremely engaging and attractive wines are fresh and light, early ready and not particularly long lived. The *Bischöfliches Priesterseminar,* is the best known grower, but the *Friedrich Wilhelm Gymnasium, Josef Milz Jr., Dr. Ronde* and a few others are also worthy of confidence. The outstanding vineyards are:

Trittenheimer Apotheke   Trittenheimer Altärchen

* *Neumagen* (875 acres of vineyards; this includes Dhron since the two villages were consolidated). An interesting little village, dating from Roman days and said to be the oldest wine-producing town in Germany. Charming wines, not unlike those of Trittenheim, but in some instances with even more bouquet. *Dünweg, Dr. Ronde* and *Milz* are reliable producers. The best known vineyards are:

Neumagener Rosengärtchen   Neumagener Engelgrube
Neumagener Laudamusberg   Neumagener Sonnenuhr

** *Dhron.* Another sound and honorable Weinberg, although not one of the truly great ones; here again you can count on the bottlings of the *Priesterseminar* and on those of *Dünweg, Dr. Ronde, Erz* and *Lehnert-Matheus.* The best known vineyards are *Dhroner Hofberger* and *Dhroner Roterd*

*** *Piesport* (1,250 acres of vineyards). The bustling town, hemmed between the river and vineyard is in quality and quantity one of the most important towns of the Mosel. Behind the town, and on both sides, the high precipitous hill that forms the north bank of the Mosel curves like the inside of a vast green bowl; its steep and rocky face, looking south, is covered with a mile-long expanse of unbroken vineyards. With such an exposure Piesport could hardly fail to produce fine wines, and there are many experts who will describe the Piesporters of great vintages as the Queens of the Mosel. Certainly there are very few that are better for they are wonderfully delicate and fragrant wines, never heavy, never coarse, with an incomparable distinction of their own. In great years they may be the greatest Mosels of them all, but in wet years they are usually less good than some of their famous neighbors.

The main producers are *Vereinigte Hospitien, Bischöfliches Konvikt, Tobias, von Kesselstatt, Dr. Hain,* and a few smaller dependable ones—*Haart, Lehnert, Weller, Reuscher, Veit, Franzen* and *Kettern.* By far the most famous vineyard is the *Goldtröpfchen* which is in the center of that huge green bowl and catches the reflected sunshine from the river. Also a considerable amount of wine is marketed under the name of the *Grosslage Piesporter Michelsberg,* since many growers have a few rows of vines in several vineyards and would find it too complicated to sell their wines in small lots under several names.

Here are the main vineyards:

Piesporter Goldtröpfchen   Piesporter Treppchen
Piesporter Günterslay   Piesporter Falkenberg

Mienheim (475 acres of vineyards). Small wines usually sold in bulk, and perhaps some as *Piesporter Michelsberg. Rosenberg* and *Burglay* are the best known vineyards. The village also sells some wines under the name of *Piesporter Günterslay,* which is a vineyard that Mienheim shares with Piesport. Piesport is challenging this practice but the matter has not yet been decided by the courts.

GROSSLAGE KURFÜRSTLAY

*   *Wintrich* (675 acres of vineyards). From a distance, the vineyards of Wintrich look like rocky stairways, with buttressed terrace walls holding up little green patches of vines. The wines have their full share of bouquet and breed, but are sometimes hard and lacking in charm except in great vintage years. *Stephanus Von Schorlemer-Lieser* is the best known producer and there is a good *Winzergenossenschaft* called St. Stephanus and many good smaller growers.

The best known vineyards are:

Wintricher Ohligsberg   Wintricher Sonnseite
Wintricher Grosser Herrgott   Wintricher Stefanslay

*   *Kesten* (313 acres of vineyards). You are not likely to see the name of Kesten on a wine list. One vineyard, however, the Paulinshofberg, is justly famous. It belongs to Franz Josef Liell of Bernkastel, its wines are sold as *Kestener Paulinshofberger,* and they bring high prices.

*** *Brauneberg* (758 acres of vineyards). Until fifty or sixty years ago this little town was known as Dusemond (from the Latin *mons dulcis,* "Sweet mountain"—supposedly so called because of the excellence and sweetness of its wines). In the middle of the last century Brauneberger was the most celebrated and highly prized of all the wines of the Mosel. But fashions change in wines as in so many other things and Brauneberger today no longer rates in popularity with Piesport, Bernkastel and Wehlen. Nevertheless the wines are remarkable—together with the Zeltingers, they are about the fullest-bodied of all the Mosels, fine, rich, with surprising authority and long life. They are particularly good in wet years and less so in dry ones. The vineyard slope, the Brauneberg, or "brown hill," is almost as impressive as Piesport's, not curving but long, straight and high, and facing slightly east of south.

There are many good producers—*Stephanus von Schorlemer-Lieser, Ferdinand Haag,* the *St. Nikolaus Hospital, Licht-Bergweiler, Karp-Schreiber Conrad* and *Wwe. Dr. H. Thanisch.*

The vineyards led by the famous Juffer and Juffer Sonnenuhr are:

Brauneberger Juffer	Brauneberger Juffer Sonnenuhr
Brauneberger Mandelgraben	Brauneberger Kammer
Brauneberger Klostergarten	Brauneberger Hasenläufer

Mülheim (215 acres of vineyards). Good secondary wines.

Veldenz (350 acres of vineyards). Not in the Mosel Valley proper but some two miles to the east, in a tributary valley, or *seitental*. In good years, and in good years only, it produces wines of remarkable freshness and bouquet that deserve to be better known than they are and that somewhat recall those of the Saar and the Ruwer. A *Veldenzer Kirchberg* of a good year is worth looking for.

* *Lieser* (Some 500 acres of vineyards). Like most of the "near greats" of the Mittelmosel, Lieser has everything necessary to deserve top rank—except full southern exposure. The village consists of a few houses and an imposing 19th Century Schloss which belongs to the Von Schorlemer family, important wine-producers and bottlers. The St. Nikolaus Hospital of Bernkastel-Kues also has important holdings, and the two vineyards worthy of note are in the *Grosslage Kurfürstlay: Niederer Schlossberg* and in the *Grosslage Beerenlay,* which is exclusively composed of Lieser vineyards: *Lieserer Niederberg-Helden.*

*** *Bernkastel* (425 acres of vineyards). This is about the most celebrated single name of the Mosel, though whether its wines on the whole are better than those of Piesport and Wehlen and Zeltingen is, I think, rather open to question. But few towns in Germany command such a magnificent view over river and vineyard, and few towns in the whole Mosel Valley are so quaint and charming; thanks to these advantages and to its excellent hotels and collection of picturesque little Weinstuben, or restaurants, both in Bernkastel and in Kues, directly across the river, its good road connections, and the well-known hospitality of its vintners, it has become a tourist center of considerable importance—the Rüdesheim, so to speak, of the Mosel. Meanwhile, of course, the fame of its Doktor vineyard has gone round the world.

Perhaps *Bernkasteler Doktor's* reputation (like that of many another wine) owes as much to the fact that the name is amusing and easy to remember as to the fact that the wine is good. The exceptional favor which it has long enjoyed in England dates, it is said, from a visit which Edward VII made to Bad Homburg, where he tasted the wine, liked it and ordered some "for home." But in the past few years it has become equally popular in America, and I rather suspect that over half the total production now crosses the Atlantic, where people still seem willing and able to pay the extraordinarily high price which it invariably commands, even in years of mediocre quality.

The three original owners were Deinhard, Lauerburg and Thanisch. Under the new German Wine Law of 1971 no vineyard property could be less than 12.5 acres. The Doktor vineyard, being under the minimum, was enlarged and the new vineyard is barely 12.5 acres and now has 11 owners. The original three owners are contesting this enlargement in court but the final decision on its size and owners may still take years to come.

During the last 20 years, I must have tasted Bernkasteler Doktor at least two hundred times including a number of times at Karl Heinz Lauerburg's, tasting many vintages one against the other. I have never been able to detect the famous "smoky flavor," which some connoisseurs claim unerringly to perceive. Smoky or not, the wine does have a somewhat special taste, and is usually first rate. There are, however, other Mosels that I would class at least on a par with it, or above it, and several other vineyards in the town of Bernkastel deserve, it seems to me, almost equal rank. The wines of the best vineyards of Bernkastel combine an elegance with substance.

The main reputable growers of Bernkastel are *Deinhard, Thanisch, Lauerburg, Heidemanns-Bergweiler, Zach. Bergweiler-Prüm Erben Dr. Pauly-Bergweiler, Thaprich, Joh. Jos. Prüm, Pfarrkirche St. Michael, St. Nikolaushospital, Friedrich Wilhelm Gymnasium* and the *Heilig Geist Armenspende Stiftung*. Bernkastel also has a well run *Cooperative Zentralkellerei* which vinifies wines from the whole Mosel-Saar-Ruwer region.

The best vineyards are in the Grosslage Badstube, which is reserved for five of the top vineyards and is one of the smallest *Grosslagen* on the Mosel. It is used extensively by the finest growers for their Bernkastel wine, preferring to blend the wines from small parcels in different vineyards than laboriously market small lots of wines from each individual one. As such the *Bernkasteler Badstube* should rank with all but the best of the Bernkastelers.

Here are the individual vineyards in the Badstube *Grosslage* in order of quality:

Bernkasteler Doctor   Bernkasteler Lay
Bernkasteler Bratenhöfchen   Bernkasteler Graben
               Bernkasteler Matheisbildchen

(Note: Some parts of the *Graben* are outstanding, whereas others are less good, which explains the fourth place in my ranking.) The vineyards in the Grosslage Kurfürstlay, that Bernkastel shares with 10 other communities including Brauneberg, are less outstanding, yet wines produced there are usually first class.

The vineyards in that Grosslage are:

Bernkasteler Johannisbrünnchen   Bernkasteler Schlossberg
Bernkasteler Stephanus-Rosengärtchen   Bernkasteler Rosenberg
Bernkasteler Kardinalsberg   Bernkasteler Weissenstein

This latter designation is sometimes sold as Kueser Weissenstein (the name of that part of Bernkastel which is on the left bank of the river).

The Josephshof near Graach.

GROSSLAGE MÜNZLAY

*** *Graach* (300 acres of vineyards). At Bernkastel the winding Mosel, running generally southwest to northeast, performs a major convolution and sets out northwestward. Unlike the vineyards of Trittenheim and Piesport and Brauneberg, which are on the left or north bank of the river, those of Graach and Wehlen and even Bernkastel are on the right or south bank. They overlook the river and face south; this sounds illogical, and it most certainly is.

There is nothing strange or wrong, however, about the wines of Graach—they are typical and lovely Mittelmosels, well-balanced, fragrant and fine. The three best vineyards, however, differ in style. The Graacher Domprobsts are heavy for a Mosel, the Graacher Himmelreichs have a finesse all their own, and the Josephshöfers which are sold without the name of the town and belong to the Kesselstatt Estate, resemble more the wines of Wehlen than those of Graach. They are rich and full-bodied rather than sprightly, big and fine rather than delicate. Graach, like Piesport makes superb wines in great and good years, and like Piesport makes less good wines in wet years.

• The leading producers, besides *Kesselstatt*, are *J. J. Prüm, von Schorlemer, Peter Prüm, S. A. Prüm Erben, Dr. Weins Erben,* the *St. Nikolaus Hospital,* the *Pfarrkirche Bernkastel,* the *Friedrich Wilhelm Gymnasium, Kees-Kieren, Otto Pauly, Ernst Kass, Adams Bergweiler, Pauli-Combali* and *Zach. Bergweiler-Prüm Erben, Dr. Pauly Bergweiler, Dr. Loosen.*

The best Lagen, as described above, are:

Graacher Domprobst   Graacher Himmelreich
Josephshöfer

*** *Wehlen* (398 acres of vineyards). Fifty brief years ago, Wehlen was considered by most experts to be nothing more than a *Guter Weinort,* a village of good wines that ranked considerably below Graach and by no means in a class with Bernkastel and Brauneberg. Today its best wines command higher prices even than Bernkasteler Doktor, and most German *Feinschmecker* will tell you that it is the best wine-producing village of the whole Mittelmosel. This change is largely due to the efforts of a single family called Prüm. What the DuPonts are to Delaware, the Prüms are, in their own remarkable way, to Wehlen. Their big, comfortable, old-fashioned stone houses stand one beside the other along the river, and facing them, beyond the Mosel's only suspension bridge, are the steep vineyards which have made the family fortune and its name.

In the center of these vineyards, between Graach and Zeltingen, a cliff has been cut away and painted to form an enormous white *Sonnenuhr,* or sundial. Year in and year out, for some three decades, the wines from Wehlen's Sonnenuhr vineyard have consistently brought the highest prices of any wines of the Mosel, and I think deservedly so. At their best, the Wehleners have no superiors and few equals—flowery, well balanced, with an almost supernatural combination of delicacy and richness, they are perfection itself.

Of course, this is by no means to say that all Wehleners are outstanding (for they are not) or consistently better than their neighbors, which is certainly doubtful. But the sign of Wehlen plus the name of Prüm on a wine label is what an astrologer would call a favorable combination, and it is usually the portent of something that will be well above the average when the cork is drawn.

The leading producers (mostly Prüms) are *Johann Josef Prüm,*

Sebastian Prüm, S. A. Prüm Erben, Peter Prüm, S. A. Prüm Erben.
There are four estates named *Zach. Bergweiler Prüm Erben; Dr.
Pauly Bergweiler, Dr. Adams, Dr. Heidemann* and *Dr. Pauli. C. H.
Berres Erben, Dr. Weins Erben, Hauth-Kerpen, Dietz, Baumler-
Becker, St. Nikolaus Hospital, Kesselstatt, Dr. Loosen.* The best vine-
yards are:

Wehlener Sonnenuhr   Wehlener Klosterberg
Wehlener Nonnenberg

Note: In the 1971 reorganization, the Sonnenuhr vineyard was greatly
enlarged. (This has been challenged in the courts and the exact border
may well change once a decision has been handed down.) J. J. Prüm
had the best parcels of land in the original vineyard and still has the
best parcels in the new one. The wines prove the point. He, like a
number of other Mosel-Saar-Ruwer growers, makes several qualities
of *Auslese,* the lesser one beng bottled with a short, the best with a
long gold capsule. He reserves the J. J. Prüm label for *Prädikat* wines
(*Kabinett* and better) and the Weingut Dr. Prüm label for his QbA.

The sundial in the Zeltinger Sonnenuhr (upper right).

*** *Zeltingen* (625 acres of vineyards) This is a rather dull and quiet little town, dwarfed and overshadowed by the incredible steep expanse of six hundred acres of vineyard that rise behind it. Its production is large and certainly a vast amount of "Zeltinger" is made and sold which could hardly be described as distinguished even by the most charitable of critics. On the other hand, there is probably not a single village in the whole Mosel Valley which produces wines which on the average are as good as those of Zeltingen, and I am not sure that any village, including Wehlen, produces wines better than Zeltingen's best. To get the best, needless to say, you must ask not for "Zeltinger" but for the town name plus that of a better-than-average vineyard, and for an Erzeugerabfüllung, though the name of the bottler is less important here than in most other wine-producing towns. A good many of the *Bauern,* or small producers, bottle their own wines in Zeltingen, and these quite often have the double charm of being good and most reasonably priced.

Fairly full-bodied for a Mosel, the typical Zeltinger of a vineyard such as Himmelreich or Schlossberg has a combination of qualities which is truly extraordinary—softness, breed, bouquet and a charm which even those who are not Mosel-lovers will find hard to resist. The wines of Zeltingen are as good if not better than the wines of Wehlen in wet years, and in any year they seem to mature faster than those of Wehlen, Graach, Bernkastel and Piesport.

There are 8 or 9 great producers: *J. J. Prüm, Ehses-Berres, Ehses-Geller, Merrem, Friedrich Wilhelm Gymnasium, C. H. Berres Erben, Dr. Pauly Bergweiler, Vereinigte Hospitien and von Schorlemer.* Among the *Bauern,* or farmers, with small holdings in excellent vineyards, it would perhaps be well to note the numerous members of a family called *Ames* (pronounced ah-mes). The label of the *Frühmess Stiftung* can also be counted on.

There are but four vineyards left after the consolidation of 1971 which are in order of importance:

Zeltinger Himmelreich   Zeltinger Sonnenuhr (a continuation of the
                         Wehlen vineyard of the same name).
Zeltinger Schlossberg   Zeltinger Deutschherrenberg

Note: Not an inconsiderable amount of wine comes from Zeltingen under the *Grosslage* name of Zeltinger Münzlay.

GROSSLAGE SCHWARZLAY

*** *Erden* (300 acres of vineyards). This is a small village on the right bank of the river. Its superb steep vineyards (the best is called Treppchen, or "little stairway," and that is an understatement) adjoin those of Ürzig, and are situated on the opposite side of the river from the village, with the exception of its largest vineyard, Busslay, which is on the right bank.

The vineyards are as vertiginous as any on the Mosel, and one can only be astonished at the patience and the determination of those who have created and those who cultivate them. To open a bottle of a great Erdener of a year like 1959 or 1976 is to feel that perhaps the infinite and unending labor of the Winzer or vintner has not been wasted, for the wines in great years are wholly magnificent. Even in relatively poor years, I have tasted *Auslese* and *Beerenauslese* wines from Erden which were extraordinary.

The wines of Erden are seen less and less in America, which is a pity, since an *Erdener Treppchen* from a good producer in a good year can hold the candle to any bottle of wine from the Mosel.

The best producers are: *Bischöfliches Priesterseminar, Christoffel, C. H. Berres Erben, Peter Loosen Erben., Schwaab-Scherr* and *Orthmann-Matty.*

The best vineyards are:

Erdener Treppchen   Erdener Prälat

the others: Erdener Busslay and Erdener Herrenberg

** *Ürzig* (150 acres in vineyards). After Zeltingen, the Mosel abruptly changes direction once more, and resumes its normal and proper northeasterly course toward Koblenz. The vineyards of Ürzig, like those of Erden, which are just next door, are therefore on the left, or north, bank of the river. They are among the most spectacular of the whole Mosel Valley: most of them mere patches of green, carved out of the face of a cliff-like hill which is almost the color of brick. There is said to be a good deal of iron in the soil of Ürzig, and the wines, in any case, have a quality all their own. They mature rather slowly and require a good deal of special care and handling in the cellar before bottling; like the wines of the Saar they are often slightly spritzig, which means that they have an almost imperceptible tendency to be naturally sparkling; they are sharp and hard in poor years, but in good years they have an odd and wonderful spiciness and piquancy (the Germans call them *würzig* and *pikant*) which makes them, for an expert, among the easiest to recognize and place of all German wines. Unlike Zeltinger, Ürziger is by no means a name to look for on less expensive bottles, but an *Ürziger Würzgarten* of a great vintage, particularly if it is a *Spätlese* or an *Auslese,* can hold its own against the best, and can be one of the greatest wines of Germany. The best producers are: *Ewald Pfeifer, Peter Nicolay, Eymael,* the *Bischöfliches Priesterseminar, C. H. Berres Erben, Dr. P. Loosen Erben* and *Christoffel Erben.* There are but two vineyards:

Ürziger Würzgarten   Ürziger Goldwingert

Kinheim (300 acres of vineyards). Wines of no great distinction and quality. The vineyards are Kinheimer Rosenberg and Kinheimer Hubertuslay.

Kröv (875 acres of vineyards). Another mediocre vineyard town, although a very ancient and a very pretty one. Like Zell, of which more later, it has acquired a certain rather doubtful fame on account of an unusual and comic wine label. The label in question reads Kröver Nacktarsch, or "naked bottom," and shows a boy being spanked, with his pants down. The wines of Kröv are better than the label. Nacktarsch is the Grosslage which covers all the vineyards of Kröv and I dare say many wines are easier to sell with this colorful label and name than under the individual vineyards name from which it was harvested. The vineyards in Kröv are:

Kröver Burglay   Kröver Herrenberg
Kröver Steffensberg   Kröver Letterlay
Kröver Kirchlay   Kröver Paradies

*   *Traben-Trarbach* (790 acres of vineyard). In reality, two villages, as the name would indicate—Traben on the left bank of the Mosel, and Trarbach on the right. Both little towns are picturesque, and are important tourist centers; and both are important in the Mosel wine trade as well. In general, the wines of Traben are small, but fresh and agreeable and charming; those of Trarbach have a little more authority, and in particularly good years a fine bouquet and a certain real distinction. *Dr. Melsheimer* is a reliable producer, and the following vineyard names are worth noting:

Trarbacher Schlossberg   Trarbacher Ungsberg
Trarbacher Hühnerberg   Trarbacher Königsberg

The Mosel at Kröv.

Enkirch (525 acres of vineyards). Enkirch marks the end of the district of great wines. For although there are vineyards along the slopes all the way down to Koblenz, the best of these hardly yield anything better than *Konsum-Weine*—those fresh and fragrant little carafe wines that are drunk when less than a year old. There are a few exceptions, of which Valwig, Winningen and Zell are the most important; the first two produce some really excellent bottles in great years, and Zeller Schwarze Katz, with the familiar black cat on its label, is one of the most famous of all German wines, although a long way from one of the best. (Zell is one of the largest wine producing towns on the Mosel with 1,570 acres of vineyards. 98% of the vines are Riesling and with the ever-increasing popularity of the Zeller Schwarze Katz the vintners have made money which they have used to make even better wines.) Enkirch, however, is another matter—its delicate wines are true products of the Mittelmosel, and I have tasted some that were genuinely outstanding. The better vineyards:

Enkircher Steffensberg   Enkircher Batterieberg
Enkircher Herrenberg   Enkircher Monteneubel

THE SAAR (as described by Frank Schoonmaker)

The Mosel's largest tributary, which hurries down to join it west of Trier, is the silvery, winding and shallow Saar. Here in Germany, hardly more than a stone's throw from the border of Luxembourg, this famous little river runs through a green and smiling countryside—all fresh meadows and fruit trees and wide expanses of steep hillside vineyards—and it looks like anything but what it is: the stream that drains the celebrated Saar Basin, which is one of the most important centers of heavy industry in Western Europe.

Here, the blast furnaces and rolling mills of the upper Saar seem a thousand miles away, and from picturesque Saarburg, with its ruined castle, all the way down to the rather dreary little town of Conz, where it meets the Mosel, the river runs past a succession of sleepy villages. On every slope that faces south, or nearly south, you can see the orderly green pattern of perfectly tended vines.

This whole district was nevertheless the scene of heavy fighting during the early spring of 1945. The anti-tank defenses, the so-called "dragon's teeth" of the Siegfried Line, ran through some of the best vineyards, and when I visited the Saar for the last time before the War, in the summer of 1939, pill-boxes were even being constructed in the gardens of my good friend, Herr Koch, of Wiltingen. I remember that I congratulated another friend, in Oberemmel, on the completion of a magnificent new barn, which looked most impressive from a distance; he winked and whispered to me that it was a very wonderful barn indeed, with "walls of concrete one and a half meters thick."

When I returned in 1946, the pill-boxes, like the "barn," had been destroyed, but the whole Saar Valley was still littered with the ugly debris of war. There were still brass cartridge cases in the grass along the roadsides, and there was still a fighter plane which had crashed and miraculously not burned, smack in the center of the Scharzhofberg vineyard. A good many of the villages had been damaged by shellfire, many of the vines overrun by tanks, and there were plenty of others that had been neglected and seemed lost beyond repair.

Fortunately, Nature, when aided by a good deal of hard work on the part of humans, has a way of covering and obliterating these scars. Today the Saar Valley looks very much as it did when I first visited its cellars over forty years ago. Most of my old friends (or their sons) are at work in their reconstructed vineyards; the War is largely forgotten, and the best Saar wines are magnificent, just as they were when I first made their acquaintance in the 1930's.

These wines of the Saar, it may be well to point out, are not to everybody's taste. The Germans have a saying that "in poor years the Saarwein is a beggar and in good years a noble lord." To be more specific, they are even more subject than the other wines of the Mosel to the caprices of weather and season. The Saar Valley is a cold little land of late spring and frequent sudden frosts; even in mid-May and early October it has far more than its share of hailstorms and icy days. At least three years out of ten produce wines that have to be "sugared" and many can only be used for the manufacture of *Sekt*, or sparkling wine. In two or three more years per decade, the wine is so hard and sharp (the Germans call it *stahlig*, or steely, and the adjective is well chosen) that only the local enthusiasts can tolerate it. Perhaps two other years out of ten yield wine that is sound and good but not extraordinary. But once, twice, or at most three times in a decade, nature is kind. And in such years the Saar produces a certain number of wines which are, to my palate, the noblest and most remarkable white wines in the world.

This, I realize, is not something one should say lightly. Wine experts, after the fashion of sailors, are supposed to have their loves in every country, and to promise undying fidelity to each one, impartially, every time they taste it. But with all due respect to Chateau d'Yquem and to Montrachet, to Marcobrunner and Imperial Tokay, I still say, give me a perfect Scharzhofberger (or a Wiltinger or an Ockfener) of a great year.

In these great and exceedingly rare wines of the Saar, there is a combination of qualities which I can perhaps best describe as indescribable—austerity coupled with delicacy and extreme finesse, an incomparable bouquet, a clean, very attractive hardness tempered by a wealth of fruit and flavor which is overwhelming—and all this in a wine which hardly exceeds 10% of alcohol by volume (whereas Montrachet and Yquem are rarely under 13% and frequently much higher). Let me say once more that only the greatest Saar wines deserve this sort of praise, that there is far more bad Saar wine than good, and that the best is never inexpensive. On the whole, the wines of the Mittelmosel are a much safer bet. But the Saar . . . is the Saar.

Here, as one goes up the Saar from its junction with the Mosel, are the principal wine-producing towns and their vineyards, with an idea of their acreage under vines.

The entire Saar is in the Grosslage Scharzberg:

Filzen (145 acres of vineyards). Undistinguished, except in the greatest years. *Piedmont Erben* and *Reverschon* are dependable producers and the best wines are:

Filzener Pulchen   Filzener Urbelt

* *Wawern* (103 acres of vineyards). On the west or left bank of the Saar. Good but not great. *Dr. Fischer* is a reputable and important vineyard owner and the Wawerner Herrenberger is entirely owned by him. The other well-known grower is *Egon Muller,* who owns the LeGallais Estate in Wawern. The best vineyards are:

Wawerner Herrenberger   Wawerner Goldberg

* *Kanzem* (185 acres of vineyards). The village is on the west side of the Saar, but the vineyards across the narrow river, cover a great steep hillside and face south. The wines in good years are excellent, with special spicy flavor and a great deal of charm. The leading producers include the *Vereinigte Hospitien,* the *Bischöfliches Priesterseminar, Kanzemer Berg, Maximilian von Othegraven,* with some of the best vineyards in Kanzem; and *H. J. Patheiger.* The vineyard names are: Kanzemer Altenberg, Kanzemer Horecker, Kanzemer Schlossberg, Kanzemer Sonnenberg.

*** *Wiltingen* (790 acres of vineyards). Ranks with Piesport, Bernkastel, Wehlen and Zeltingen as one of the incomparable best. One of its wines is so famous that it never carries the name of the village but is sold as Scharzhofberger. The Scharzhof itself is a lovely old manor house, which has been the property of the Müller family for generations. Three or four other vineyards in Wiltingen are quite in the class with the Scharzhofberg, and produce, like the Saar as a whole, wonderful wines in good years and wines of little or no interest in years of insufficient sunshine.

The original Scharzhofberg was almost entirely owned by Egon Müller and the Hohe Domkirche. Here as elsewhere in the great consolidation of vineyards, the most famous name became the most desirable, and the vineyard was consolidated with several less famous and is now 68 acres in size.

The famous producers are *Egon Müller* (owner of the Scharzhof), *Apollinar Joseph Koch*, the *Hohe Domkirche* or *Cathedral of Trier* (producer of Dom Scharzhofberger), the *Vereinigte Hospitien*, the *Bischöfliches Priesterseminar*, *Otto van Volxem*, *LeGallais*, the *Bischöfliches Konvikt*, *Kesselstatt*, *Graf zu Hoensbroech* and *Von Hövel*. The vineyards are the following: (with Scharzhofberger and Braune Kupp being the acknowledged best, followed by Kupp and Braunfels):

Scharzhofberger (always without Wiltingen)

Wiltinger Braune Kupp	Wiltinger Schlossberg
Wiltinger Rosenberg	Wiltinger Sandberg
Wiltinger Hölle (entire vineyard is owned by	
Vereinigte Hospitien)	
Wiltinger Kupp	Wiltinger Gottesfuss
Wiltinger Klosterberg	Wiltinger Braunfels
Wiltinger Schlangengraben	

** *Oberemmel* (625 acres of vineyards). Just east of Wiltingen, another village which in great years produces wines that can only be described as extraordinary. *Von Hövel, Kesselstatt, Otto van Volxem* and *Friedrich Wilhelm Gymnasium* are the most important vineyard owners. The vineyards are:

Oberemmeler Karlsberg	Oberemmeler Altenberg
Oberemmeler Hütte	Oberemmeler Raul
Oberemmeler Agritiusberg	Oberemmeler Rosenberg

* *Mennig* (275 acres of vineyards). Another good little vineyard town which deserves to be better known. *Kesselstatt* is a major producer. The vineyards are:

Menniger Herrenberg	Menniger Sonnenberg
Menniger Euchariusberg	Menniger Altenberg

** *Ayl* (270 acres of vineyards). This little village west of the Saar owes its fame to one magnificent hillside facing south and completely planted in vines. The *Bischöfliches Konvikt* and the *Bischöfliches Priesterseminar* are labels to look for, and there is also an important cooperative (*Winzerverein*). The best Lagen are:

Ayler Kupp   Ayler Herrenberger

** *Ockfen* (195 acres of vineyards). Produces a few wines which, in years such as 1959 and 1976, are truly superb and among the best of the whole Saar Valley. The top producers are the *State Domain (Staatsweingut)* who own the entire Happenstein vineyard, *Dr. Fischer, Adolf Rheinart Erben, Forstmeister Geltz, Karl Ludwig Gebert, Friedrich Wilhelm Gymnasium* and *Freiherr von Solemacher*. Here are the vineyards, of which the top two are Bockstein and Geisberg:

Ockfener Kupp	Ockfener Herrenberg
Ockfener Heppenstein	Ockfener Bockstein
Ockfener Zickelgarten	Ockfener Neuwies
Ockfener Geisberg	

* *Saarburg* (185 acres of vineyards). Saarburg has become to the Saar what Bernkastel is to the Mittelmosel, the center of the wine trade as well as a bustling, picturesque little town that attracts tourists. The wines are quite remarkable in good and great years, though not as outstanding as the wines of Ockfen. They are worthy representatives of the Saar.

The main growers are *Forstmeister Geltz, Adolf Rheinart Erben* and *Freiherr von Solemacher*. The best known vineyards are:

Saarburger Antoniusbrunnen	Saarburger Klosterberg
Saarburger Fuchs	Saarburger Schlossberg
Saarburger Rausch	

* *Serrig* (233 acres of vineyards). As you go up the Saar valley, the climate becomes increasingly unfavorable almost from one mile to another, and the vineyards are less and less dependable as far as quality is concerned. Wiltingen, for example, will make good wine perhaps two or three years out of five, but Saarburg and Serrig only about three times in a decade. A great Serriger of a great vintage (1949, 1959, 1976) is something quite remarkable. Today of course with the better methods of deacidification, the good growers make a dependable wine in most years. In the 1970s they were blessed by many good harvests and three great ones so far.

The major producers are the *Staatliche Domäne,* the *Vereinigte Hospitien,* sole owners of *Schloss Saarfelser Schlossberg, Bert Simon,* an extraordinarily dynamic and good wine grower who has in recent years built a major Estate under the name of *Weingut Herrenberg,* and

D. Ebert who as a refugee from Eastern Germany acquired Schloss Saarstein and built it into a reputable vineyard. The main vineyards are:

Serriger Antoniusberg
Serriger Schloss Saarfelser Schlossberg
Serriger Kupp
Serriger Heiligenborn

Serriger Schloss Saarsteiner
Serriger Herrenberg
Serriger Vogelsang
Serriger Würtzberg

THE RUWER AND THE DISTRICT OF TRIER

Grosslage Romerlay

The venerably and colorful little city of Trier, which was to a large extent in ruins in 1945, has risen miraculously from its ashes, like all of Western Germany. Its daily market is bright with flowers again, its streets in summer are full of tourists, and the dining-room tables of its hotels are heavy with good food and slender green bottles of Mosel, just as they were twenty years ago. In the center of town stands Trier's most impressive relic of Roman days, the Porta Nigra, a three-story fortified gateway of dark stone, which survived the last war as it has survived other wars without number in the eighteen hundred years of its existence; northeast of the city a whole new district of small homes is under construction, and there is even a traffic circle, in the American style.

Some two or three miles beyond the traffic circle, on the road that leads downstream toward the vineyards of the Mittelmosel, the valley narrows and a little river tumbles down to join the Mosel out of the high, cold, pine-covered hills of the Hunsrück. This is the Ruwer (pronounced *Roo-ver*)—it looks a good deal more like a trout stream than like a river, but its wines are famous. The Ruwer (it has of course nothing to do with the Ruhr, which is northeast of Cologne) runs north, and since the vineyards face south, they are not visible until you start up the valley; then, off to the left and right of the winding road and the narrow stream, you see one wide steep hillside after another planted with vines. The soil, as on the Mittelmosel and the Saar, is largely slate, and the construction and cultivation of the vineyards require an amount of hand labor which is almost incredible.

Happily, at least in good years, the Ruwer wines are worth all this effort. Hard and even acid in years like 1972 and 1978, they have a wonderful lightness and an exquisite flowery fragrance when they are at their best, and I have tasted marvelous wines from Eitelsbach, and Grünhaus and Kasel which were well under 9% of alcohol by volume. This means that they are in general the lightest of all the fine wines of the world, and an obscure local poet has described them as a combination of "the fire of the sun, the gold of the stars and cool moonlight"—"*Sonnenfeuer, Sternengold, kühler Mondlichtschein.*"

In the Ruwer Valley proper there are only three wine-producing villages of more than passing interest, and perhaps a half-dozen major producers in all. The two of Zeltingen alone produces as much as the whole Ruwer Valley. Here are the three villages:

** *Maximin Grünhaus* (150 acres of vineyards). The largest estate is that of the celebrated Von Schubert family, and their lovely old-fashioned label is a welcome and reassuring sight on a wine bottle. The vineyards are on the left, or west, bank of the Ruwer, and the wines are sold as Maximin Grünhäuser, plus in many cases the name of the specific *Lage* such as Herrenberg, Bruderberg and Abtsberg.

** *Eitelsbach* (187 acres of vineyards). Facing Maximum-Grünhaus across the valley, the ancient Carthusian Monastery of Eitelsbach has become Eitelsbacher Karthäuserhofberg, and when you add to this not inconsiderable mouthful a vineyard name, plus Erzeugerabfüllung Werner Tyrell, vorm. Rautenstrauch (the owners) you get something very nearly unpronounceable by American standards. Here, too, the label is an unusual and an interesting one—a sort of elaborate little collar around the neck of the bottle—and there used to be a joke to the effect that the wine in Germany with the longest name had the smallest label. But the wine is admirable, delicate and well-balanced. Apart from Tyrell, the *Bischöfliches Konvikt* of Trier is the principal producer, and the best vineyards include:

Eitelsbacher Karthäuserhofberger Kronenberg	Eitelsbacher Karthäuserhofberger Sang
Eitelsbacher Karthäuserhofberger Burgberg	Eitelsbacher Marienholz

* *Kasel* (220 acres of vineyards). The largest and most important vineyard town of the Ruwer. The Kaseler wines, while rarely great, are almost unfailingly pleasant, light and fresh and full of bouquet and

charm. The *Bischöfliches Priesterseminar,* the *Bischöfliches Konvikt, von Beulwitz Erben, v.* Fumetti, *von Nell* and *Kesselstatt* are major producers, and the vineyards are the following:

Kaseler Herrenberg	Kaseler Dominikanerberg
Kaseler Kehrnagel	Kaseler Hitzlay
Kaseler Nieschen	Kaseler Paulinsberg
Kaseler Timpert	

Waldrach (300 acres of vineyards). Upstream and back of Kasel, the little town of Waldrach produces wines in good years as good as Kasel. The two main producers are *Schloss Marienlay* and *Scherf's Mühle* and the best known vineyards are:

Waldracher Krone	Waldracher Laurentiusberg
Waldracher Jesuitengarten	Waldracher Hubertusberg
Waldracher Sonnenberg	

* *Avelsbach* (Kurenz) (120 acres of vineyards). As might be expected, the Avelsbachers have all the faults as well as a good many of the virtues of the wines of the Ruwer and the Saar. They are exceedingly hard and acid except in great vintage years; they have a superb bouquet; they are very light, very pale, very fresh, rather tart; in a fabulous year such as 1976 they are magnificent, but even in a great year like 1975 the average consumer is likely to find some of them, although of course not the *Spätlesen* and *Auslesen,* a little too steely for his taste. The largest vineyard owners are the German Government (*Staatsweingut*) and the Cathedral of Trier (*Hohe Domkirche*). The Cathedral's wines are sold as "Dom-Avelsbacher." And the best *Lagen:*

Avelsbacher Herrenberg	Avelsbacher Hammerstein
Avelsbacher Altenberg	Avelsbacher Rotlay

4

RHEINGAU

ONCE it leaves the Swiss border at Basel, the Rhine runs almost due north toward Holland and the North Sea; it flows tranquilly but swiftly down that splendid and fertile valley, that vast flat trough which it has cut for itself between the Black Forest and the Alsatian Vosges; it passes within sight of the Haardt Mountains of the Palatinate on its left, and the wooded hills of Baden on its right; it skirts the red, terraced vineyards of Nierstein and Nackenheim and sweeps majestically on northward down to Mainz.

At Mainz this steady northerly progress ends abruptly, and the face of the river changes. Directly in its path rises the high, forest-covered barrier of the Taunus Hills; the Rhine broadens and curves west, and for twenty miles, from Mainz to Rüdesheim and Bingen, it flows, not north, nor even west, but actually south of west. And the lower slopes of these same Taunus Hills are the one great vineyard. This is the Rheingau—the Weingau, as the Germans call it—and among celebrated viticultural districts of the world, it has the Burgundian Côte d'Or for its only real rival.

Unlike Bordeaux, unlike Champagne, unlike the Mosel Valley even, this is not a whole wine-growing region—it is a single hillside, steeper to be sure in some places than in others, cut by its minor depressions and little valleys, but protected everywhere against the cold north wind by the wooded mass of the Taunus, and everywhere, or almost everywhere, facing due south over the river, so that its Rieslings get the full benefit of the southern sun.

There are other sections of this incomparable Rhine Valley which are perhaps more impressive than the Rheingau, but none, surely, more gracious and more beautiful. The quiet, shady terraces of its little vineyard towns overlook the river; they are fragrant in summer with linden blossoms—wonderfully inviting places to sit and relax over a good bottle or two. The Rhine, among other things, is one of the great commercial arteries of Western Europe, and the constant river traffic gives the whole scene a special liveliness and charm. There are barges and strings of barges—French and sometimes Belgian, Swiss and Dutch and German; there are sailboats and excursion steamers, canoes and kayaks, and patrol-boats flying the German flag. The narrow river road, the Rheinstrasse, is busy too—crowded all summer long with tourists, youngsters on bicycles, buses from every part of Western Germany and even from Scandinavia, cars with the license plates of a dozen different countries.

Behind all this bustle and activity, and wholly unaffected by it, but constituting the real life of the Rheingau, is the old and solid and sound tradition of good wine. In almost every one of the little river towns there are one or two old patrician families who, for generations, have owned their famous vineyards and made their famous wines, and whose labels are known from Chicago to Cape Town, and from Manila to Maine. In Eltville is the gracious, ancient home of the Von Simmern family; the old Baron, whom I knew before the war spoke half a dozen languages and had been German Ambassador to Spain. In Erbach, and directly on the river, is Schloss Reinhartshausen, the celebrated estate of Prince Heinrich Friedrich of Prussia, a cousin of the last Kaiser. In Hallgarten there is the estate of Prince Löwenstein, and in Hattenheim that of Graf von Schönborn, one of whose ancestors signed, in nearby Geisenheim, the treaty ending the Thirty Years' War. Schloss Johannisberg, of course, has been owned by the Metternich family since 1816, and the late Graf Matuschka, of Schloss Vollrads, was President of the German Wine Growers Association. The Von Brentanos of Winkel were friends of Goethe. In Rüdesheim and Kiedrich are the estates of Baron von Ritter zu Groenesteyn, and in Lorch there is Graf von Kantz. These are only a few of the more illustrious, for there are fifty or sixty major producers in all and of course literally hundreds of smaller ones.

A good many of these smaller growers, fortunately for us as well as for themselves, have set up cooperative cellars—*Winzervereine* and *Winzergenossenchaften*—and are thus able to afford the presses and other expensive equipment without which modern wine-making is scarcely possible. A list of such cooperatives and a reasonably complete roster of major growers has been included farther on in this chapter.

At the head of any such list, of course, must come the State, which here, as in Rheinhessen and on the Mosel, is by far the largest single vineyard owner, with some three hundred acres in the best towns and best *Lagen* of the whole Rheingau. The most interesting and most celebrated building of the Rheingau, Kloster Eberbach (an ancient, secularized Cistercian Monastery), is also state property, as are a whole series of modern cellars in Eltville, Rüdesheim, Hochheim, etc., all superbly equipped and magnificently run.

Compared to other wine-growing districts of Germany, let alone those of France, the Rheingau is a very small area indeed, with 7,105 acres of producing vineyard; the Mosel has four times, the Rheinhessen almost eight times and the Rheinpfalz seven and one half times as much. But nowhere else is the average quality so high. To begin with, 78% of the vines are Rieslings and in all the better Lagen there is practically nothing else. The large estates have experimented with other grape varieties that might yield riper juice for blending with the Riesling in bad years. These plantings only represent 5% of the better Estates, but because they have proven unsatisfactory, they are being largely reconverted into Riesling. There are some new grape varieties, particularly "Ehrenfelser," which may some day play an important role in the Rheingau. At present there are only 118 acres in Ehrenfelser, a mere 1.7% of total plantings, whereas Müller-Thurgau accounts for slightly over 10% and Silvaner for 4%. The plantings of Müller-Thurgau and Silvaner are largely in sections of heavier soil and lower lying vineyards, for example around Hochheim and Lorch. Second, the Rheingau's boundaries are so rigidly fixed by nature (Rhine on the south and cold, wooded hilltops on the north) that there is no possibility of the growers' expanding their plantings, even if they were tempted to do so. Third, and no one knows why, this seems to be one of those rare corners of the earth that ranks as a sort of Vintner Mother Lode where sun and soil and one special variety of grape combine with man's help to produce a miracle which cannot be performed or repeated elsewhere.

In what might be called the geographical Rheingau—the lower slopes of the Taunus between where the Rhine turns west at Mainz and where it turns north once more at Bingen; or, stated otherwise, between where it is joined by the Main and where it is joined by the Nahe—there are fourteen villages, nine strung along the river and five set back in the hills. The names of at least ten of the fourteen are well-known to wine-lovers the world over.

Oddly enough, perhaps the most famous of all (and one which has given a portion of its name—*"Hock,"* from the name "Hochheim"—to Rhine wines as a whole), is only in the Rheingau by courtesy so to speak. It lies well to the east of the fourteen, and overlooks the Main, rather than the Rhine, but its wines are Rheingau wines all the same, not only legally, but in taste and flavor and class. Similarly, the villages of Lorch and Assmannshausen, both in the Rhine gorge north of Rüdesheim and Bingen, are rated as part of the Rheingau, and so is the big, popular resort of Wiesbaden, which was an important American headquarters after the war.

It must not be thought that even in so small a district as the Rheingau all the wines are alike or have more than a certain superficial family resemblance. Experts can name almost unfailingly the village that a particular wine comes from, and sometimes even the precise vineyard, or Lage. Each has its somewhat different character, and to tasters who live with them and see them daily they are as familiar as the faces of old friends. Thus the Hochheimers are full and fruity, sometimes with a trace of earthy taste, or Bodenton; the Rauenthalers are distinguished by their fruit, and an almost spicy quality of flavor; the good, familiar Eltvillers are well-balanced, consistently pleasing, rarely great; the Erbachers are sturdier; with more backbone, and the finest of them the Marcobrunners, can be incomparable; the wines of Hattenheim, which is just next door, run to finesse and delicacy and bouquet, whereas those of the Steinberg, on the hill behind Hattenheim, are forthright, masculine, overpowering, and in great years perhaps Germany's best. The Hallgarteners are extremely full-bodied, and I have heard them called "clumsy" and "graceless," although these are not wine-tasters' terms; the Johannisbergers and the best wines of Winkel, such as Schloss Vollrads, have great "elegance" and "distinction"—these are true wine-tasters' words, and high praise. The Geisenheimers have a rather special taste, by no means

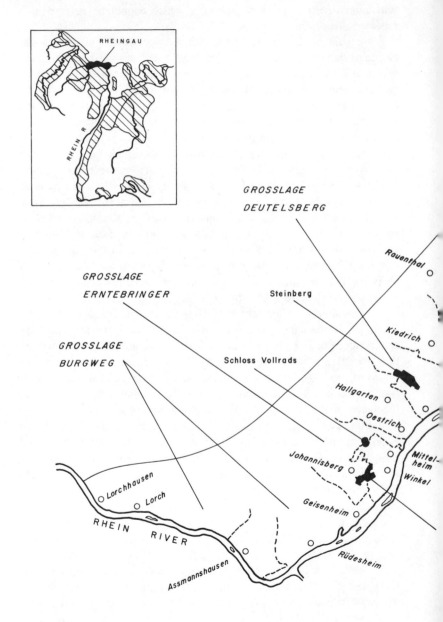

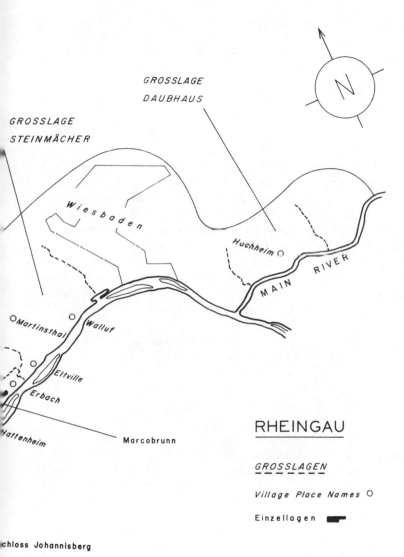

GROSSLAGE
DAUBHAUS

GROSSLAGE
STEINMÄCHER

N

W i e s b a d e n

Hochheim ○

MAIN   RIVER

○ Martinsthal   ○ Walluf

○ Eltville

○ Erbach

Hattenheim ———— Marcobrunn

RHEINGAU

GROSSLAGEN

Village Place Names ○

Einzellagen ▬

chloss Johannisberg

0   5 Miles

disagreeable but usually not too hard to recognize, and the Rüdesheimers, finally, are a law unto themselves; generally full and rich and
fine, they rank in poor or fair years as the best of the Rheingau, but
they are sometimes almost too heavy and too high in alcohol, with an
underlying dryness, in years rated as great.

So much for a quick glance. The full story is a good deal more
complicated as we shall soon see.

Here in the Rheingau, as on the Mosel, there are only a few of
the great vineyards, or Lagen (four to be exact: Schloss Vollrads,
Schloss Johannisberg, Steinberg and Schloss Reichartschausen), which
are not partitioned, are named after the Estate, and belong to a
single owner. The rest are called after myriad names and are jointly
owned by many growers. This is much closer to the system which
prevails in Burgundy than to that which prevails in Bordeaux, where
Chateau Lafite is Chateau Lafite, and no nonsense about it. Here,
therefore, the producer's name is quite as important as the vineyard
name, and I am giving lengthy and rather detailed lists of the major
producers for this exact reason. No such lists can hope to be complete,
but there are certainly no major omissions in those farther on in this
chapter.

And now to a closer examination of the Rheingau. Due to its geographical limitations and its comparatively large Estates, it is the one
wine-growing area in Germany that has changed the least. As a matter
of fact it plants more Riesling today than it did thirty years ago, and its
wines have become if anything, better than they were. The cooperatives, Estates and growers have benefited from the research at Geisenheim, the famous viticultural school and experimental station, which is
the pride of the Rheingau, and an example of how science can improve winemaking. It is a standing joke that the centrifugal separator
is the Mercedes of the wine grower in the Rheingau; since the separator which has contributed so much to the high quality of the wine, is
as expensive as the status symbol car.

The wine law of 1971 consolidated the geographical nomenclature of the Rheingau vineyards into one Bereich (Subdistrict): Bereich
Johannisberg, ten Grosslagen (general vineyard sites), and 120 Lagen
(single vineyard sites) extending over 28 winegrowing communities,
that include the cities of Frankfurt and Wiesbaden. As a result of this
consolidation there are fewer vineyards for every community, with the
better known often absorbing the less well known neighbors; also the

The Domdechaney vineyard in Hochheim.

grower has become if anything even more important, with the bigger
ones owning the better and original portions. The consolidation furthermore has made it necessary to mention, in the case of the more
famous communities, the names of all their vineyards, since after all
there are only 120 in the whole region.

Going from east to west in the Rheingau, here are the main communities with their best vineyards and growers:

*** *Hochheim,* Grosslage Daubhaus, a good ten miles east of the
Rheingau proper, overlooks the Main, some three miles upstream from
its junction with the Rhine. The country round about is gently rolling
farm and orchard land, and Hochheim's 524 acres of vineyard form
what amounts to an astonishing little island of vines in a district where

there are no grapes at all. It is even more amazing that these vines planted on relatively flat ground, as they are, yield wines which are not only comparable in quality to the Johannisbergers, for example, but which have the same essential characteristics of bouquet and texture and taste. For they are Rheingau wines and no mistake about it, and those from the eight or ten best vineyards—especially, oddly enough, in fair and good rather than great years—have the finesse and fruit and balance which are the marks of greatness in a wine. In Hochheim, more than in most other Rheingau towns, there is a striking difference between the wines of the better and those of the lesser vineyards. The former have an attractive softness; the latter, particularly in warm, dry years, lack class and have a trace of commonness. The best *Lagen* (as their names would indicate) are those that directly adjoin Hochheim's pretty Gothic church, for *Kirchenstück* means "church-piece" and Domdechaney means "deanery."

No less famous than these, but certainly much less good, is the "Königin Victoriaberg," which was named after Queen Victoria when she visited Hochheim in 1850. If, as has been reported, this was her favorite wine, as Bernkasteler Doktor was Edward VII's the Queen had certainly a less good palate for German wines than her son, for the Victoriaberg is a long way from being Hochheim's best vineyard.

The leading producers of Hochheim are as follows:

Domdechant (which means Dean) *Werner'sches Weingut.* 32 acres including holdings in almost all of the better *Lagen.*

Geh.-Rat Achrott'sche Gutesverwaltung. 33 acres equally well placed.

Graf von Schönborn (see Hattenheim). Portions of Kirchenstuck, Domdechaney, Stein, etc.

Staatsweingut (the German State Domain—see Eltville). Holdings in Kirchenstück, Domdechaney and Stein.

Weingut der Stadt Frankfurt (the city of Frankfurt). 37 acres in the better Lagen.

Weingut Königin Victoriaberg. Sole owner of the 15 acre vineyard by the same name.

SOLE AGENTS FOR THE U.S.A.
IMPORTERS · WILE · NEW YORK, N.Y. ESTABLISHED 1877

PRODUCED, BOTTLED & SHIPPED BY DEINHARD & CO., KOBLENZ GERMANY

KOBLENZ · DEINHARD · AM RHEIN & MOSEL

RHEINGAU
OESTRICHER LENCHEN
RIESLING AUSLESE »EISWEIN«
ERZEUGER-ABFÜLLUNG DEINHARD
QUALITÄTSWEIN MIT PRÄDIKAT · A.P. Nr. 2902405876

Deinhard

PRODUCT OF GERMANY CONTENTS 1 PINT 7 FLUID OUNCES ALCOHOL 9% BY VOLUME

SCHLOSS VOLLRADS

Erzeuger-abfüllung
Graf Matuschka-
Greiffenclau
Oestrich-Winkel
Rheingau

Deutschland
A.P.Nr.
27074 006 79

RHEINGAU
1978er QUALITÄTSWEIN
grün · Riesling

e 75 cl
Alc. 10,1%
by Vol.

VERBAND DEUTSCHER
PRÄDIKATSWEINGÜTER
E.V.
Unsere Mitglieder besitzen
Lagen von Weltruf!

V D P

QUALITÄTSWEIN
MIT PRÄDIKAT
aus eigener Erzeugung eines
unserer Mitgliedsbetriebe.

A.P.Nr.
40 083 007 77

Domdechant Wernersches Weingut
seit 1780 im Familienbesitz

1976er
Hochheimer Domdechaney
Riesling Spätlese
ERZEUGERABFÜLLUNG
RHEINGAU

RHEINGAU
Qualitätswein mit Prädikat
1971er
Steinberger
Riesling
Großer Preis · Bundesweinpr. der DLG 1973
EISWEIN-AUSLESE
Erzeuger-Abfüllung – Amtl. Prüf.-Nr. 33050 052 72
Verwaltung der Staatsweingüter, Eltville

QUALITÄTSWEIN
MIT
PRÄDIKAT
RHEINGAU
A. P. Nr. 26026 007 77

1976er
Schloss Johannisberger
Rotlack
KABINETT

Erzeuger-Abfüllung
Fürst von Metternich-Winneburg'sche
Domäne Schloß Johannisberg/Rheingau

Qualitätswein RHEINGAU mit Prädikat
Freiherr Langwerth von Simmern · Eltville
Erzeuger-Abfüllung
Rauenthaler
Riesling 1971er Baiken Riesling
A. P. Nr. 33045 007 72

RHEINGAU
Schloss Schönborn
1976er
Erbacher Marcobrunn
Riesling
Trockenbeerenauslese
A.P. Nr. 31.052.011.77
Erzeugerabfüllung der Gräflich von Schönborn'schen Kellerei Hattenheim
QUALITÄTSWEIN MIT PRÄDIKAT

Smaller producers of excellent reputation include a *Winzergenossenschaft, Jean Quink-Klein, Christian Duchmann, Walter Velten, Peter Velten, Franz Künstler, Willi Orth, Wilhelm Joseph Schäfer* and *Werner Hueck.*

All the vineyards of Hochheim are part of the Daubhaus Grosslage (general vineyard site), which also has vineyards in nearby Kostheim, Flösheim and Wicker, communities which rarely, if ever, export wines under their name; they are most likely to blend them under the general vineyard site name of Hochheimer Daubhaus.

Here, in approximate order of quality, are the better vineyards of Hochheim:

Hochheimer Domdechaney	Hochheimer Kirchenstück
Hochheimer Hölle	Hochheimer Stein
Hochheimer Sommerheil	Hochheimer Stielweg
Hochheimer Königin Victoriaberg	Hochheimer Hofmeister
Hochheimer Reichesthal	

Wiesbaden is such an attractive town, and remembered with affection by so many Americans, that it hardly seems fair to say what I feel I must about its little vineyards, which consist of the Neroberg, plus 6 plots in the three communities of Wiesbaden-Frauenstein, Wiesbaden-Schierstein and Wiesbaden-Dotzheim. Unlike the Neroberg, which is a vineyard without a *Grosslage,* the vineyards of the other three suburbs of Wiesbaden are all in the Grosslage of Steinmächer and are more likely to be sold as Rauenthaler-Steinmächer than as Schiersteiner Dachsberg or Dotzheimer Judenkirch. All the vineyards of Wiesbaden and its suburbs are technically part of the Rheingau, and the Neroberg is owned by the city of Wiesbaden.

In Wiesbaden-Frauenstein, the *Groroler Hof* produces in great years some very creditable bottles. These like the Nerobergers, are hardly worth exporting, but there is not much chance that we could get them even if we wished, for the thirsty burghers of Wiesbaden itself, aided, it must be admitted, by American officers, and by a good many thousands of tourists every year, drink them up in short order. There are 11 acres in the Neroberg, but there are 365 acres in the vineyards of Frauenstein, Schierstein and Dotzheim, and whatever is not drunk locally will be bottled under the name of the *Grosslage:* Rauenthaler-Steinmächer.

Martinsthal, until quite recently, was called Neudorf, and the old name still appears in many wine books and on many vineyard maps.

The growers finally decided that the name Neudorf (which means "new village") had very little glamor on a wine label, and Martinsthal, it must be admitted, is an improvement. The village and its vineyards (195 acres) lie a mile or so back in the hills, not far from Rauenthal, and if the wines are a long way from equaling the astonishing quality of the Rauenthalers, they are creditable and sound, and in good years like 1976 have a considerable amount of bouquet and fruit.

The principal producers are *J. B. Becker, Singer, Arnet Erben, Adam Scherer, Diefenhardt'sches Weingut, Klaus Peter Kessler, Hirt-Gebhardt, Christian Faust* and *Werner Engelmann*. Martinsthal is part of the Grosslage Steinmächer, but most of its wines are sold under their own name, since they enjoy considerable popularity in the neighboring towns of Wiesbaden and Mainz, as well as in the many picturesque Weinstuben and Restaurants of Martinsthal itself.

The two best known Lagen are:

Martinsthaler Langenberg   Martinsthaler Wildsau

which literally means "wild sow"; it has a charging boar on the label and it is locally as well known as the Zeller Schwarze Katz on the Mosel (Black Cat of Zell).

Walluf, Grosslage Steinmächer. This is another town name that has undergone a sea-change in the last decade. Formerly there was Oberwalluf and also Niederwalluf. The two still exist as villages, Niederwalluf with a little yacht harbor and a most agreeable restaurant terrace on the Rhine, Oberwalluf back up in its narrow valley on the way to Martinsthal. As far as their wines are concerned, both now are Walluf. The better Lagen, although little known, produce something quite excellent in good years, wines that are distinguished and fine; those from lesser vineyards often have a certain amount of "soil" taste, or Bodenton. The good producers are *J. B. Becker, Singer, Arnet Erben* and *Adam Scherer,* and the superior vineyards (260 acres in all) are:

Wallufer Walkenberg   Wallufer Oberberg
Wallufer Berg-Bildstock   Wallufer Fitusberg

The above names though, can only be found in the local restaurants. Whatever is not sold locally is usually exported as Rauenthaler Steinmächer and not as Wallufer.

** *Eltville,* Grosslage Steinmächer. 600 acres of vines make it one of the larger vineyard towns of the Rheingau, and most of these vines are part of a single unbroken "Weinberg," extremely impressive in extent although not very steep, overlooking the Rhine, just east of the town. A great deal of Eltville is produced, and as a matter of fact, in the middle and lower price brackets, there is no better name to look for on German wine labels. The name is not famous enough to have been commercialized as yet, and the wines, if rarely sensational, are wonderfully consistent and pleasing, fine, soft and with good bouquet.

The town is substantial and busy, picturesque and very old. Its name does not, however, as some authorities have stated, come from the Latin *alta villa:* there were no towns on the right bank of the Rhine in Roman days, and Eltville was formerly called Ellfeld. Today it is to the wine trade what Rüdesheim is to the tourists—the Rheingau's unofficial capital—for in addition to several of Germany's most important *Sektkellereien,* or sparkling-wine houses, obvious and impressive on its main street, Eltville can also take pride in what is probably the most modern wine cellar in the world, that of the *Staatsweingut,* or State Domain, and two others hardly less famous but considerably more picturesque (Graf Eltz and Langwerth von Simmern) and in at least twenty smaller ones of honorable tradition and good name. Here is a brief list with a few details:

The *Verwaltung der Staatsweingüter,* or Administrative Office of the State Domain is in Eltville as are the main storage and bottling cellars for the seven separate estates owned by the State of Hesse in the Rheingau and the Hessische Bergstrasse. The State Domains are in Assmannshausen, Rüdesheim, Hattenheim, Steinberg, Rauenthal, Schloss Hochheim and a vine nursery on the Island of Lorch, an island in the middle of the Rhine on the very western reaches of the Rheingau. The vineyard holdings total 291 acres and each has its own press-house and cellars. The majority of the vineyards used to belong to the Church and were secularized during the French occupation of 1803: among them are some of the finest vineyard properties in the Rheingau, including the Steinberg in its entirety. The wines are mostly sold at a *Weinmesse* (wine exchange) in April, the annual sale that takes place at Kloster Eberbach at which some of the best Estates of the Rheingau offer their wines at a once a year discount. There used to be many auctions in the past but they are now reserved for older vintages and rarities and take place twice a year, in April and November. The State Domain produces one million liters of wine and sells almost all of it, from a QbA to *Trockenbeerenauslese,* as Estate bottled wine under a simple white label with a stylized eagle.

Güterverwaltung Schloss Eltz with 80 acres of vineyard in Eltville, Rauenthal and Kiedrich was formerly the property of the Eltz family. It is now owned by the government and administered by the Estate of Langwerth von Simmern. Jakob Eltz, the former owner, was for many years president of the Rheingau Winegrowers Association and is still involved with the management of the property. The wines are consistently of high quality. The name Schloss Eltz appears on the labels, together with the town and vineyard designations. Langwerth von Simmern (Freiherrlich Langwerth von Simmern'sches Rentant). 9.39 acres in Eltville, Hattenheim, Rauenthal and in the Marcobrunn of Erbach. The von Simmern home, and the cellars, are built around a beautiful, ancient, shady courtyard in the very center of Eltville. The wines, especially the Hattenheimers and the Marcobrunners are of the very highest class, and the Simmern label, to my personal taste, is the most attractive of the Rhine.

Other producers of Eltviller wine, less important but of impeccable reputation, include *Jakob Fischer Erben, Adam Hubert, C. Belz Erben, Franz Richter-Boltendahl, Erwin Vowinkel Erben, Koegler, Willi Jonas, Ems-post, Geschwister Offenstein, Weingut Klostermühle, Hans Jos. Ernst, Franz Stringens,* and *Egon Mauer.*

The best vineyards are:

Eltviller Taubenberg	Eltviller Langenstück
Eltviller Sandgrub	Eltviller Sonnenberg

*** *Rauenthal,* Grosslage Steinmächer, a modest and not particularly prepossessing little village, is some two miles north of Eltville, back in the Taunus Hills. The river road and the river traffic pass it by, and its wines, oddly enough, never seem to have found much favor with winedrinkers outside Germany. This is indeed strange for at the famous wine auctions that take place every spring and fall in the Rheingau the Rauenthalers consistently bring higher prices than the wines of any other town, and in the opinion of a majority of German experts, they are not far from the Rheingau's best. It would certainly be hard to imagine anything much better than the 1971 and 1976 Rauenthalers of the State Domain, for example, although it must be admitted that unlike the wines of Rüdesheim, the Rauenthalers are anything but outstanding in off years.

I have before me as I write these lines the notes of two German friends (great connoisseurs, both of them) with whom I tasted a group of 1953 Rauenthalers a few years ago. Their comments were like a round of applause, and by the time we finished tasting there was a broad smile on the usually impassive face of Herr Direktor Jost, who was then in charge of the Rheingau State Domains, and whose wines these were. For higher praise is hardly possible: *"pikante reife, feine Art, elegante Würze und Frucht, volle Frucht, edel feine Fülle, hochedle Frucht und Würze."* These terms are almost impossible to translate accurately, but one can say at least that distinction, ripeness and especially a piquant, an almost spicy sort of fruit and flavor, are more strikingly present in the Rauenthalers than in any other wines of the Rhine.

In addition to the State Domain (*Staatsweingut*), with holdings in Gehrn, Baiken, Wulfen and Langenstück, major producers include *Freiherr Langwerth von Simmern* and *Graf Eltz* (see Eltville). There is a *Winzerverein* and a few good small growers: *Otto Sturm und Sohn, Klein, Russler* and *Wagner.*

Here are the more celebrated vineyards out of Rauenthal's 245 acres:

Rauenthaler Baiken	Rauenthaler Gehrn
Rauenthaler Wülfen	Rauenthaler Rothenberg
Rauenthaler Langenstück	Rauenthaler Nonnenberg

** *Kiedrich,* Grosslage Heiligenstock. Kiedrich, like Rauenthal, lies back in the hills behind Eltville and faces, across a narrow valley, an enormously impressive sweep of vines, crowned by the ruined castle of the Electors of Mainz, the Scharfenstein. It is an attractive town, with a pretty church and a famous old organ, and its wines, like those of Rauenthal, deserve to be better known outside Germany than they are, for those from its best vineyards (Gräfenberg and Wasseros especially) can be truly remarkable in good years, with considerably more character and class than the wines of Eltville. The major producers include *Graf Eltz, Dr. Weil* (33 acres, mostly in Kiedrich), *Freiherr von Ritter zu Groenesteyn* (important here as well as in Rüdesheim) and the *Staatsweingut.*

Among the good small growers are *Barbeler, Brückmann, Gundlich, Geschwister Bibo, Hans Prinz, Steinmächer-Eberbacher Hof, Franz Staab, Georg Sohlbach, Winzergenossenschaft,* and *Schäfer-*

Kronenberg. There are 430 acres in all; all the Lagen are good and well known and within the community of Kiedrich. Thery are:

Kiedricher Klosterberg   Kiedricher Wasseros
Kiedricher Sandgrub   Kiedricher Gräfenberg

*** *Erbach,* Grosslage Deutelsberg (675 acres). Half a mile west of Eltville, and directly below Kiedrich, on the river, Erbach deserves top rating and three stars if only because of one vineyard, the Marcobrunn. This, one of the Rheingau's three or four most celebrated Lagen, is an absurdly narrow little strip of land, bounded by the river road, and bisected lengthwise by railway tracks. It lies off west of Erbach, beyond Schloss Reinhartshausen, the rather modest castle of Prince Friedrich of Prussia, on the way to Hattenheim, and it takes its name from a little fountain carved out of red sandstone and called the *Marcobrunnen,* or "boundary fountain," since it marks the boundary between Erbach and Hattenheim, the next village.

Officially the fountain, and the vineyard therefore, and the wine as well, belong to Erbach, not Hattenheim. And long ago a village poet of Hattenheim complained of the fact in couplets that have become famous and which, translated, say:

To solve this thorny question
Of what is yours, what mine . . .
Let Erbach keep the water
Give Hattenheim the wine.

Until 1971 both Erbach and Hattenheim growers claimed the vineyard. In 1971 it was placed squarely into the village boundaries of Erbach and since then the name "Erbacher Marcobrunn" graces all its extraordinary bottles. Its wines, perhaps Rheingau's best, particularly in dry years, have a wonderful balance, with fruit and great breed, and a bouquet that can only be described as magnificent.

The other Erbach wines, while excellent, are hardly of this superlative class; they are firm and fine, usually with a good deal of body, often somewhat hard. But they are well-knit, long-lived, and if they cannot stand comparison with the illustrious Marcobrunner, neither, it must be admitted, can most of the other wines of the Rhine.

All of the major producers listed below have holdings in the Marcobrunn and most of them in other Erbach vineyards as well:

Schloss Reinhartshausen (Prince of Prussia). The wines are sold as *Schloss Reinhartshausener Erbacher Marcobrunn* (or Erbacher Siegelsberg, etc.) which scarcely has the virtue of making them easier to order from a wine waiter. The Estate has two labels, one for white, which is white with orange border, and one for red wines, orange with gold border. The Domain consists of 150 acres of vines largely in Hattenheim and Erbach. *Freiherr Langwerth von Simmern* (See Eltville) *Graf von Schönborn-Wiesentheid* (See Hattenheim) *Staatsweingüter, Max Ritter und Edler von Oetinger, Winzergenossenschaft,* and *Josef Kohlhaas.* Smaller growers of note include: *H. Tillmanns, Erben, Crass, Detlev von Oetinger, Wagner-Weitz, Weingut Martin, Phil. Debo, Weingut Jung-Dahlem, Christof Jung, Heinrich Lebert,* and *Johann Nikolai.*

The following are the Erbach Lagen:

Erbacher Marcobrunn	Erbacher Siegelsberg
Erbacher Honigberg	Erbacher Rheinhell
Erbacher Steinmorgen	Erbacher Hohenhrain
Erbacher Michelmark	Erbacher Schlossberg

*** *Hattenheim,* Grosslage Deutelsberg. Of all the little towns of the Rheingau, Hattenheim is perhaps the prettiest, for there are dozens of quaint old half-timber houses clustered along its narrow streets, and a wide green meadow extends from the village down to the Rhine. With one outstanding exception, its best vineyards adjoin those of Erbach-Wisselbrunnen, Nussbrunnen and Mannberg almost as extensions of the Marcobrunn, and produce wines of the same surpassing quality, though perhaps a little more delicate and less firm. The exception, and a major one at that, is the incomparable Steinberg, on a hill a mile behind Hattenheim. This, together with its wonderful adjoining monastery, Kloster Eberbach, is technically within Hattenheim's town limits, but it is important enough to deserve treatment apart, and even without it, Hattenheim has its full share of good things. In bouquet, in those subtle qualities which go to make up what experts describe as "texture," in finesse, the best Hattenheimers of great years are simply unbeatable, and I, for one, have never tasted wines more flawless than the 1949 Hattenheimer Nussbrunnen Auslese of Langwerth von Simmern, or the 1953 Hattenheimer Engelmannsberg Spätlese of the State Domain. If the lordly Steinbergers can be called the kings of the Rheingau, these, surely, are the Rheingau's queens—feminine rather than powerful, but indescribably charming.

Hattenheim's most important cellars are those of *Graf von Schönborn-Wiesentheid,* where all of the wines of this Domain (the Rheingau's second largest—148 acres in all) are aged and bottled—not only Hattenheimers, but wines from Rüdesheim, Johannisberg, Erbach, Hochheim, etc. Other major producers include *Freiherr Langwerth von Simmern, Schloss Reinhartshausen,* the *Pfarrgut, "Georg Müller Stiftung"* (a charitable foundation now administered by the town of Hattenheim) and the *Staatsweingut,* or State Domain. And among the good smaller ones are *Adam Albert, Gossi, Gerhard, Diefenhardt, Ettinghausen, Adolf Horne, Ludwig Horne, Winzergenossenschaft, Anton Doufrain, Karl Molitor, Karl Bausch, Paul Geipel,* and *Ewald Claudy.*

If experts the world over were asked to name Germany's greatest vineyard, it is more than possible that a majority would choose the ***Steinberg:*** Here, back of Hattenheim, as at Vougeot, in Burgundy, in France, Cistercian monks created, some seven hundred years ago, a unique, walled, hillside vineyard. Clos Vougeot today is divided among some sixty owners, but the 79-acre Steinberg is still intact—a single parcel, owned by the German State, cultivated and managed with the most scrupulous care. Although part of Hattenheim, its labels never so state, and its wines are sold simply and proudly as Steinberger, or Steinberger Kabinett, or Steinberger Spätlese or Auslese or Trockenbeerenauslese, etc.

Between these various grades and classes, rigorously kept separate and never blended, there are, of course, enormous differences, even in the wines of a given year.

All of them will, to be sure, have a certain family resemblance, and to a greater or lesser extent the unmistakable Steinberger characteristics: full body, steely acidity, great class, power and depth of flavor sometimes at the expense of subtlety, forthrightness sometimes at the expense of charm. Yet the wines labeled simply Steinberger may go to the consumer at $4 a bottle while the *Trockenbeerenauslesen* may bring, and have brought, $150 a bottle at auction. Steinberger 1953 is not one wine, but a dozen or more quite different wines and the designations that follow the name Steinberger on its label are of an importance hard to exaggerate.

The Steinbergers are not likely to be distinguished below the level of "Riesling Kabinett," and since a number of grape varieties other than Riesling have been planted in the Steinberg in recent years, the "Riesling" is as important for the label as is the *"Kabinett."* In ex-

Old winepresses at Kloster Eberbach.

tremely dry years like 1959 they sometimes have a trace of bitterness and lack of fruit; in poor years like 1972 and 1978 they can be hard and unattractive, though with time they are likely to become wines of a rather haughty elegance. When nature smiles, however, as in 1975 and 1976, they are the true glories of the Rheingau.

The same Cistercian monks who created the Steinberg and surrounded it with its mile-and-a-half-long wall, also constructed in a wooded valley nearby a magnificent Gothic monastery, long since secularized, but remarkably preserved—Kloster Eberbach. This was actually founded by Augustinians in 1116, but was taken over by Cistercians, under the direction of St. Bernard de Clairvaux, less than twenty years later, and within a century it had become the principal center of German viticulture and the German wine trade, with a branch in Cologne and a fleet of wine ships on the Rhine. In the old monastery buildings, which are extraordinarily picturesque with their vaulted ceilings and ancient wine-presses, some of the major German wine auctions take place.

Including the Steinberg, Hattenheim has 574 acres of vineyard and here is a list of the better Lagen:

Hattenheimer Nussbrunnen	Hattenheimer Hassel
Hattenheimer Engelmannsberg	Hattenheimer Pfaffenberg
Hattenheimer Wisselbrunnen	Hattenheimer Schützenhaus
Hattenheimer Mannberg	

* *Oestrich,* Grosslage Gottesthal, (except for portions of the Klosterberg vineyard, which are in Mehrhölzchen). Oestrich with 1108 acres, has the largest extent of vineyards of the Rheingau, a wide, gently sloping semicircle of vines extending along the Rhine for well over a mile, and swinging back into the hills to the west of Hallgarten. The wines are full-bodied, and not unlike those of Hallgarten but with considerably less class, soft and in certain vintages even a little coarse.

Lenchen is by all odds the best Lage, though the consolidation of 1971 has mixed some of its 363 acres with not so good ones, the price for simplification. The top producer is *J. Wegeler Erben.* The smaller ones are *Gebrüder Walter, Fischbach, Freymuth, Kunz Fetzer, Kühn Erben,* and a number of growers by the name of *Eser: August, Hermann, Josef,* etc.

Oestrich like Erbach has one vineyard that does not carry the name of the community: Schloss Reichartshausen; it is only 9.5 acres, of which .625 are in the Hattenheimer Pfaffenberg and the rest in the Oestricher Doosberg. As most old and famous vineyards, it belonged to the church (the same Cistercians from Kloster Eberbach) and has preserved its individuality through all vagaries of simplification and politics.

Here are the vineyards of Oestrich:

Oestricher Lenchen	Oestricher Doosberg
Oestricher Klosterberg	Schloss Reichartshausen

* *Mittelheim.* Here, some vineyards are in the Erntebringer and some in the Honigberg Grosslage. (418 acres). The wines are very similar to Oestrich, perhaps a little more full bodied. They are hardly ever exported, though as worthy as those of Oestrich, and because they are not as well known, offer better value for money. Reliable growers are *Reitz, Hupfeld, Henner, Schonleber, Hermann Kunz, Beisgen* and *Rainer Sieben*.

The Lagen are:

Mittelheimer Goldberg (entirely in the Grosslage Erntebringer)
Mittelheimer Edelmann ⎰ The two vineyards are partially in the
Mittelheimer St. Niko- ⎱ Grosslage Erntebringer and partially
laus   in Honigberg.

** *Hallgarten,* Grosslage Mehrholzchen is another one of the upland villages, as distinguished from the river towns of the Rheingau; it is about a half mile west of Kloster Eberbach and some of its best vineyards are only a stone's throw from the Steinberg. With such a situation, Hallgarten could hardly fail to produce, especially in great years, wines of extraordinary quality, and the Hallgarteners of 1921, 1945, and 1949, were and still are famous. They are tremendous wines, fuller in body even than the Rüdesheimers, although drier, and generally with less alcohol. The Hallgarteners of poor or fair years are another matter, and I cannot say that I find them attractive.

The most important producer is *Prince Löwenstein,* or as it reads on the label, the *Fürstlich Löwenstein-Wertheim-Rosenberg'sches Weingut,* but *Karl Franz Engelmann* is quite in the same class.

There are two cooperatives with rather amusing names, that produce good wines from major holdings. They were originally three all founded during the Boer War. The larger and richer growers formed the *"Vereinigte Weingutsbesitzer,"* and were promptly called *"die Engländer"* (the Englishmen) by their poorer neighbors who formed their own association, a *Winzergenossenschaft* named *"die Buren"* (The Boers). A third, a *Winzerverein* named *"Die Deutschen"* (The Germans) was formed later. In the meantime *"die Deutschen"* have merged with *"die Buren,"* so that now there are only two cooperatives left. There are a few additional small producers worth noting: *Josef Bug, Stettler, Strieht, Hugo Wolf, Oswald Ruhl Erben, Kempenich, Songen, Jakob Riedel* and *Josef Semmler. Hallgarten has 523 acres under vines and the Lagen are:*

Hallgartener Schönhell   Hallgartener Hendelberg
Hallgartener Jungfer   Hallgartener Würzgarten

Schloss Vollrads with its vineyards.

*** *Winkel,* Grosslage Honigberg, except for the Dachsberg vineyard, which is in the Grosslage Erntebringer. The word *Winkel* in German means "angle" (as well as "nook" or "quiet corner") and the "angle," looking very much like a carpenter's square, appears in the coat-of-arms of Winkel and on the wine labels of several of its good producers. In summer, at least, the village is anything but a "quiet corner," for it is practically indistinguishable from Mittelheim two rows of houses strung along the noisy, busy, and unfortunately very narrow Rheinstrasse, the river road.

Winkel's greatest glory is ****Schloss Vollrads,* the venerable and famous estate of the Matuschka-Greiffenclau family, a half mile back in the hills and reached by a narrow road up a long alley of poplar trees. This, with its 91.5 acres of vineyards is one of the largest privately owned estates and one of the loveliest houses in the Rheingau. Apart from the picturesque central tower, which dates from the year 1335, it is more of a manor house than a Schloss, or castle, built in the baroque style, out of a red sandstone that complements the green of the huge trees in its central courtyard, and the dark slate of its high roofs.

The present Graf Matuschka personally supervises both vineyard and cellar operations, and has greatly publicized the fact that German white wines, though slightly sweet at times are ideal with food.

In good and great years (for this is a vineyard which requires sunshine) the wines of Vollrads are unsurpassed—they have ripeness, great fruit, and an extraordinary distinction. They are classified and labeled in a rather special way which merits a few lines of explanation.

All the wines of the estate have the same labels, with only their capsules indicating their particular style and quality. *"Qualitätswein bestimmter Anbaugebiete"* (QbA) bear green capsules for the lowest quality and green with gold stripe for the better ones. *Kabinett,* similarly is categorized into two qualities: blue capsules for the ordinary, blue with gold stripe for the better quality. *Spätlese* and *Auslese* are similarly treated with rose for *Spätlese* and white for *Auslese,* their better qualities again deserving a gold stripe on the basic color. The *Beerenauslese* and *Trockenbeerenauslese* carry gold capsules, with the *Trockenbeerenauslese* bottles having neck labels in addition, the only wines of Vollrads that do.

Unfortunately the estate makes distinctions between different qualities which in the modern market place make no sense, the differences being too esoteric to justify the complex system of capsules.

The prosaic little town of Winkel has four or five other vineyards of almost equal distinction and fame (658 acres in all including Vollrads). Most of these (Hasensprung is the best of them) lie between Schloss Vollrads and Schloss Johannisberg, and one could hardly rub shoulders with better neighbors. The principal producers of Winkel are as follows: *Graf Matuschka-Greiffenclau'sche Kellerei und Gutsverwaltung-Schloss Vollrads. Landgräflich-Hessiches Weingut* (formerly *Kommerzienrat Krayer Erben*). 33 acres in Winkel and Johannisberg. *Von Brentano'sche Gutsverwaltung.* 19 acres in Winkel. *Geromont'sche Gutsverwaltung.* 10 acres in Winkel and Johannisberg. *Weingut Jakob Hamm.* 10 acres in Winkel and Johannisberg.

There are at least a dozen smaller growers worthy of confidence: *Hans Krayer, Hans and Gerhard Blümlein, Johannes Grün, Sterzel, Faust, Derstroff, Kremer, Basting-Gimbel, Hans Ohlig & Sohn,* and *Fritz Allendorf.*

The *Lagen* in Winkel are:

Schloss Vollrads	Winkeler Hasensprung
Winkeler Bienengarten	Winkeler Dachsberg
Winkeler Klaus	Winkeler Gutenberg
Winkeler Schlossberg	Winkeler Jesuitengarten

*** *Johannisberg,* Grosslage.Erntebringer, is by all odds the greatest name of the Rheingau. Whether it is the best wine can perhaps be argued, and even pleasantly and profitably argued, after the fashion of the French judge, who, being asked whether he preferred Burgundy or Bordeaux, replied, "My friends, this is a case in which the evidence on both sides is so interesting that I shall probably spend most of my life examining it, and allow my decision to be made public only after my death."

But it is a fact that even the Riesling grape is known in a number of countries, including Switzerland, and the United States, as the Johannisberg, or Johannisberger, and when one speaks of Rhine wine, the name Johannisberger comes almost automatically to mind. And principally, of course, and first of all, ****Schloss Johannisberg* itself.

There is no other vineyard quite like it; none with the same immensely regal look, as if it had been planned on a vast scale, by some enormously talented landscape gardener. Its great steep hill, isolated, symmetrical, crowned with its castle, set in a sort of green amphitheater of the Taunus, is as dramatic as a stage setting, and whether seen from the river road, or from across the Rhine, dominates the whole landscape. The view from the castle terrace, whether by day or in the evening, is no less splendid—the vines fall away from the terrace edge like a green wave, and one has the impression that the Rhine, and its fertile, busy valley, are directly at one's feet.

It may or may not be true that it was Charlemagne himself who ordered the first vines planted on Johannisberg's steep hill. In any case, a Benedictine monastery had been constructed there by the year 1100, and when the church properties were secularized in 1803, it became the property of Prince William of Orange. The Congress of Vienna, after the fall of Napoleon, ceded it to the Emperor of Austria, and he in turn bestowed it as a fief on Prince Metternich, reserving, however, in perpetuity, one-tenth of its production of wine. This *"Zehntel"* (or *Zehent"*) is still paid (though generally no longer in the form of wine) to the Habsburg heirs, by Fürst von Metternich, the present owner.

The present castle is new. The previous *Schloss* was bombed with incendiaries by the R.A.F. during the War, and, except for its cellars, almost entirely destroyed. The reconstruction has been carried out with good taste and the castle is quite as handsome as it was before.

The Schloss Johannisberg vineyard consists of 86.5 acres, directly in front of the castle, and its exposure could not conceivably be better. The press-house is modern, and the deep, vaulted cellars directly under the castle are models of what cellars should be.

Prince Paul Metternich is often absent and the day-to-day management of the estate is entrusted to the capable hands of Josef Staab, whose signature appears on the labels. His predecessor, Christian Labonte, was responsible for the introduction of certain modern techniques of agriculture and of wine-making which have perhaps shocked a few traditionalists, but have proved eminently successful none the less.

It is nevertheless true that for nearly a decade-beginning with the 1954 vintage, which was poor everywhere and ending with the 1962, which should have been better here than it was—Schloss Johannisberg went through a period of lean years. Its wines seemed somehow to have lost the special elegance which distinguished them; they were sound, even fine Rheingau wines like their neighbors, but the old unmistakable superiority was no longer there. Happily it is now possible to report that the eclipse is over and the bad days are past. In 1963 and again in 1964 there were no better wines made in the whole Rheingau than here, and the devoted partisans of Schloss Johannisberg have at last had their patience rewarded and their faith restored.

Perhaps the most flattering thing one can say about Schloss Johannisbergers when they are as they should be, is that they are worthy of their reputation, which is second to none. Less full-bodied than the Steinbergers, less overwhelming in fruit and flavor than the Marcobrunners, less piquant and spicy than the Rauenthalers, often with a taste of flinty slate reminiscent of the best Mosels, they are clearly the "first gentlemen" of the Rheingau and their distinction, their class, is both obvious and incomparable.

Like Schloss Vollrads, Schloss Johannisberg continues to label and capsule their wines without compromises to the German wine law of 1971 or for that matter to logic. With the exception of *Trockenbeerenauslese* and *QbA* (Yellow capsule), all other wines have two standards at every level and two different labels: the coat-of-arms of the Metternichs for the lower quality wines with red capsule for *Kabinett,* white for *Spätlese,* rose for *Auslese,* and rose/gold for *Beerenauslese.*

The picture of the Castle for the finer qualities with orange capsule for *Kabinett,* white for *Spätlese,* light blue for *Auslese,* blue/gold for *Beerenauslese* and gold for *Trockenbeerenauslese.*

I remember discussing this label and capsule idiosyncracy a couple of years ago with Herr Staab and meeting with very little understanding; even after I pointed out that the system divided the crop of some 25,000 cases in a good year, into ten categories and unnecessarily confused the consumer.

Directly behind the Schloss, and out of sight of the river road, is the tiny village of Johannisberg, with 206 acres of vineyard surrounding the central 87.5 acres of the castle's Schlossberg. These, too, particularly in good years produce wines of wonderful finesse and bouquet, often quite comparable in quality to those of the Metternich domain. The leading producers, all of them deservedly famous, are: *Landgräflich-Hessisches Weingut, G. H. von Mumm'sche Gutsverwaltung, Graf von Schönborn-Wiesentheit.*

Less important, but well worth noting, are a number of good small growers such as *Karl Zerbe, Peter Schamari, Erben, Moos Erben, Eser, Josef Klein Erben, Winzergenossenschaft, Karl Gross, Helmut Hanka,* and *Odernheimer.*

The best *Lagen* are:

Schloss Johannisberg	Johannisberger Klaus
Johannisberger Hasenberg	Johannisberger Hölle
Johannisberger Vogelsang	Johannisberger Mittelhölle
Johannisberger Goldatzel	Johannisberger Schwarzenstein

** *Geisenheim,* Partially in Grosslage Erntebringer and partially in Grosslage Burgweg. Geisenheim is even more celebrated for its school, the *"Forschungsanstalt fur Weinbau, Gartenbau, Getränketechnologie and Landespflege,"* than for its wines, excellent as they are. This "Research institute for viticulture, horticulture, technology of beverages and care of the land" as it is succinctly called, is one of the great wine schools of the world, responsible in no small measure for the remarkably high level of wine technology in Germany.

The school property includes extensive vineyards from which the wines are made, as might be expected, with scrupulous care, and the school label is one of the most respected of the Rheingau. The town is prosperous and attractive, with a Gothic cathedral, a castle belonging to Graf Schönborn, and a famous 600-year-old linden tree.

The vineyards extend from within a few hundred yards of Schloss Johannisberg to what used to be the village of Eibingen, and is now part of Rüdesheim, or for nearly two miles; they comprise 1,075 acres.

Like the Rüdesheimers, the wines of Geisenheim have the considerable virtue of being good and sometimes even excellent in vintage years ranked as fair; unlike most Rüdesheimers, they achieve surprising heights in great years as well and the *Beerenauslesen* and *Trockenbeerenauslesen* of Geisenheim rank with the very best. A Gesienheimer Mäuerchen, for example, was rated as the Rheingau's finest wine in the superb 1893 vintage, and the 1945's, too, were remarkable.

Leading producers include the *Hessische Forschungsanstalt fur Wein-, Obst- und Gartenbau'*, *Weingut Zwierlein, Hebauf, Rammersbach Erben, Dr. Werthmann Erben, Phillip Graf, Karl Heinz Brunk, Jakob Holschier, Sons, Corvers, Dieter Oschmann, Reiner Schmitt, Freimuth, Vollmer* and *Wilhelm Göttert*.

The vineyards in the Grosslage Burgweg are:

Geisenheimer Fuchsberg   Geisenheimer Mäuerchen
Geisenheimer Mönchpfad   Geisenheimer Rothenberg

And in the Grosslage Erntebringer:

Geisenheimer Schlossgarter   Geisenheimer Kläuserweg
Geisenheimer Kilzberg   Geisenheimer Klaus

The vineyard Klaus is in three communities: Johannisberg, Winkel and Geisenheim.

*** *Rüdesheim,* Grosslage Burgweg, is the westernmost town of the Rheingau proper—beyond it not even an Arizona cliff-dweller would attempt to construct a village. Its principal buildings and main streets occupy the last few acres of flat land at the foot of the Rüdesheimer Berg, and some of its narrow "Gassen," or alleys, wind and clamber like the streets of a hill town in Italy.

Seen from across the river, from Bingen, at the mouth of the Nahe, Rüdesheim and its Berg present an extraordinary impressive picture: a smiling and pretty little town; next to it and behind it, an almost perpendicular hill, cut and terraced into what looks like a gigantic stairway, with wall above wall above wall, each supporting its little patch of vines, as the vineyards climb on past Rüdesheim's ruined castle, the Ehrenfels, to the trees of the Niederwald at the hill's crest.

The Rhine, once it has been joined by the Nahe, picks up speed, and narrows, then swings in a great swift curve around the Rüdesheimer Berg to plunge into the veritable canyon through which it runs northward to Koblenz. This stretch of fast and often turbulent water, dangerous and difficult to navigate, is the so-called *"Binger Loch,"* the "hole of Bingen," and on a little island a picturesque old tower, the *Mäuseturm,* stands guard over it. Near here, too, are the famous "Hunger Stones"—rocks in the bed of the Rhine that are visible only in years of extreme drought and low water—their appearance is supposed to presage a poor harvest, but great wine.

Situated in a sort of bottle-neck of road and rail and river traffic, Rüdesheim was heavily bombed and badly damaged in the War, although its great railway bridge over the Rhine survived, and was only destroyed by the retreating German army, at the end. Many of the good vineyards too were severely battered but they and the town itself have largely been restored, and Rüdesheim is once more a major tourist and excursion center boasting an excellent Wine Museum among its many attractions. An auto-ferry runs across to Bingen, there are passenger steamers in both directions on the Rhine, and a new cable railway carries its baskets of visitors high over the vineyards to the Niederwald. Here a hotel and restaurant have been installed in what was once the hunting lodge of the Dukes of Nassau, and here, too, is the National Denkmal, the "Germania Monument," a graceless pile if there ever was one, which, however, commands a truly magnif icent view over the Rhine Valley.

Most of Rüdesheim's best vineyards (there are 819 acres in all) are somewhat west of the village, on the terraced face of the Berg, and wines from these have the word *"Berg"* as part of their name as Rüdesheimer Berg Rottland, for example, but not Rüdesheimer Rosengarten, nor Rüdesheimer Klosterlay. These Berg wines have the typical Rüdesheimer characteristics to a pronounced degree: an extraordinary richness and ripeness, full body, a somewhat more golden color than most other Rheingau wines, slightly more alcohol, somewhat less finesse. Because of the incomparable exposure of the vineyards, and the shallow, rocky soil on which they are planted, the vines often suffer from drought, particularly in great or sunny years. In vintages considered fair or good, the Rudesheimers are frequently the best wines of the Rhine; in great vintages they are often less outstanding, lacking in balance and sometimes in fruit, and this is even more true

The vintage at Rüdesheim.

of the Berg wines than of the others. Many of the 1950 Rüdesheimers were better than the '49s, and in a year ranked as superlative, particularly if it is a dry one, the wines from the valley are better than from the hillside. The latter are likely to be too alcoholic and lacking in fruity acidity.

The top producers of Rüdesheim are not very numerous, nor are their holdings very large. All the following produce wines of the highest class, and their labels can be counted on absolutely.

Schloss Groenesteyn, Weingut des Reichsfreiherrn von Ritter zu Groenesteyn. Important holdings, 44.5 acres in all, in seven of Rüdesheim's ten vineyards including Berg Rottland and Berg Roseneck.

Staatsweingut (the State Domain). Important acreage (58 acres in all) in Berg Schlossberg, Berg Rottland, Berg Roseneck and Bischofsberg.

Domäneweingut Schloss Schönborn. Holdings in Berg Schlossberg, Berg Rottland and Bischofsberg.

Geh. Rat Julius Wegeler Erben. Important holdings in Berg Rottland and Berg Schlossberg as well as lesser holdings in others.

G. H. von Mumm'sches Weingut: Important holdings in Berg Roseneck, Bischofsberg and Drachenstein, as well as lesser holdings in other vineyards.

Hessische Forschungsanstalt fur Wein-, Obst- und Gartenbau. Important holdings in Magdalenenkreuz and Klosterberg. There are a good number of dependable growers. For example: the *Pfarrgut,* the *Frühmessereigut, Philipp Veith, Wallenstein Erben, Dadischek, Geschwister Hess Erben, Josef Philipp, Geschwister Erhardt, Jakob Lill IV, Jakob Christ, Karl Heinz Hirsch, Karl Heinz Glock, Franz Böhner* and *Fendel Hetzert.*

The following are the vineyards of Rüdesheim, and they rank more or less in this order of quality:

Rüdesheimer Berg Rottland	Rüdesheimer Drachenstein
Rüdesheimer Berg Roseneck	Rüdesheimer Kirchenpfad
Rüdesheimer Berg Schlossberg	Rüdesheimer Bischofsberg
Rüdesheimer Klosterberg	Rüdesheimer Klosterlay
Rüdesheimer Berg Magdalenenkreuz	Rüdesheimer Rosengarten

Assmannshausen, Grosslage Steil and Burgweg lies north of the Binger Loch, beyond the Rüdesheimer Berg, and for a boatman it is therefore outside the Rheingau, whatever we wine-drinkers may say. Actually, in terms of wine, too, it is a region apart, since it produces more red than white. This red Assmannshäuser, can best be described as tasting in a good year like the lightest wine from the côte de Beaune in Burgundy.

The vineyards (435 acres) are directly north of, and parallel to, those of Rüdesheimer Berg; they are on a slope almost equally steep, overlooking a little side valley running back to Aulhausen, behind the National *Denkmal* of Niederwald; 38% are planted in Riesling and over 60% in Pinot Noir (here called the Spätburgunder) cuttings of which were brought from France by St. Bernard de Clairvaux over 800 years ago. Outside of one excellent hotel, the Krone, there is nothing much to the town. By a very large margin, the most important producer is the *State Domain,* or *Staatsweingut;* smaller growers with a good reputation include *Hufnagel, Wittman, Dr. Jung, Eulberg, König, Schön* and *Michael Schön.*

The vineyard names in the Grosslage Steil are:

Assmannshäuser Hinterkirch   Assmannshäuser Höllenberg
(40% Riesling, 60% Pinot Noir)   (90% Pinot Noir)
Assmannshäuser Frankenthal
(50% Riesling, 50% Pinot Noir)

In the Grosslage Burgweg:

Assmannshäuser Berg Kaisersteinfels

(entirely planted in Riesling).

Lorch and Lorchhausen, Grosslage Burgweg.

Here, north of Assmannshausen, the official Rheingau comes to what can only be described as a rather inglorious end. One excellent producer, *Gräflich von Kanitz' sche Weingutsverwaltung,* whose holdings are 47.6 acres in Lorch, makes excellent wine, but the soil and growing conditions, in the best Lagen are quite different and, however good, these are Rheingau wines in name only and could better be described and listed as the outstanding products of another and adjoining district, the Mittelrhein. *Graf Schönborn* has holdings here as well as a number of smaller and dependable growers amongst which are *Troiztsch, Vellenzer, Mohr Erben* and a good *Winzerverein.*

Lorch and Lorchhausen together have 680 acres of vines of which some are in Lorchhausen:

Lorchausener Rosenberg   Lorchhausener Seligmacher

And in Lorch:

Lorcher Schlossberg   Lorcher Kapellenberg
Lorcher Krone   Lorcher Pfaffenweis
Lorcher Bodental-Steinberg

5

THE NAHE

SEVENTY years ago, when German wines were at the height of their pre-World War and pre-Prohibition popularity, the wines of the Nahe occupied an honorable and important place among them. This was particularly true in and around St. Louis, and the fact that several of the leading Nahe producers were called Anheuser, and were actually cousins of the Anheusers of Anheuser-Busch and Budweiser fame, gave them an immediate entrée. At the turn of the century no good New York wine list was complete without its Nahe wine listings. Yet all this has changed and for years after Prohibition and after the second World War, Nahe wines were hardly known in America.

Recently however, they are once again finding their way into leading wine lists throughout the country. They are certainly much better now than in the days of our fathers and grandfathers; as a matter of fact, one of the best vineyards of all (Schloss Böckelheimer Kupfergrube) did not even exist in 1900 and was later created by the State on a steep hillside originally covered with scrub and brush. Today the wines of the Nahe fully deserve a place alongside those of the Rheingau and Rheinpfalz, of the Mosel and Rheinhessen.

Here, as in other parts of the left bank of the Rhine, Muller-Thürgau is the predominant grape variety. It accounts for over 31% of the total plantings, followed by 24.3% Silvaner and 22.5% Riesling. There is a good sprinkling of new crossings; almost 5% Scheurebe, 2.5% Kerner and 2.1% Bacchus and Faber respectively. The traditional Ruländer (Pinot Gris) has 2.5% of the total plantings.

The soil and climate of the Nahe, particularly on the precipitous valley upstream and southwest from Bad Kreuznach, lend a considerable distinction and breed, not only to the Rieslings but to all other varieties as well. All Nahe wines, being more akin to Rhine than to Mosel, are shipped in brown bottles.

Because of the fact that the valley of the Nahe lies between that of the Mosel and the Rhine valley proper, some writers have chosen to say that the wines, too, are midway between the Mosels and Rhines in character. This seems to me a poor way to describe them: their qualities are their own; the best of them are grown on red sandstone soil very different from the slate of the Mosel, and their bouquet, however admirable, is not a Mosel bouquet by any means. It is, as a matter of fact, more like that of a good Niersteiner, though some of the fine Rieslings from Kreuznach, Niederhausen, Norheim and Schloss Böckelheim have a greater resemblance to a Rheingau than a Niersteiner.

Typical vineyard on the Nahe.

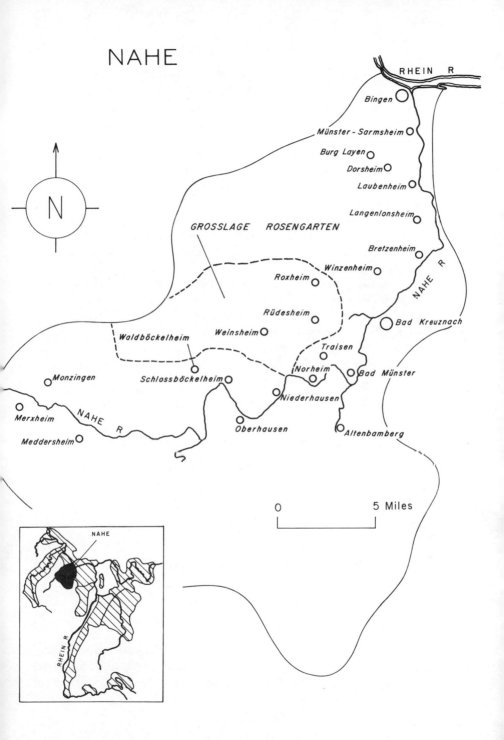

NAHE

We have had occasion before to mention the mouth of the Nahe—it is directly opposite the Rheingau's Rüdesheimer Berg, and almost in the shadow of the Binger Scharlachberg, the westernmost vineyard of Rheinhessen. Actually four districts—Rheingau, Rheinhessen, the Mittel-rhein and the Nahe—come together at this point; what are officially classified as the Nahe vineyards begin a little further south, half way between Bingen and Bad Kreuznach.

Bad Kreuznach is the county seat and the center of the wine trade. A bustling town, attractively situated on both sides of the Nahe, it is the home of the famous Seitz Werke, one of the great innovators in the art of winemaking. Its filtering and bottling equipment is to be found around the world wherever man is dedicated to making fine wine.

All the leading producers of the region, with the exception of the *State Domain* in Schloss Böckelheim, are based in Bad Kreuznach and own vineyards in at least three or four different communities. The eight great producers of the district are:

Paul Anheuser. Vineyards in Kreuznach, Schloss Böckelheim, Norheim, Niederhausen, Monzingen and Altenbamberg.

Weingut Herf und Engelsmann Erben. Holdings in Kreuznach, Winzenheim, Rotenfels, etc.

Weingut Gutleuthof, Carl Andres. Kreuznach, Roxheim, Etc.

Weingut August Anheuser. Vineyards in Kreuznach, Winzenheim, Schloss Böckelheim, Niederhausen, Norheim, etc.

Reichsgräflich von Plettenberg'sche Verwaltung. Holdings in Kreuznach, Norheim, Bretzenheim, Winzenheim, etc.

Staatsweingut Weinbaulehranstalt (the Provincial Wine School). Kreuznach, Norheim, Niederhausen, etc.

Staatlich Weinbaudomänen, Niederhausen-Schloss Böckelheim, (the State Domain). Vineyards in Schloss Böckelheim, Niederhausen, Münster, Rotenfels, etc.

And finally two absolutely first class cooperatives: the *Zentralkellerei der Nahewinzer*, Bad Kreuznach with new and modern cellars in Bretzenheim. This central cooperative makes every bit as fine wines as the other principal producers on this list and the *Winzergenossenschaft*

Rheingrafenberg in Meddernsheim which handles only wines of the upper Nahe. This cooperative has greatly contributed to the high quality image of this part of the region.

Kreuznach is not only the commercial but the geographical center of its district, and in its own right a wine-producing town of absolutely first rank. The nearby villages that belong in the same high category are all further upstream, which here means south, and they are all strung along the narrow, winding Nahe Valley: Münster (or Bad Münster-am-Stein), Norheim, Niederhausen, Schloss Böckelheim, Altenbamberg and Monzingen.

The rolling hills west and northwest and north of Kreuznach are also for the most part covered with vines, and in this essentially secondary area three or four towns are truly outstanding—Roxheim is certainly the best of them, with Bretzenheim fairly close behind.

The Nahe from Bad Kreuznach to Bingen, where it flows into the Rhine, has three additional villages known for their wines: Münster-Sarmsheim, Burg Layen in the picturesque valley of the rivulet Troll, and finally one of the oldest wine growing communities in Germany, Langenlonsheim with its own Grosslage Sonnenborn.

The Nahe is divided into two *Bereiche:* Schloss Böckelheim and Bad Kreuznach. (Although *schloss* is the German word for castle, as in the French *château,* here it is only the name of the town, which was originally built around a castle.)

The two *Bereiche* are subdivided into seven Grosslagen encompassing 321 individual vineyards and located in 80 wine growing communities.

The following is a brief summary of the towns and their best vineyards:

BEREICH SCHLOSS BÖCKELHEIM:

1) *Grosslage: Burgweg:*

*Altenbamberg	Rotenberg
***Niederhausen	Hermannshöhle, Hermannsberg, Steinberg
**Norheim	Delichen, Kafels
***Schlossböckelheim	Kupfergrube, Königsfels Felsenberg
**Traisen	Bastei

2) *Grosslage: Paradiesgarten:*

**Meddersheim	Rheingrafenberg
**Merxheim	Römerberg
**Monzingen	Frühlingsplätzchen

3) *Grosslage: Rosengarten:*

*Roxheim	Höllenpfad
Rüdesheim	Goldgrube

(wines from this vineyard are usually sold under the name of the Grosslage as Rüdesheimer Rosengarten).

BEREICH KREUZNACH:

1) *Grosslage: Kronenberg:*

***Bad Kreuznach	Hinkelstein, Krötenpfuhl, Brückes Narrenkappe, St. Martin, Mollenbrunnen Rosenheim
*Bretzenheim:	Pastorei, Hofgut

2) *Grosslage: Schlosskapelle:*

**Dorsheim	Goldloch
***Münster-Sarmsheim	Dautenpflänzer, Rheinberg Pittersberg, Kapellenberg

3) *Grosslage: Sonnenborn:*

*Langenlonsheim	Löhrer Berg, Steinchen

4) *Grosslage: Pfarrgarten:*

Wallhausen	Felseneck, Johannisberg, Pastorenberg
Sommerloch	Steinrossel
Gutenberg	Schloss Gutenberg

6

RHEINHESSEN

RHEINHESSEN is a little rectangle of rather bare, rolling country, about thirty miles by twenty, bounded on the east and north by the Rhine and on the west by the Nahe. An old Roman road runs diagonally across it and the cities of Worms and Mainz and Bingen mark three of its four corners; all three are on the Rhine. Rheinhessen is the largest of the wine areas in acreage and second only to the Rheinpfalz in production.

Rheinhessen, as far as Americans are concerned, is perhaps best known for its Hessians, those mercenary soldiers of the King (fortunately for us, not too good ones) in our Revolutionary War, or War of Independence. But this is not the whole story by any means. Gutenberg, the father of printing, was born and died in Mainz. Worms is famous for its "Diet of Worms" which as I learned long ago, to my considerable disappointment as a schoolboy, does not mean what it seems to and is connected instead with the history of the Reformation. Bingen, in turn, is celebrated for its "Bingen pencils," which is another and amusing word for "corkscrews" in colloquial German. (The term Bingen pencils originated during a city council meeting in Bingen. The mayor asked one of the city councilors for a pencil, and it turned out that none of the city councilors had pencils, but they all had

0   5   10 Mi

N

RHEIN R.

MAIN R.

Bingen

Büdesheim

Gau - Algesheim

Ingelheim

Mainz

Laubenheim

Bodenheim

Nackenheim

NAHE R.

Ebersheim

Gau - Bischofsheim

Harxheim

Jugenheim

Saulheim

Nierstein

Oppenheim

Dexheim

Dienheim

Gau - Bickelheim

Dalheim

Guntersblum

Alsheim

Alzey

Mettenheim

Weinheim

Bechtheim

Westhofen

Osthofen

RHEIN R.

RHEINHESSEN

Flörsheim - Dalsheim

RHEIN R.

RHEINHESSEN

corkscrews. Hence the origin of the word Binger pencil). A surprisingly large number of the Germans who came to America during the 19th Century were from Rheinhessen, and finally, of course, Rheinhessen is the home of Nierstein and Liebfraumilch. It could almost properly be called Liebfraumilchsheim.

Just as a matter of record, there are 167 villages in Rheinhessen which produce wine; it is safe to say that 99% of them produce Liebfraumilch, or something eventually sold as such; what is more astonishing is that 120 out of the 167 have names that end in *"heim."* Home, or *"heim,"* is something important to all of us, but this would seem excessive, and it is certainly confusing. The custom has spread to neighboring provinces, witness Rüdesheim in the Rheingau, Norheim on the Nahe, Deidesheim and Wachenheim in the Pfalz, and even, to go farther afield, Bergheim in Alsace and Anaheim in Southern California. But the Hessians are easily the champions.

"Home" and "Mother" are so often coupled together in common speech that it is hardly surprising to find Hessia (the home of *"heim"*) specializing in a wine called "Milk of the Blessed Mother," for this, precisely, is what Liebfraumilch means.

The name "Liebfraumilch" or "Liebfrauenmilch" was used centuries ago to name the wines that came from the vineyards surrounding a church called "Liebfrauenkirche" in Worms. With time the name was given to wines growing in the general area of Worms. By 1910 it had assumed such general use that the Chamber of Commerce of Worms issued a regulation that limited the use of the name to Rheinhessen wines of a certain standard of quality. (The German Chamber of Commerce, unlike ours, have certain official governmental functions).

On August 12, 1971, the Land Government of Rheinland Pfalz extended the area by provisional decree to include all "Qualitätsweine" from the Nahe, Rheingau, Rheinhessen and Rheinpfalz.

At this stage the German government is trying definitively to regulate the use of the name, since under E.E.C. law a quality wine can only come from one designated area of origin. Therefore there are two solutions to the problem: either to form a 12th designated area of origin, which would include certain parts of the Rheinhessen and Rheinpfalz or to give the sole right of the name to only one of the two traditional areas. It is likely that a decision will be made before this book goes to print.

Liebfraumilch is to German wine what Port is to Portuguese and

Champagne to French wines: a large enough geographical area enabling the exportation of a consistent produce under one geographical name of origin. It is no wonder that Liebfraumilch accounts for 50% of German wine exports. Its name is often combined with a brand name such as Hans Christof, Crown of Crowns, Madrigal, Glockenspiel, Madonna and Blue Nun. Each brand owner markets his particular blend, just as each Champagne House markets its particular Cuvée.

The wine of Rheinhessen, like those of the Rheingau, the Nahe, and the Pfalz, come in brown bottles, and apart from those called Liebfraumilch, they are labeled according to the same system—town plus vineyard name, and all of the rest—as other German wines.

The wines of Rheinhessen are grown in different soil and under different microclimatic conditions than all the others on the Rhine. This being a large area, there are actually seven different districts each with its own distinct character.

In the Western part of the district along the Rhine, in Bingen and its surrounding region, they are similar to the wines of the Nahe. There, the Rieslings have elegance and style, and even the Silvaners tend to develop some. Around Ingelheim, halfway between Bingen and Mainz, there are a handful of communities—Ockenheim, Gau-Algesheim, Kleinwinternheim, Appenheim and Jugenheim—that are primarily a red wine district. The area is well known for its Pinot Noir, which here makes a rather light and pleasant red wine. Then there are the communities along the so called Rhine front, that area which goes from Mainz through Laubenheim, Bodenheim, Nackenheim, Nierstein, Oppenheim, Dienheim, Guntersblum to Alsheim and Mettenheim. This area has the largest proportion of Riesling in Rheinhessen, and all its wines, not only the Rieslings, are the most elegant of the entire region.

"In the Bereich Wonnegau around communities such as Bechtheim, Osthofen, Dittelsheim-Hessloch and Westhofen, all the wines even the Rieslings, are full bodied and clumsy, and as the natives say, *"volles maul"* a mouthful. Then there is an area called Rheinhessische Schweiz, the Switzerland of Rheinhessen, in the northwest corner of the region and around the communities of Frei-Laubersheim, Biebelsheim, Wonsheim and Neubamberg where the wines are lighter and fruitier. Worms with its surrounding communities, villages that all have become suburbs in the urban spread —Pfeddersheim, Herrnsheim and Leiselheim forms yet another microregion with rather flat and dull wines. Finally there is the interior which is called the *Hügelland*—hill country—where the wines are less full bodied, they are juicy, fresh and balanced. Centered around Alzey, the county seat, this area includes Weinheim well known for its Riesling, Albig, Flonheim, Bornheim, Gaubickelheim, Gau-Odernheim, Saulheim, Wörrstadt and Framersheim.

Here, as elsewhere in Germany, the best wines are made from the Riesling grape, but the overwhelming majority of the Rheinhessens are made from the Müller-Thurgau. Actually, of the 55,360 acres of vineyards, 36.4% are planted in Müller-Thurgau, 28.7% in Silvaner and only 5% in Riesling. The latter are concentrated in the best vineyard towns and Lagen. Actually Rheinhessen has become one of the two regions (the Rheinpfalz being the other) where new crossings are very important and make up 18.9% of total plantings. The Scheurebe accounts for 6% and the Morio-Muskat occupies the same acreage as Riesling. Though lately it seems to be in distavor, since it only makes good wines from ripe grapes and rather bitter ones from unripe ones.

There seem to be fashions for grape varieties, as for everything else, and the present fashion tends towards two derivatives of the Riesling—Kerner and Bacchus, (the latter has a grapefruit-like bouquet)—and two varieties unrelated to the Riesling—Faber and Huxel. They were both developed by Georg Scheu in Alzey, and the Huxel is only used in the best of vineyards to make top *Prädikat* wines, *Auslesen, Beerenauslesen* and *Trockenbeerenauslesen.*

The Müller-Thurgau, because of its flowery and juicy qualities has replaced many acres of the once dominant Silvaner and the newer varieties have helped to produce juicy, soft and fruity wines, even when blended with a broader and milder Silvaner. Modern techniques in Viticulture have helped produce excellent wines throughout the Rheinhessen, while a mere thirty years ago few wines of the interior were thought good enough to travel far from their native villages.

Today, many of the 167 wine producing villages of Rheinhessen have added their names to winelists that formerly only carried wines from Nierstein and Bingen. The best wines still come from the *"Rheinfront,"* those villages south of Mainz either on the river or on the escarpments that overlook the river, and from Bingen with its "Scharlachberg" or Scarlet hill, at the mouth of the Nahe. These wines have a good deal in common; softer and fuller than the Rheingaus, they usually accompany a meal while the Rheingaus are drunk alone.

Although the wines from the interior share these characteristics, they often lack the ripeness and fullness of their neighbors that profit from the reflected sunshine of the vineyards that overlook the great river, particularly in Nierstein.

The bulk of the wines from the interior are used in average years as the backbone of the better known Liebfraumilch, yet in good years a lot of them represent the extraordinary bargains of *Spätlese* and *Auslese* from such little known villages as Alsheim, Dienheim and Albig.

This improvement in wine growing and winemaking was promoted by the viticultural experimental station in Oppenheim and the vine propagation station in Alzey and is generously supported by the government. The large commercial cellars that give long term contracts to wine growers and cooperatives were equally instrumental in improving the quality and stabilizing the wine market.

The wine law of 1971 consolidated this large region into three Bereiche (Bingen, Nierstein and Wonnegau), 24 Grosslagen and 446 individual vineyards distributed over 167 communities. Here is a short description of the principal communities, the important and better vineyards and growers:

Bereich Bingen is the subdistrict which covers a large area, all the way from Bingen to the city borders of Mainz some 20 miles away. The area is Germany's orchard, cherry, apple, pear and plum trees growing alongside vineyards. The orchards grow in the fertile Rhine valley, the vineyards on the low hillsides bordering the valley. This stretch of Rheinhessen has only two communities noteworthy of its wines; Bingen and Ingelheim.

** *Bingen,* (Grosslage Sankt Rochuskapelle), directly opposite Rüdesheim, occupies a narrow triangle of flat land, formed by the junction of the Nahe and Rhine, at the extreme northwestern corner of Rheinhessen. Behind it rises the vast red buttress of the Scharlachberg, or "scarlet hill" (although its color is rather dusky brick than scarlet), a good part of which, particularly the slope that faces south, and away from Bingen, is covered with vineyards that, though little known outside Germany, produce some of Rheinhessen's best wines.

Originally and not too long ago, three separate towns were involved—Bingen itself, Rüdesheim and Kempten—but the two latter are now part of what might be called "greater Bingen."

The wines of Bingen are fuller and heavier, almost more concentrated than the average Rheinhessen wines. Like the Rüdesheimers across the river, they profit from a warmer microclimate that, in a good year, gives them a special fullness and ripeness.

The leading producers in Bingen are the *Staatsweingut,* the *Villa Sachsen* (that belongs to Nestlé) and *P. A. Ohler.*

Here are the best vineyards of Bingen out of a total of 1,832 acres:

Binger Schlossberg-Schwätzerchen	Binger Bubenstück
Binger Kirchberg	Binger Rosengarten
Binger Kapellenberg	Binger Scharlachberg

The Bereich Bingen has six *Grosslagen,* besides Sankt Rochuskapelle: they are Abtey, Rheingrafenstein, Adelberg, Kurfurstenstück and Kaiserpfalz. The main wine producing villages in these Grosslagen are Ockenheim, Gau-Algesheim, Sprendlingen, Wollstein, Flonheim, Gau-Bickelheim (the seat of the Central Cooperative for all of Rheinhessen), Jugenheim, and finally, in the Grosslage appropriately called Kaiserpfalz:

* *Ingelheim,* now an industrial town, is reputed to have been one of the birthplaces claimed for Charlemagne as well as the site of one of his palaces. It is from Ingelheim that Charlemagne supposedly noticed the early melting of snow on the opposite side of the Rhine and ordered a vineyard to be planted on that spot. This same hill is today the vineyard surrounding Schloss Johannisberg. The town still has its medieval walls intact and boasts some impressive ruins.

Ingelheim has approximately 1,737 acres planted in grapes, about a third of which is red, both Pinot Noir and Portugieser. The rest is largely Müller-Thurgau and Silvaner. Ingelheim is mainly known for its red wine for which there is a good market in Germany. The wines are light, often slightly sweet and rarely exported. Only in great years do they approach the taste of a light Burgundy.

Bereich Nierstein, with 11 Grosslagen.

The best vineyards in Rheinhessen are in the Bereich Nierstein which includes the magnificent Western bank of the Rhine from Mainz to Guntersblum and the hills just west of the river overlooking the valley.

The better vineyards in this area are invariably terraced and face south and southeast in order to take advantage of the reflected sun on the great river. The red slate soil is largely responsible for the substance, fullness and elegance of the wines, qualities that come out even in the Scheurebe and Kerner and Silvaner varieties in good years. The Riesling that is planted in Nierstein, the premier town of the region, approaches, in a ripe year that is blessed with enough rain the elegance and style of the great Rieslings of the Rheingau. The Bereich starts at the city of *Mainz, long one of the principal centers of the German wine trade. The city, like Frankfurt and Wiesbaden owns vineyards at its suburbs of Harxheim and Eversheim. The Harxheim vineyards, chronically unprofitable, were finally leased to a grower by the name of Husar while the wines from the Ebersheim vineyards still carry the legend *"Weingut der Stadt Mainz"* or Estate bottled by the City of Mainz—on their labels and are invariably served at official functions.

Mainz is in the Grosslage Sankt Alban and most of the wines from the vineyards south of the city, mainly from a community called Laubenheim, are more likely to be sold under the name of the Grosslage than the village and vineyard with the exception of Bodenheim.

** *Bodenheim* marks the real beginning of the wine country. Its eminence is due, as far as modern times are concerned, principally to the efforts of two vineyard owners, the heirs of the late Lieutenant-Colonel Liebrecht, and the State Domain. Both have important holdings on the hillsides well back from the alluvial soil along the river and both produce wines with little or none of the heavy, earthy flavor (called *Bodenton* or *Bodengeschmack*) which used to be typical of the average vintages of this rather unfortunately named village before modern technology eliminated it. The truth is of course that these deprecatory terms have only an accidental connection with the name of Bodenheim.

The two leading producers, as mentioned above, are the *Oberstleutnant Liebrecht's Weingutsverwaltung* and the *Staatsweingut Bodenheim;* both, in years such as 1971 and 1976 produced some extraordinary wines. There are 1,300 acres of vines, with a small proportion of Rieslings.

The better *Lagen,* or individually named vineyards are:

Bodenheimer Hoch	Bodenheimer Silberberg
Bodenheimer Westrum	Bodenheimer Leidhecke
Bodenheimer Burgweg	Bodenheimer Ebersberg
Bodenheimer Mönchpfad	

After Grosslage Sankt Alban the official vineyard registry lists the Grosslage Domherr, which encompasses all the villages south of Mainz and west of the hills that border the Rhine. None of the wines produced in these villages is likely to find its way to America under the village name.

Most of the great vineyards of Rheinhessen are within the boundaries of seven Grosslagen: Gutes Domtal, Spiegelberg, Rehbach, Auflangen, Güldenmorgen, Krötenbrunnen and Vogelsgärten. The first of these vineyards is in the village of Nackenheim.

* *Nackenheim* is unknown beyond the frontiers of Germany. The vineyards are not very large but the best of them, Rothenberg, forms the northern cusp of the extraordinary crescent of red hillside soil overlooking the Rhine which has made the reputation and the glory of Nierstein. This is the finest soil of Rheinhessen, and unfortunately there is precious little of it; it is unmistakable, and as red as brick. Nackenheim's portion is very small indeed, about 150 acres, and it is not by chance that the best vineyard of all is called Rothenberg, or "red hillside."

The four "great" estates listed below are actually holdings of between twelve and thirty acres each and sell their annual output so easily that they scarcely need to develop an export market for their wines. The wines have great bouquet, and are remarkable for what German experts call "elegance"—finesse and class.

Nackenheim has only 370 acres under vine, about a third of them Riesling, but here even the Silvaners seem to surpass themselves.

The leading producers are: *Gunderloch-Lange, Gunderloch-Usinger, Staatsweingut Nackenheim* and *Dr. Dietrich* and the better *Lagen:*
Nackenheimer Rothenberg   Nackenheimer Engelsberg

To illustrate the complexity and yet the logic of the new German wine law, Nackenheim is situated in two Grosslagen: Spiegelberg which encompasses the above great vineyard sites and Gutes Domtal in which Schmittskapellchen, the one remaining and largest vineyard of Nackenheim is located. It is no accident that the names of the *Grosslagen* in this area originally belonged to individual vineyards that were consolidated in the great regrouping of 1971. Spiegelberg, Rehbach, Anflangen and Güldenmorgen were proud names of famous vineyards that today lend their names to the best *Grosslagen.*

Weingut
Hermann Franz Schmitt
Hermannshof
Nierstein am Rhein
1978
Niersteiner Pettenthal
Riesling Spätlese
Qualitätswein mit Prädikat
RHEIN-
HESSEN
A. P. Nr.
4382 423 / 1979 0,75 L e
Erzeuger-Abfüllung

Anno 1654
RHEIN-   HESSEN
Qualitätswein   A. P. Nr.
mit Prädikat   4382 022 / 12 77
1976
Niersteiner Rehbach
Riesling Auslese
ERZEUGERABFÜLLUNG
ESTATE-BOTTLED · PRODUCE OF GERMANY
e 0,7L   WEINGUT   700 ml e
BÜRGER-   NIERSTEIN
MEISTER Anton Balbach Erben AM RHEIN

GUNTRUM
FAMILIENWAPPEN VERLIEHEN   DURCH KAISERLICHEN WAPPENBRIEF
ANNO 1545   DES 31. MAI
RHEINHESSEN   750 ml e
RHEINHESSEN   RHEINHESSEN
QUALITÄTSWEIN   MIT PRADIKAT
WHITE QUALITY RHINE WINE ALCOHOL 10% BY VOLUME
Oppenheimer Sackträger
Riesling u. Silvaner Auslese
A. P. Nr. 4382 083
SOLE AGENTS Dreyfus Ashby & Co NEW YORK, N.Y.
PRODUCED AND ESTATE-BOTTLED BY:
WEINGUT LOUIS GUNTRUM ERZEUGER-ABFÜLLUNG
NIERSTEIN AM RHEIN   GERMANY

Amtl. Prüf. Nr. 4 589 083 18 72
1971er   Rheinhessen
Niersteiner Brudersberg
Riesling Spätlese
QUALITÄTSWEIN MIT PRADIKAT · ERZEUGERABFÜLLUNG
Weingut Freiherr Heyl zu Herrnsheim · Nierstein a. Rh.

Bezirks-Winzergenossenschaft
Rheinfront eG
Nierstein-Rhein
RHEINHESSEN
QUALITÄTSWEIN MIT PRADIKAT
Amtliche Prüfungsnummer 4382031 3977
1976er
Niersteiner Auflangen
Riesling Auslese
ERZEUGER-ABFÜLLUNG

Weingut
J. u. H. A. Strub
Nierstein a. Rhein
ERBHOF ULFENHOF
ERBHOF CHATTENHOF
Qualitätswein mit Prädikat
Amtliche Prüfungsnummer 4 382 288 / 17 77
1976er Niersteiner Rehbach
Riesling Auslese
Erzeuger-Abfüllung
RHEINHESSEN

*** *Nierstein* is easily the foremost wine town of Rheinhessen fame, first by far in total production, and usually first in quality as well. It is a busy and cheerful little place, with a mineral spring, the *Sironabad,* which was known even in Roman days, and an important anchorage much used by Rhine barges. The town and the better vineyards are directly on the river and it is believed that the reflected morning sunlight off the Rhine plays a major role in the development of that extraordinary ripeness which is the distinguishing mark of the best Niersteiners. They are very great wines indeed, in some years quite similar to the great Rheingaus yet in others quite different in character from them or from the other great wines of the Rheinpfalz.

There is an old saying that all Liebfraumilchs would be Niersteiners if they could, and it is fairly safe to assume that the really distinguished ones are either straight from some good Nierstein vineyard, or are blends of Niersteiner and something else.

This is not at all to say that everything that Nierstein produces is great wine, for such is a long way from being the case. Well over half of the 2,250 acres of vineyard is in Müller-Thurgau and not all ideally situated. The celebrated Lagen, the ones that have made Nierstein's reputation are on two narrow hillsides—most of them on the "Rheinfront," facing southeast along the river, the others face almost due south over a shallow tributary valley. In the case of no other German wine, therefore, is a vineyard name so important. Nierstein's average production is in the neighborhood of 2,000,000 gallons a year, of which, of course, a good share is consumed locally, and a substantial part labeled simply Bereich Nierstein or Liebfraumilch. The cream, marketed under a vineyard name, amounts to only about 15% or 20%.

Three producers and estate bottlers are internationally known, and the label of any one of them is almost in the nature of a diploma. They are *Franz Karl Schmitt, Hermann Franz Schmitt-Hermannshof* and *Freiherr Heyl zu Herrnsheim Mathildenhof.* In addition there is a well-run *Winzergenossenschaft* or cooperative and about a dozen reputable growers who also bottle their wine: *J.H.A. Strub, Louis Guntrum, Geschwister Schuch, Bürgermeister A. Balbach Erben, Georg Harth, Staatsweingut, Weingut Jakob Gerhardt, Gustav Adolf Schmitt, Reinhold Senfter, Kurfürstenhof, Hath, Heinrich Seebrich* and *Eugen Werheim.*

The vineyards of Nierstein, with the exception of one, which is in the Grosslage Domtal, are divided into three *Grosslagen:*

1. Spiegelberg: where the best vineyards are: (in rough order of quality)

Niersteiner Brückchen   Niersteiner Paterberg
Niersteiner Hölle   Niersteiner Rosenberg
Niersteiner Bildstock   Niersteiner Klostergarten
          Niersteiner Findling

2. Rehbach: with three famous ones:

Niersteiner Pettenthal   Niersteiner Brudersberg
          Niersteiner Hipping

and the small Niersteiner Goldene Luft which is owned entirely by Winzermeister Heinz Seip and is sold under the label of Kurfürstenhof.

and

3. Niersteiner Auflangen, with its vineyards going from the center of the little town to the hills that almost form a gorge facing the Rhine, all of them producing superb wines under the names of:

Niersteiner Kranzberg   Niersteiner Zehmorgen
Niersteiner Bergkirche   Niersteiner Heiligenbaum
Niersteiner Ölberg   Niersteiner Schloss Schwabsburg
Niersteiner Orbel   Niersteiner Glöck

Perhaps the greatest mark of Niersteiners is that they are more often shipped under the name of the famous Grosslagen Spiegelberg, Rehbach and Auflangen than their individual vineyard names and therefore their marketing is simpler.

In a good year there is a cornucopia of wine in every category of the complex scale of quality. Niersteiners are futhermore long-lived and I can well remember a 1911 *Kabinett* which we drank in 1975 and a 1921 *Trockenbeerenauslese* I served on a special occasion in 1971. The first was old but still recognizable, the second gloriously mature and balanced, with the bouquet of a rare nectar.

Oppenheim, Dienheim and Guntersblum are three communities that make excellent wines; Oppenheim just as good as Nierstein, the others just a shade less superb.

Though Dienheim and Guntersblum are the lesser known of the three, they share the same soil and exposure as Oppenheim and many of the Oppenheim growers also own vineyards in Dienheim and Guntersblum.

*** *Oppenheim,* very picturesque and pretty little town, with a fine Gothic church, is set on a low hill well behind the river, and commands a charming view over the green fertile bottomland of the Rhine Valley. The 560 acres of vineyard, about a third in Riesling, are mostly south of the town, on gentle hills that slowly diminish into the flat plain at Dienheim in the direction of Worms. Not long ago, in an old book on the wines of Rheinhessen, I ran across a description of the wines of Oppenheim obviously written by one of their most faithful lovers and most determined champions. Practically every favorable adjective in the German language, conceivably applicable to wine, is included, and the list runs as follows: *"rassig, reintönig, reingärig, elegant, sauber, spritzig, stahlig, blumig, saftig, bukettreich, glatt, kernig, süffig, vollmundig, duftig, zart, rund, reif, gross, hochedel."* Obviously no such paragon among wines ever existed.

The best Oppenheimers are as good as the best Niersteiners, and in dry years even better. In dry years, which often are also the great years, the Niersteiners are broad and flabby, whereas the Oppenheimers have style and elegance. In Nierstein only the low vineyards and the flat land do well in dry years, as they are able to get enough moisture from the soil. On the other hand in average years, and even less good years, Nierstein tends to make finer and more elegant wines than Oppenheim.

The vineyards of Nierstein.

The leading producers are the *Landes-Lehr-und Versuchanstalt* (a Provincial wine school) which also runs the vineyards of the State Domain in Nierstein and Oppenheim, *Louis Guntrum, Carl Koch Erben, Carl Sittmann* and *Dr. Dahlem Erben.*

There are 2 *Grosslagen* in Oppenheim: The better vineyards are in the Grosslage Güldenmorgen:

Oppenheimer Herrenberg	Oppenheimer Gutleuthaus
Oppenheimer Sackträger	Oppenheimer Daubhaus
Oppenheimer Kreuz	Oppenheimer Zuckerberg

The other Grosslage is Krötenbrunnen, the vineyards of which are:

Oppenheimer Schlossberg	Oppenheimer Paterhof
Oppenheimer Schloss	Oppenheimer Herrengarten

Here, as in the case of Nierstein, most of the wines are sold under the name of the *Grosslage.* So that the Dienheim wines can take advantage of the Oppenheim Grosslagen, and the wines of Guntersblum, that are situated in the Krötenbrunnen Grosslage can similarly profit from the better known name. It is, therefore, just as likely that an Oppenheimer Krötenbrunnen originates in the vineyards of Dienheim and Guntersblum as in the vineyards of Oppenheim proper.

** *Dienheim.* Something over a mile farther south on the road to Worms, is Oppenheim's immediate neighbor and within its communal limits are portions of two of Oppenheim's Lagen, Schloss and Paterhof.

The quality of the wines, however, is not as good since some of the 1,150 acres of vineyards of this community are on the plain. Most, if not all of the growers listed in Oppenheim are also vineyard owners in Dienheim. In addition we have the following dependable growers: *Johann Walz und Sohn, Bürgermeister Steinfurth* and *Martinshof Hermann Martin & Sohn.*

The three vineyards of Dienheim which are in the Grosslage Krötenbrunnen are shared with Oppenheim:

Dienheimer Schloss	Dienheimer Paterhof
Dienheimer Herrengarten	

and in the Grosslage Güldenmorgen, similarly, two vineyards are shared with Oppenheim:

Dienheimer Kreuz   Dienheimer Herrenberg

There are four additional vineyards worthy of note in this Grosslage:

Dienheimer Tafelstein   Dienheimer Siliusbrunnen
Dienheimer Falkenberg   Dienheimer Höhlchen

** *Guntersblum* is a large producer of wine. Its 1,550 acres of vineyards make it the fifth major community within a large uninterrupted wine producing area, which starts with Nackenheim, Nierstein, Oppenheim and Dienheim in the north, continues to the south through the small village of Ludwigshöhe into Guntersblum, and ends into two neighboring communities: Alsheim and Mettenheim.

Half of Guntersblum is in the Krötenbrunnen and half in the Vogelsgärten Grosslage. The wines are sometimes as good as those of Oppenheim and I dare say that some of the best Oppenheimer Krötenbrunnen comes from Guntersblum.

In good years, furthermore, it can produce very elegant and fine wines not only from the Müller-Thurgau and Silvaner, but also from Gewürztraminer, Pinot Gris and many of the newer crossings.

The foremost growers are *Schlossgut Schmitt, Ernst Küstner, Schmitt-Dr. Ohnacker, Julius Hiestand, Dr. Muth* and *Friedrich Frey.*

There is no doubt that some of the better Liebfraumilch is blended with Guntersblum, but the choice wines of Guntersblum find their way to the market under the names of the individual vineyards, the best of which are in the Grosslage Krötenbrunnen:

Guntersblumer Steinberg   Guntersblumer Sonnenberg
Guntersblumer Eiserne Hand

and in the Grosslage Vögelsgarten:

Guntersblumer Steig-Terrassen   Guntersblumer Authental
Guntersblumer Himmelthal   Guntersblumer Bornpfad

* *Alsheim* was an unimportant village thirty years ago but enterprising growers, as well as the new crossings have made it a community of 1,500 vineyard acres. The leading grower is *Dr. R. Muth Rap-*

penhof who specializes in stylish Riesling alongside Gewürztraminer and some new crossings. He is also in the forefront of making Trocken and Halb-Trocken or Dry and Half-Dry wine. Other dependable growers are *Peter Balzhauser, Arno Balz Nibelungenhof,* and *Hans Eckelmann.*

Alsheim and the bordering community of Mettenheim (800 acres) share a large vineyard called either Alsheimer or Mettenheimer Goldberg.

The vineyard is in the Krötenbrunnen Grosslage while the rest of Alsheim and Mettenheim are in the Rheinblick Grosslage, where the best vineyards are:

Alsheimer Fischerpfad	Alsheimer Sonnenberg
Alheimer Frühmesse	Mettenheimer Michelsberg
Alsheimer Römerberg	Mettenheimer Schlossberg

Between Oppenheim and Worms the river bends out into a large half circle and the vineyards form an almost straight line from Oppenheim, through Dienheim, Guntersblum, Alsheim, and Mettenheim, through the two villages of Bechtheim and Osthofen, before they end in Worms, the southermost wine producing community on the Rhine in Rheinhessen. This half circle is unsuitable for vines since it is subject to spring frosts and a good five kilometers of truck farms, fruit orchards and wheat fields separate the vineyards from the river. The wines of *Osthofen* and *Bechtheim* are very similar to the ones of *Alsheim* and *Mettenheim*. Both communities have about 1,250 acres in vine. The vineyards, however, belong to a different Bereich, with the poetic name of Wonnegau which literally means "province of great joy."

The best growers of Bechtheim are *Richard Beyer, Dr. Schickert Erben, Brenner'sches Weingut, Manfred Kochler* and *Geil-Bierschenk:* the best growers of Osthofen: *Weingut Weisser, Ross Alfred Müller, Ahnenhof Hermann Müller, Erhard Glaser* and *Hans Melloth.* The best *Lagen* of these two communities are:

Osthofener Goldberg	Bechtheimer Hasensprung
Osthofener Hasenbiss	Bechtheimer Rosengarten
Osthofener Gotteshilfe	Bechtheimer Stein

Not an inconsiderable amount of wine is sold under the Grosslage name of Osthofener Pilgerpfad.

* *Worms,* before the War, was a pleasant small city of red sandstone buildings and a green belt of grass and trees had replaced most of its old walls; unfortunately it was also a focal point of rail and road traffic along and across the Rhine. As such it was heavily bombed, to the point that it was hardly recognizable in 1945. It has been attractively rebuilt and the scars of war can no longer be seen.

To the casual visitor, Worms looks about as unlike a town famous for its wine as a town well could. According to official records there are 2,400 acres of vineyard within the city limits but there is nothing which could be called a hillside within two miles or more, and most of the country round about is in sugar beets or potatoes, and as flat as a potato pancake. The one celebrated vineyard, which consists of only 26 acres, is in the northern part of the town, and it is easy to miss it if one is traveling by car. This is the "Liebfrauenstift-Kirchenstück" and it surrounds the Liebfrauenkirche, the Church of Our Lady. In all probability this gave its name to Liebfraumilch, but the wine it produces is sold as Liebfrauenstift-Kirchenstück, not Liebfraumilch, today. The vineyard is divided between two growers, both substantial and important, and it certainly produces the best wines which such alluvial soil is capable of yielding under any circumstances. Nevertheless Liebfrauenstift-Kirchenstück is no Niersteiner or Nackenheimer; I have tasted far better wines called simply Liebfraumilch than any it has ever produced or is even likely to produce. But such Liebfraumilchs, of course, did not come from Worms. The two producers in question are Valckenberg and Langenbach, and the Liebfrauenstift-Kirchenstück that carries their labels is authentic—as good as any wine from Worms can be.

When this book was last revised Worms had only 412 acres in vines. The city has encroached on its neighboring suburbs and has incorporated 7 villages with their vineyards. The new and old vineyards of Worms form the Grosslage Liebfrauenmorgen, a name more likely to appear on the label of a Worms wine than any of the 20 individual vineyard names within the Grosslage, with the exception of Liebfrauenstift-Kurchenstück which is proudly marketed by the two important wine shippers who own it jointly.

We have passed through the communities that lie on the Rhine or border the valley and own the majority of the fine vineyard land of Rheinhessen. Most of the communities, however, that produce the bulk of the wine of Rheinhessen, which alone produces twice as much as Alsace and Beaujolais, comes from the interior of the province.

Protected from the west winds by the two small mountains of Donnersberg and Soonwald, the gently rolling countryside is covered with vineyards on the hillsides while on the plain wheat and sugar beet fields alternate with farms and orchards. It is a fertile land with village names such as Weinheim, Westofen, Dittelsheim-Hessloch, and Albig.

Only three communities in the interior deserve mention:

* *Alzey:* the county seat famous as the home of a vine cultivation institute which for many years was directed by Dr. Scheu, one of Germany's foremost viticulturists. He developed there the grape variety that is named after him, the Scheurebe, as well as the variety he named Faber.

It is no accident that Alzey's 1,800 acres of vineyards have a good proportion of these two grape varieties which seem to prosper here. The Scheurebe, in particular, develops its typical blackcurrant-like taste. Alzey is also in the Bereich Wonnegau and it is more likely that you will find its wines either under the name of the *Bereich,* or the Grosslage Sybillenstein, or blended into a quality Liebfraumilch, rather than under one of its 11 individual vineyard names.

The other two communities worth mentioning are:

* *Flörsheim-Dahlsheim,* about half way between Alzey and Worms. Three growers, *Dr. Kurt Becker, Rodensteiner Hof Ludwig Scherner* and *Schales* have made this community of 1,500 acres of vineyards known beyond its borders. The vineyards are all in the Grosslage Burg Rodenstein and there is a good deal of Riesling planted, particularly by Dr. Becker.

The best vineyards are:

Flörsheimer Bürgel   Flörsheimer Hubacker
Flörsheimer Sauloch

A great deal of wine is also sold under the prestigious sounding Grosslage: Burg Rodenstein.

* *Weinheim,* a community just southwest of Alzey is blessed with soil similar to Nierstein's. The local growers have planted a large percentage of Riesling and produce wines of style and elegance. The best growers are *Winzermeister Karl Matheis, Gernot Gysler* and *Winzermeister Karl Marx.* The best vineyards are:

Weinheimer Mandelberg   Weinheimer Hölle

7

RHEINPFALZ

THE Rheinpfalz, or Palatinate, as it is called in English, is full of surprises and contradictions, and full of an odd sort of earthy charm. Once rather inaccessible, with small roads dating from the Roman and Napoleonic times, it now boasts two superhighways or *"autobahn"* to the centers of the Mittelhaardt and Landau. A well marked road the "Weinstrasse," the "wine road" winds through the sea of vineyards that extend almost without interruption for 50 miles; through immaculate and picturesque villages, country inns serving the hearty specialties of the region and colorful signs inviting you to sample the wine and buy it directly from the local grower. The people are friendly and it is no wonder that an increasing number of visitors come to enjoy the food, the hospitality and last but not least the wine.

The Rheinpfalz is second only to Rheinhessen in vineyard acreage but as it regularly produces more, it is recognized as Germany's largest wine producing area.

To begin at the very beginning: the word *Pfalz*, in German is a variation of Palast or palace, and all three derive from the Roman word *"Palatium"* which also gave its name to the "Palatine" Hill, on which the Roman emperors constructed the first of their imperial residences, over two thousand years ago.

In the Holy Roman Empire the title *"Pfalzgraf"* (*comes pala-tinus*) was originally conferred on members of the court who acted for the King as Judges. The most important of these was the *Pfalzgraf bei Rhein* (*comes palatinus Rhein*), who eventually was given the temporal and worldly power over Southern Germany. The present Rheinpfalz is but a small part of the original *"Kurpfalz,"* the area the Pfalzgraf ruled over until it was reduced to its present size at the Congress of Vienna. Since 1100 the best vineyards in the Pfalz belonged to the Prince Bishop (*Kurfürst*) of Speyer, like most of the better German vineyard land which was church property from the middle ages until the German occupation by Napoleon.

The Rheinpfalz is bound on the south and southwest by France, and on the west by the Territory of the Saar. Being a border province it has seen more than its share of wars, and having been repeatedly invaded and ravaged and burned, especially during the 17th and 18th centuries, in quarrels that were none of its making, it has largely lost its taste for things military.

For this is a very peaceful and peaceable country, very like Alsace, almost a northern prolongation of Alsace. The hills of its Haardt range, pine-covered with innumerable ruined castles, are really a northern extension of the Alsatian Vosges, and the two provinces have much in common—nature has been kind to both. The Mittelhaardt, the section of the Rheinpfalz that grows the finest vines, has the warmest climate in Germany and the lowest rainfall during the growing season. Like Alsace, it is a country of wonderfully prolific orchards, famous not only for their cherries, their peaches and their plums, but even for their apricots and figs and almonds, which at this latitude is rare. Like Alsace, it is a land of plentiful game and trout streams, of old walled villages and half-timber houses, steep roofs and wrought-iron tavern signs and window boxes full of flowers. Both are districts of white wine, of pale fresh Müller-Thurgau and Silvaners, "spicy" Traminers, and noble Rieslings. Both are districts of copious meals and stout trenchermen. And if there is no cuisine in the Pfalz to equal that of Strasbourg and Colmar and Ammerschwihr, there are no wines in Alsace to equal the best of Deidesheim and Forst and Wachenheim.

The good people of the Pfalz are notoriously fond of their own wines and they drink them plentifully, at all times and in all seasons. First, just after the vintage, in the form of what they call *Federweisser* (or "feather-white"—though it is certainly no beverage for anyone who wears the white feather of a temperance organization); at this stage it is half grape juice and half wine, still a little cloudy, still a little sweet, young and blond and innocent-looking, but as treacherous as a knife in the back. Second, they drink it, all year long and happily and properly as *Schoppenwein,* which means something like *"vin de carafe"* but sounds a little less elegant. And finally they drink it, when they find it above average quality and worth bottling, as *Flaschenwein,* a year or many years later, on real occasions, with their friends.

Happily, we are never likely to see the explosive Federweisser outside of Germany. And we are hardly likely to get much Schoppenwein either, unless it is disguised as one of its betters; all of it is more agreeable when its age can be counted in months, not years; none of it is of really outstanding quality, and if it is called *Schoppenwein* to begin with, we may be fairly sure that it is better thus than prepared and bottled for the export market. (*Schoppen* is the German measure for half a liter).

Only about 14% of the Rheinpfalz vineyards, are planted in Riesling. The dominant grape variety is Müller-Thurgau with almost 25% of total acreage, followed by Silvaner with 20%. It is interesting that only 25 years ago, Silvaner accounted for more than half of total plantings! 15 years ago it had dropped to 39% and five years ago to 23.4%. The red Portugieser accounts for 10.3%, followed by Morio-Muskat 7.6%, Kerner 5.5, Scheurebe 5.5% and Rulander (Pinot gris) 2.9%. The only other grape variety worth mentioning is the Gewürztraminer, which, with only 1.7% of total plantings, still accounts for some of the finest wines of the region.

Nowhere else in Germany has the research in Viticulture and Vinification made a bigger impact than here. When this book was first written, the Rheinpfalz produced a total of 15,000,000 gallons annually and its author described the bulk of its wines as *"Schoppenwein,"* the ordinary wine of the local bar, with an almost indescribable, heavy flavor which the Germans called a *Bodengeschmack,"* a taste of earth." He continued that "it is not very agreeable to an educated palate, just as a cheap cigar is not very agreeable to a lover of fine Havana Tobacco." By 1977, the production had climbed to 60,000,000 gallons and I doubt if much of it had any Bodengeschmack.

The last 25 years have seen a veritable revolution. Whole vineyards were uprooted, the earth rearranged by gigantic earth moving machines and replanted with clonally selected root stock. The smaller farmers joined some of the most advanced cooperatives in the world,

equipped with modern presses, centrifugal separators and trained oenologists guaranteeing the cleanest and most scientifically fermented
grape juice. The growers have prospered and, next to their fine old
cellars with the wooden casks in which the Rieslings still spend their
infant months, they now display stainless steel tanks and those little
Westphalia separators that cost many times that of the Mercedes or
BMW parked outside the Manor Houses.

All this was made possible not only by the longest period of pros-
perity the country has ever seen, but also by an ever increasing demand for finer wines in a marketplace unfettered by protectionism,
duties or wine taxes. With this vast improvement, this coming of age,
the Rheinpfalz has not only secured the domestic market, but it has in-
augurated the exportation of meaningful quantities of German wine to
France.

The better Rheinpfalz wines, the Rieslings especially, are perhaps
the best of all German wines to drink with the best of German food.
Considerably fuller in body than the wines of the Mosel, less mild and
soft than the wines of Rheinhessen, perhaps less overwhelming in
bouquet than the great Rheingaus, they have a remarkable and attractive balance, and they are as easy to drink with food as the fine white
Burgundies of France. The *Auslesen* and *Beerenauslesen* are of course
another matter—these are dessert wines, and among the most distinguished in the world.

The vineyard district of the Rheinpfalz, like many another great
vineyard district, consists essentially of the lower slopes of a single
range of hills; like the vineyards of the Burgundian Cote d'Or, they
face east over a plain, and are between five and seven hundred feet
above sea level. The hills, "the *Haardt Gebirge*," run from a thousand to twelve hundred feet higher at their wooded summits, and extend from Herxheim, north of Bad Dürkheim, almost to the French
frontier.

At the foot of the hills, threading its way through the vineyards
and vineyard towns, running fifty miles from Kleinbockenheim, on the
border of Rheinhessen south to Schweigen, on the French frontier, is a
famous road. This, as unlike an Autobahn or superhighway as a road
well could be, is the *Deutsche Weinstrasse,* the "German Wine
Road." It is certainly no route for a person in a hurry, but to a lover of
good wine, picturesque villages and enchanting countryside, it would
be hard to recommend a more rewarding journey. There are thirty-five
little vineyard towns on the road itself, and at least a dozen others, all
worth seeing, within two or three miles of it.

Traveling the *Weinstrasse,* it is easy to recognize the three main sections into which the Rheinpfalz vineyards are divided. First, the less steep, rolling country from the border of Rheinhessen down to Herxheim; this, formerly called Unterhaardt, is a country of average, rather undistinguished wines, unlikely to be exported under their name of origin at this stage. The area is now part of the northern Bereich, which is called *"Mittelhaardt Deutsche Weinstrasse."* Here, as elsewhere in the reorganization of 1971, the growers of the lesser district, the former Unterhaardt, were incorporated in the Bereich of the finer vineyards. It would have been better to create three Bereiche instead of two and preserve the logical division that has existed for a long time: Unterhaardt, Mittelhaardt and Oberhaardt. But there are only two: the *"Mittelhaardt Deutsche Weinstrasse"* and the *"Südliche Weinstrasse."* The former and classical Mittelhaardt is the area between Herxheim and Neustadt; this is the district of great wines, the center and kernel of the Rheinpfalz, and we shall have considerably more to say about it in a moment. Third, extending south from Neustadt almost to the French frontier, is the former Oberhaardt now the *"Bereich Südliche Weinstrasse."* This was *Schoppenwein* country where quantity rather than quality counted; but the modern cooperatives, the new grape varieties and last but not least the new breed of oenologists have changed all that. It has become an area of even larger production, but of good enough quality to have made friends in Germany and abroad. Without any doubt however it is the old Mittelhardt, the southern portion of the present Bereich Mittelhaardt, between Herxheim and Neustadt, which produces the wines that have made the Rheinpfalz world famous.

It is eighteen miles from Herxheim to Neustadt, and the vineyards run like a green ribbon, a mile to two miles wide, between the dark pine forests above and the flat farmland below.There are seventeen villages in all in this section of Edelweine; Seven of the seventeen produce wines that are better than average, but you will rarely see their names—Herxheim, Freinsheim, Leistadt, Friedelsheim, Niederkirchen, Mussbach, and Haardt—on labels of wine bottled for the export market. Six others—Kallstadt, Ungstein, Bad Durkheim, Gimmeldingen, Königsbach and Neustadt—produce wines that are excellent and in some instances great. The last four, in the exact middle of the Mittelhaardt, are the incomparable ones—from north to south, Wachenheim, Forst, Deidesheim, Ruppertsberg.

From Wachenheim to Ruppertsberg it is only about three miles, even by way of the curving *Weinstrasse,* and some four square miles

of vines—roughly 4,000 acres are alone responsible for the
Spitzenweine, or "peak" wines of the Rheinpfalz.

These 4,000 precious acres are divided into 40 individual vineyard sites or *Lagen,* each one with its well known, well established
name and its legal boundaries. The largest is 475 acres, the smallest
only 10. Some 20 producers own vines in that small, extraordinary
parcel called Forster Ungeheuer, for example, and it is therefore possible to buy estate bottled Forster Ungeheuer under 20 different labels,
and they will be 20 quite different wines; they will have been pressed,
fermented and aged in twenty different cellars according to ideas of
twenty different cellar-masters, and bottled under wholly dissimilar
conditions and at different times.

In order to buy Rheinpfalz wines intelligently, it is essential,
therefore, to be familiar not only with the town names and the vineyard names, but with the producers' names as well. Fortunately, this is
not as difficult as it sounds. Most of the really small producers have
banded themselves together into cooperatives—*Winzervereine* or *Winzergenossenschaften*—and offer their better wines under the cooperative label.

Apart from those there are only 12 major producers which include
4 cooperatives, who own more than 25 acres of land and produce at
least 7,000 cases of wine a year. Eleven others own between 10 and
25 acres (between 3,000 and 7,000 cases) and those that produce less
will either sell their wines through the excellent cooperatives or not
export them at all. The thirteen are:

Weingut Geheimer Rat Dr. v. Bassermann-Jordan	100 acres in Deidesheim, Forst, Ruppertsberg, Bad Dürkheim and Ungstein
Weingut Dr. Bürklin-Wolf	250 acres in Wachenheim, Forst Deidesheim, Ruppertsberg and Bad Dürkheim
Weingut Reichsrat v. Buhl	265 acres in Deidesheim, Forst Wachenheim, Ruppertsberg and Königsbach and Friedelsheim
Dr. Deinhard	80 acres in Deidesheim, Forst, and Ruppertsberg
Georg Siben Erben	29 acres in Deidesheim, Forst and Ruppertsberg

Wilhelm Spindler	43 acres in Forst, Deidesheim, Ruppertsberg and Wachenheim
Eugen Spindler-Weingut Lindenhof	33.4 acres in Forst, Deidesheim, Ruppertsberg and Wachenheim
Weingut Hahnhof	66.5 acres in Deidesheim, Forst and Ruppertsberg.

Winzergenossenschaft Wachtenburg-
Luginsland in Wachenheim

Winzerverein in Forst

Winzerverein in Deidesheim

Winzerverein in Ruppertsberg

Josef Biffar

Dietz-Matti

Herbert Giessen Erben

Dr. Kern

Jul. Ferd. Kimich

Heinrich Spindler

Mehling

Werle

Mosbacherhof

Magin

Sieben Erben

Producers owning between 10 and 25 acres in great vineyard towns

It should not be imagined that these estates consist of large holdings or of entire vineyards. With a very few exceptions ALL of the better vineyards of the Rheinpfalz are divided among a number of different owners, and the acreages given above, far from representing unbroken areas of vineyard, are made up, literally, of scores of tiny portions of different Lagen, often of an acre or less, and often four or five miles from one another. The famous Bassermann-Jordan family, for example, owns portions of over 12 different Lagen in Deidesheim, of ten in Forst and six in Ruppertsberg. Dr. Bürklin-Wolf is the sole owner of the Rechbächel vineyard in Wachenheim and the Gaisböhl vineyard in Ruppertsberg, but has holdings in twenty others.

Some of the producers with only ten acres in all will actually make 20 different wines from 20 different vineyards in three or four different townships. These of course are rarely blended but are scrupulously kept separate, and it is hardly surprising that the quantity of wine available from a given vineyard, producer and year, is in almost all cases extremely limited, and often amounts to no more than a single cask of 300 gallons. This, from a commercial viewpoint, may seem hardly sensible, but there is an old adage about the proof of the pudding, and it is hard to imagine how the great Rheinpfalz wines could be any better than they are.

Needless to say, there is an enormous amount of Rheinpfalz wine produced and sold and even exported which is not handled in this way at all.

It goes in tank truck, not long after the vintage, from the producer to one of the many shippers in Neustadt or Bad Dürkheim or even Worms or Mainz. There, if it is a Ruppertsberger Linsenbusch, for example, it will be blended with one or more of the other 20 vineyards comprising the Grosslage "Deidesheimer Hofstück."

Under the present system the bottler can use the name of any community within the Grosslage as the name for this wine. The Grosslage Hofstück, for example, encompasses vineyards in Ellerstadt, Gonnheim, Friedelsheim, Hochdorf-Assenheim, Rödersheim-Gronau, Niederkirchen, Deidesheim, Ruppertsberg and Meckenheim. Logically the bottler will choose a well known and prestigious community rather than an unknown one. This liberal practice is being challenged by the Common Market wine authority and it is not certain if it will continue in future.

It would certainly be a mistake to suppose that such wines are necessarily inferior to unblended estate-bottlings, for this is not by any means the case, whatever the purists may say. A shipper's wine may be magnificent, or may be worthless, but wine merchants by and large, are as honest as other people, and a shipper who makes a practice of selling bad wine will not be successful in the long run. On the other hand, what is true in Germany as a whole is true no less in the Rheinpfalz: almost all of the best vineyards are owned by producers who bottle their own wines, and if they sell part of their production in bulk and part in bottle, it is safe to assume that the best goes to market under their own name and label. This may mean, and it generally does, more trouble for the consumer, who cannot be assured of a continuing supply of a favorite wine, and who has to work his way through all the complexities of vineyard names, producers' names and the like. But the game is worth the candle.

It would be too bad to conclude even a brief chapter such as this without at least a word about the innumerable wine-and-vintage festivals of the Rheinpfalz. The Pfälzer love their wines, and they are never happier than when they can find an excuse for opening a few special bottles for friends or appreciative guests. Over a hundred thousand visitors usually attend the so-called *"Wurstmarkt,"* or "sausage sales" in Bad Dürkheim, in September, which has a great deal more to do with wine than with sausages, and when the Wine Queen of the Rheinpfalz is crowned in Neustadt in October, the whole Palatinate is there. But there are literally dozens of others, since nearly every village has its *"Fest,"* and they run from Whitsuntide through all the good weather until after the vintage.

THE RHEINPFALZ VINEYARDS

The following is a rather more detailed summary of the major Rheinpfalz vineyards and their wines, as one encounters them traveling south along the *Weinstrasse,* from Böckenheim on the border of Rheinhessen to Schweigen, and the French frontier.

The area as stated before, is subdivided into two Bereiche, 26 Grosslagen and 335 Individual Vineyard Sites distributed over 170 communities; a total of 55,500 wine producing acres.

Bereich Mittelhaardt/Deutsche Weinstrasse

The northern part of Bereich Mittelhaardt/Deutsche Weinstrasse produces little or nothing in the way of wine fit for bottling and export. The only possible exception is one wine grown largely from Gewürztraminer grapes along the Rheinhessen border in the two villages of Zell (which should not be confused with Zell on the Mosel) and Harxheim (which should not be confused with Herxheim near Bad Dürkheim). It is marketed under the extraordinary name of Zeller Schwarzer Herrgott, no doubt in order to compete with the Mosel's Zeller Schwarze Katz. It is not very distinguished.

Southern Part of Bereich Mittelhaardt

Eleven of the seventeen villages and towns of this southern section of the Mittelhaardt are listed below, together with their better-known producers and Lagen. Asterisks have been used as indications

RHEINPFALZ

SÜDLICHE

WEINSTRASSE

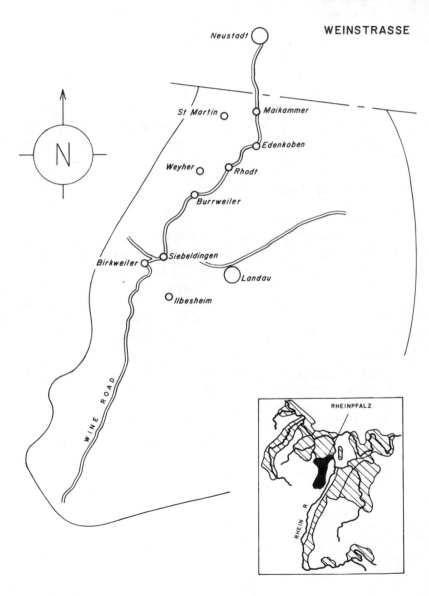

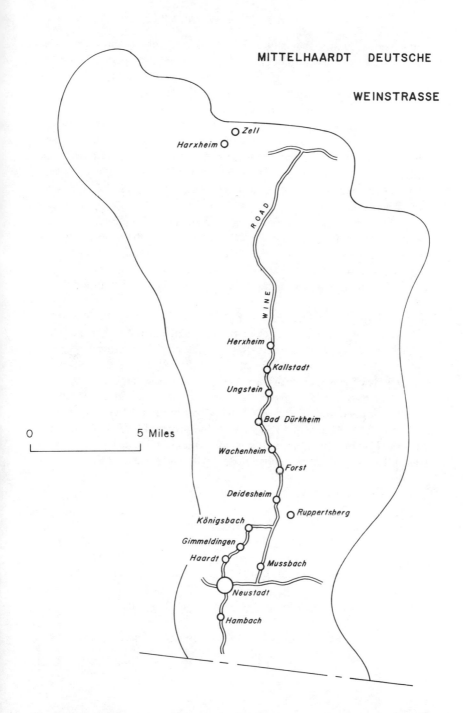

MITTELHAARDT DEUTSCHE

WEINSTRASSE

Zell

Harxheim

ROAD

WINE

Herxheim

Kallstadt

Ungstein

Bad Dürkheim

0   5 Miles

Wachenheim

Forst

Deidesheim

Ruppertsberg

Königsbach

Gimmeldingen

Haardt

Mussbach

Neustadt

Hambach

of superior quality, but any such ratings are only generalizations at best, and I have tasted (though not often) exceedingly poor wines from villages to which I have given three asterisks (***) such as Deidesheim, and also (though not often) excellent wines from villages to which I have given no asterisks at all.

Although only about one-sixth of the Rheinpfalz's great acreage of vines is in Riesling, you will find little else planted in the best Lagen, and in general the towns where the Riesling predominates, or at least runs well over the 15% average, are those that produce the best wine. (The Rheinpfalz has 35% more acreage planted in Riesling than the Rheingau.)

The Rheinpfalz also produces 21% of the red wine of Germany, but a good deal of this is drunk by the *"Winzer"* themselves, or sold as *Schoppenwein,* as it properly should be. The best of it, compared to the fairly good wines of France, is poor stuff indeed.

Here then is a brief roster of what has made the Rheinpfalz famous:

The first major Grosslage is Kobnert and it is likely that the wines of Herxheim, will be sold under the Grosslage name rather than one of the three vineyard names of the Community. The same applies to the neighboring villages of Leistadt and Freinshem, and even to the vineyards of Kallstadt that are in the Kobnert Grosslage.

There is a *Winzergenossenschaft* (cooperative) in Herxheim as well as a good size *Winzerverein* (cooperative) named Liebfrauenberg in Freinsheim. There is also a dependable grower by the name of Lehmann-Hilgard. Freinsheim has some vineyards actually in another Grosslage called Freinsheimer Rosenbühl, and a total of 950 acres in vines.

The first major vineyard town is:

*   *Kallstadt,* with 875 acres and a number of hillside vineyards that produce honorable and at times excellent wines, a good number of them made from Riesling. Dependable growers are *Stumpf-Fitz, Koehler-Ruprecht, Arthur Bender, Eduard Schuster* and a good *Winzergenossenschaft.* The three best vineyards are small and make up the total of the Kallstädter Saumagen Grosslage. They are:

Kallstädter Nill   Kallstädter Kirchenstück
Kallstädter Horn

Most of the wines from these vineyards would probably be marketed under the famous name of the Grosslage.

*　*Ungstein*, like Kallstadt is situated in two Grosslagen: Hochmess which has vineyards from Ungstein and Bad Dürkheim and Honigsäckel reserved solely for three comparatively small vineyards.

Ungsteiner Weilberg　Ungsteiner Herrenberg
Ungsteiner Nessriegel

The best of the three is Herrenberg and it is likely that most of the wine from the other two will be sold under the prestigious Grosslage. The wines of Ungstein have a certain elegance and breed. The three best growers are *K. Fitz-Ritter*, *v. Bassermann-Jordan* and *Julius Koch* together with the *Winzergenossenschaft Herrenberg-Honigsäckel*.

*　*Bad Dürkheim*, has actually annexed Ungstein as a suburb but Ungstein has kept its name solidly anchored to its vineyards and Grosslage. Dürkheim together with its suburbs has 3,200 acres of vineyards within its new city limits. It is indeed a bustling spa. Nestling among its vineyards, at the foot of the forest-covered hills of the Haardt, with mineral springs, many hotels, and even a gambling casino, Bad Durkheim is a popular resort town, and a very pretty one.

Among its minor attractions is the so-called *"Dürkheimer Fass"* ("Wine-Vat"), a restaurant in the form of a barrel—which could, theoretically, hold half of Dürkheim's annual wine production. This production, incidentally, is very large. The white wines from its better vineyards, while rarely of the highest class, are good and widely known, and deserve their reputation. Leading producers include *Fitz-Ritter*, (sole owner of Dürkheimer Abtsfronhof) *Julius Koch*, *Karl Schäfer*, *Basserman-Jordan* and a large and excellent *Winzergenossenschaft* called *Vier Jahreszeiten-Kloster Limburg*. First among many good smaller growers are: *Gebr, Barth, Karl Fuhrmann* and *Joh. Gg. Zumstein*.

Bad Dürkheim is located in three *Grosslagen:*
(1) Feuerberg, with three vineyards:

Dürkheimer Herrenmorgen　Dürkheimer Steinberg
Dürkheimer Nonnengarten

RHEIN PFALZ

Weingut Dr. Bürklin-Wolf
WACHENHEIM/WEINSTRASSE

Wachenheimer Gerümpel
Riesling Auslese

Erzeugerabfüllung · A. P. Nr. 5 142 043 82 77

QUALITÄTSWEIN MIT PRÄDIKAT

Weingut **Deidesheim**

Reichsrat v. Buhl **Rheinpfalz**

1976er **Forster Ungeheuer**
Riesling Trockenbeerenauslese
Qualitätswein mit Prädikat   A. P. Nr. 5 106 044 26 77
ERZEUGERABFÜLLUNG

Aus dem **Rheinpfalz**
Weingute **Deidesheim**
Geh. Rat **Dr. v. Basser-** **mann-Jordan**
IN VITE VITA

1978er Forster Jesuitengarten Kabinett
Riesling

Qualitätswein mit Prädikat
A. P. Nr. 5 106 064 13 79

e 75 cl   Erzeugerabfüllung
Weingut v. Bassermann-Jordan, Deidesheim   RHEINPFALZ

RHEINPFALZ
ERZEUGERABFÜLLUNG

Winzergenossenschaft

Wachtenburg-Luginsland
WACHENHEIM A. D. WEINSTRASSE

Qualitätswein mit Prädikat
Wachenheimer Mandelgarten
Scheurebe Kabinett

0,7 l. e   A. P. Nr. 5 142 373 77 79

RHEINPFALZ

Riesling
QUALITÄTSWEIN
ERZEUGERABFÜLLUNG
GEBIETS-WINZERGENOSSENSCHAFT DEUTSCHES WEINTOR EG
ILBESHEIM · SÜDL. WEINSTRASSE

e 0,7 l

(2) *Hochmess,* with four vineyards:

Dürkheimer Michelsberg   Dürkheimer Spielberg
Dürkheimer Rittergarten   Dürkheimer Hochbenn

(3) *Schenkenböhl* with three vineyards:

Dürkheimer Abtsfronhof   Dürkheimer Fuchsmantel
Dürkheimer Fronhof

** *Wachenheim,* 1,250 acres. Northernmost of the four great wine producing villages of the Pfalz, and directly adjoining Forst, one of the most highly rated of all, Wachenheim has at least half a dozen vineyards that have acquired international fame. The best Wachenheimers of great years are among the most sought-after wines of Germany for they combine substance and bouquet with extraordinary finesse yet are the lightest in body. *Dr. Bürklin-Wolf,* the most active figure in Rheinpfalz wine affairs, is the leading producer. His 250 acres of vineyards include substantial portions of five Wachenheimer Lagen listed below, plus important holdings in Ruppertsberg and smaller ones in Forst and Deidesheim.

Similarly excellent Wachenheimers are grown and bottled by *von Buhl, Wilhelm Spindler, J. L. Wolf Erben,* and the *Winzergenossenschaft,* one of the oldest and best equipped in Germany, "*Wachtenburg-Luginsland,*" which at times makes as fine wines as the growers.

Wachenheim has three *Grosslagen,* but its most famous vineyards are in the Mariengarten, a Grosslage that Wachenheim shares with Forst and Deidensheim.

The best vineyards in this Grosslage are:

Wachenheimer Böhlig   Wachenheimer Altenburg
Wachenheimer Gerümpel   Wachenheimer Goldbächel
Wachenheimer Rechbächel

Goldbächel and Gerümpel are the best two Wachenheim vineyards in all of its three Grosslagen.

The other two Grosslagen are:

(1) (*Wachenheimer*) *Schenkenböhl* with the best vineyards of:

Wachenheimer Fuchsmantel   Wachenheimer Mandelgarten
and

(2) (*Forster*) *Schnepfenflug* with its number one vineyard of

Wachenheimer Luginsland

*** *Forst,* 510 acres. 70% Rièslings. Although it has less than 800 inhabitants and a single street (which appropriately enough, is called Deutsche Weinstrasse), Forst is one of the most famous wine-producing towns of the world. Through its high, arched doorways of red sandstone you can get a glimpse of prosperous-looking flower-grown, shady courtyards, and of the press-houses to which the grapes are brought in autumn. Everywhere else—around the church, in the very back yards of the village buildings—there are vines. This is hardly surprising, since many of the best vineyards plots of Forst are practically in the village itself, and two of them, Jesuitengarten and Kirchenstück, are rated about the most valuable agricultural land in Germany.

The unusual quality and bouquet of the Forster wines is said in large part to be due to certain outcroppings of black basalt which exist in the vineyards of Forst, but not elsewhere in the Rheinpfalz nor, to my knowledge, elsewhere in Germany. All of the "great" wine growers of the Rheinpfalz have holdings in Forst, even if their homes and principal cellars are in Wachenheim or Deidesheim, and you will see their names and labels on "Forster" wine. They are: Reichsrat von Buhl, Dr. von Bassermann-Jordan, Dr. Bürklin-Wolf, Dr. Deinhard, Hahn, Wilhelm Spindler, Heinrich Spindler. Less important but equally reputable are: J. F. Kimich, Kern, Magin, Mosbacherhof and the Forster Winzerverein.

The great controversy has always been whether Forst or Deidesheim produce the greatest wines. Both are incomparably better than their neighbors and each has its staunch supporters. The answer seems to be in both. Deidesheimers grow on lighter soil than Forsters and lighter soil makes more elegant wines. Since lighter soil, furthermore, usually makes for a quicker ripening process, it assures Deidesheim of riper grapes, in other words better wines, in less good years. There is, however, one disadvantage to lighter soil: it requires more water since it does not retain moisture as well as heavier soil.

The heavier clay soil of Forst is rich in minerals. It may take longer to warm up but retains moisture even in dry years. Therefore in dry years, which often are great years, Forsters are usually greater than Deidesheimers, though in lesser years they tend to be somewhat steely and austere.

Forst, and particularly its most famous vineyard, Jesuitengarten, was completely uprooted and replanted in the *"Flurbereinigung"* or

Wachenheim vineyard.

"Rearrangement." Only now, and slowly at that, have the new vines reached enough maturity to make once again great wines.

Forst has three vineyards in the Grosslage Schnepfenflug:

Forster Bischofsgarten   Forster Süsskopf
Forster Stift

and seven vineyards in the Grosslage Mariengarten:

Forster Musenhang   Forster Pechstein
Forster Jesuitengarten   Forster Kirchenstück
Forster Freundstück   Forster Ungeheuer
Forster Elster

Without any doubt the three greatest Forst vineyards are Jesuitengarten, Kirchenstück and Ungeheuer, in that order.

*** *Deidesheim,* 1,255 acres. 60% Riesling. With such a large area in vineyard even for a town of the Rheinpfalz, Deidensheim is easily first in the production of great wine—in quality it is on a par and often surpasses Forst, and there is no higher praise possible. The little town itself is extraordinarily charming—with old patrician homes built out of red sandstone, a lovely, ancient *Rathaus,* or Town Hall, a score, at least, of winding, narrow streets and alleyways, picturesque and full of the flavor of the past, and gardens green with figs and apricots and vines.

Although less important than Bad Dürkheim as far as the general wine trade is concerned, it is the undisputed fine wine center of the Rheinpfalz, and the home of all of the really great producers with the exception of Bürklin-Wolf (Wachenheim) and Wilhelm Spindler (Forst).

The "great producers" include first of all, the heir of the late dean of German wine growers, *Dr. Friedrich von Bassermann-Jordan,* who was honorary president of almost every Palatinate wine organization and author of many erudite volumes on the history of the vine, whose museum of antiquities and library of books and bottles are world famous and who was the sole owner of Forster Jesuitengarten. His son, Dr. Ludwig von Bassermann-Jordan, is a worthy heir who is continuing to improve the wine museum and is keeping the old traditions where they benefit his wines best, but adopting the new methods of viticulture and vinification where they profit the wines most. His Rieslings are the most elegant of the Rheinpfalz and his scholarship the perfect continuation of his father's life work.

Second, *Reichsrat von Buhl,* whose cellars are many hundreds of meters under the town, and whose 265 acres of vineyard constitute the largest privately owned domain in Germany.

Third, a half dozen others, less large perhaps but of no less impeccable reputation: *Dr. Deinhard, Sieben Erben, Biffar, Hahn.* It should also be noted that several producers listed above under Wachenheim and Forst have important holdings in Deidesheim as well, e.g., Bürklin-Wolf.

The *Winzerverein* in Deidesheim ranks as a major cooperative, and good smaller growers are: *Dietz-Matti, Josef Biffar, Giessen Erben, Dr. Kern and Kimich.*

Deidesheim has vineyards in three *Grosslagen,* one each in Schnepfenflug (Deidesheimer Letten) and Hofstück (Deidesheimer Nonnenstück). Many growers from the villages of Ellerstadt, Gonnheim, Friedelsheim, Hockdorf-Assenheim, Rodersheim-Gronau, Niederkirchen and Meckenheim, market their wines under the well known Deidesheimer Hofstück Grosslage rather than under their unknown village names. This is indeed reflected glory and an easy way for a worthy wine to find its way to the market. The best *Lagen* of Deidensheim, however, the ones that have made it famous, are in the Mariengarten Grosslage, which has within its borders all the great vineyards of Deidesheim, Forst and Wachenheim. The nine vineyards in order of quality are:

Deidesheimer Hohenmorgen   Deidesheimer Kalkofen
Deidesheimer Grainhübel   Deidesheimer Paradiesgarten
Deidesheimer Kieselberg   Deidesheimer Maushöhle
Deidesheimer Leinhöhle   Deidesheimer Langenmorgen
Deidesheimer Herrgottsacker

** *Ruppertsberg*, 950 acres. About 40% Riesling. Only about a half mile from Deidesheim, its vineyards forming part of the same incomparable slope, Ruppertsberg is another one of the Palatinate's great names. For all its reputed Roman origin, the village is a great deal less interesting than its wines, and the more important vineyard owners, without exception, live elsewhere—mostly in Deidesheim and Wachenheim. This in no way detracts from the admirable quality of Ruppertsberg's wines and any of the following names on a bottle of Ruppertsberger can be considered a virtual guarantee of superior quality. *Bassermann-Jordan, Bürklin-Wolf, von Buhl, Dr. Deinhard, Dietz-Matti, Sieben Erben and Biffar.* Ruppertsberg has also an important *Winzerverein.*

All the vineyards of Ruppertsberg are in the Hofstück Grosslage. The six vineyards led by the two best are:

Ruppertsberger Reiterpfad   Ruppertsberger Gaisböhl
Ruppertsberger Hoheburg   Ruppertsberger Spiess
Ruppertsberger Linsenbusch   Ruppertsberger Nussbien

Neustadt is in the southern part of the Mittelhaardt what Bad Durkheim is in the northern part: a busy bustling market town, a major center of the wine trade and the seat of the Rheinpfalz Viticultural and Oenological school and experimental station. In the continuing urban spread, it has incorporated a number of villages to the north and with its 5,325 acres, it has become the biggest wine community not only in the Rheinpfalz but probably in all of Germany. If one considers that the whole of the Rheingau only has 7,105 acres, one can visualize the sea of vineyards that stretch from Neustadt to the north, through Muss-bach and Haardt, through Gimmeldingen and Königsbach, to the very borders of Ruppertsberg. There are only two of these communities worthy of mention:

* *Königsbach*, 30% Riesling. Although a great deal less famous than Ruppertsberg, Königsbach produces wines that are quite in the same class with those of its illustrious neighbor. The village is west of the Weinstrasse on the edge of the woods—above, rather than below its vineyards. *Reichsrat von Buhl* (see Deidesheim) is the major pro-ducer, but there is also a good *"Weinzerverein."*

It has four vineyards all in the Grosslage (Gimmeldinger) Meer-spinne, a popular name for the marketing of wines from these parts. Their names are:

> Königsbacher Oelberg   Königsbacher Idig
> Königsbacher Jesuitengarten   Konigsbacher Reiterpfad

Gimmeldingen is a pretty village with some good vineyards. *Mugler* is a dependable producer and there is a large and well-run *Winzergenossenschaft* called *"Weinbiet"* Mussbach-Gimmeldingen. Gimmeldingen is in the Grosslage (Gimmeldinger) Meerspinne and most of its wines are sold under this popular *Grosslage* name which, before 1971, was the name of a single vineyard. Of its four individual vineyards, only one is worthy of mention:

> Gimmeldinger Mandelgarten

BEREICH SÜDLICHE WEINSTRASSE

Between Neustadt and the French border there are almost a hundred villages, subdivided into nine Grosslagen, that produce wine. Until about 30 years ago this wine was either shipped in the barrel or in unlabeled liter bottles. It was drunk within the year as the daily wine of the Weinstuben or used for blending. It all too often had the earthy taste that became the hallmark of the wines of the Oberhaardt, the southern portion of the Rheinpfalz. Perhaps the most significant reason for this was the lack of demand for quality wines. Wine writers often forget that at times economics can be more important for making good wine than soil, grape or climate. Without an ever expanding market demanding finer wines and willing to pay for them, this area would still be making unlabeled white wine. But the opening of new markets, and the increasing sophistication of the consumer precipitated the change that put the wines of this region on the map.

Germany's wine industry has developed the most advanced enlightened cooperative system through Governmental support, scientific management and access to cheap credit. There are today 388 local, regional and Provincial cooperatives, with some 63,000 grape farmers as members, owning roughly a third of all planted vineyards in Germany. The combined storage capacity of these cooperatives is close to 20,000,000 gallons, their turnover close to one billion D. Mark a year. It is big business and it has given the farmer the scientific management that can tell him what grape and clone to plant where, and advise him on fertilizing, pruning, spraying and picking. More than half the sins of bad wine were committed between the period of harvest and the end of fermentation and they were all eliminated with technical management and modern equipment which the individual farmer would never have been able to afford by himself.

The two areas that have benefited the most from the modern cooperatives are Baden and the Südliche Weinstrasse. Two regional, highly modern cooperatives: the *Gebietswinzer-genossenschaft Deutsches Weintor in Ilbesheim and the Gebietswinzer-genossenschaft Rietburg* in Rhodt, have managed to put S*üdliche Weinstrasse* wines literally on the map. Gone is the heavy *"Bodengeschmack"*—the wines are clean, with a certain elegance and can compete with all but the top wines of the Region.

A good number of the wines are sold as varietals: Müller-Thurgau, Silvaner, Morio-Muskat, Kerner, Gewürztraminer and the like. Some wines are sold with village and vineyards names but most go to the market as "Südliche Weinstrasse" on the label of the regional cooperative. They find their way to supermarkets all over Germany and now even to France.

The following villages have the best vineyards: Maikammer, St. Martin, Rhodt, Weyher, Burrweiler, Siebeldingen and Birkweiler. The *Grosslagen* to watch for are Königsgarten and Ordensgut and the Lagen: Birkweiler Kastanienbusch, Rhodter Rosengarten and Weyherer Michelsberg. There is a dependable grower, *Rebholz,* in Siebeldingen and another, called *Beyersdorfer* in Birkweiler.

8

FRANCONIA

(Franken)

THE lovers of Frankenwein, or, as some like to call it and not always accurately, *Steinwein,* or *Stein-in-Bocksbeutel,* have made almost a cult of their devotion to their special favorites among these wines of the Main Valley. They are quick to point out that Goethe, who drank German wines with great gusto and rather copiously all his life, preferred the wine of Franconia to all others; they are immensely proud of the picturesque *Bocksbeutel* (which should never be spelled "Boxbeutel"), in which these wines are shipped; they have listed and classified 155 individual vineyard plots, or Lagen, in 125 wine-producing towns, and are ready to do battle at the drop of a hat, or the pop of a cork over the relative merits of Escherndorfer Lump and Randersackerer Teufelskeller, of Iphofer Julius-Echter-Berg and the Riesling-vom-Reuschberg from Horstein.

I must admit that I cannot altogether share this boundless enthusiasm for wines which are almost always agreeable but hardly ever great, nor can I explain Goethe's preference for them except to say that they go very well with food, have a less pronounced bouquet and character than other German wines, are generally quite full-bodied and dry without being tart, and possibly taste more like Alasatian wines or white Burgundies than Mosels and Rheingaus.

The Franconian vineyards are almost all strung along the valley of the Main, upstream and well east of Mainz and Hochheim and Frankfurt. Between Aschaffenburg and Schweinfurt the river forms a sort of gigantic "W" as it cuts its way through the hills, and here, as on the Mosel, the slopes planted with vineyards are almost exclusively those that face south.

The principal center of the wine trade is Würzburg, the rather handsome, old provincial capital, which has at last recovered from the devastating bombings it underwent during the War. Oddly enough, and alone among all the vineyard towns that I know or have ever heard of, it is as celebrated for its beer as for its wine. Würzburger Edelbräu is highly regarded by experts the world over, and a stein of Würzburger (which is beer) can be quite as pleasant as a Würzburger Stein (which is wine). The first *"stein,"* of course, is a *"stone"* or earthen ware drinking-vessel; the second is Franconia's best vineyard.

As such, the Würzburger Stein has given its name to a sort of generic term (*Steinwein*) erroneously used for Franconian wines as a whole. Correctly speaking, a *Steinwein* is a wine from certain portions of an extraordinary rocky hill within the municipal limits of Würzburg. In any case, no other wine should be so labeled, or could legally be so labeled in Germany.

Fortress Marienberg with its vineyards in Würzburg.

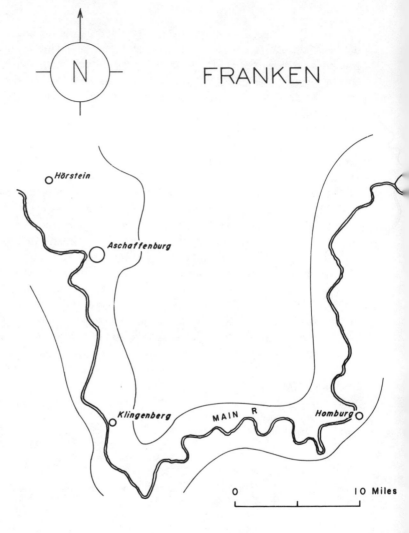

FRANKEN

N

Hörstein

Aschaffenburg

Klingenberg

MAIN R

Homburg

0   10 Miles

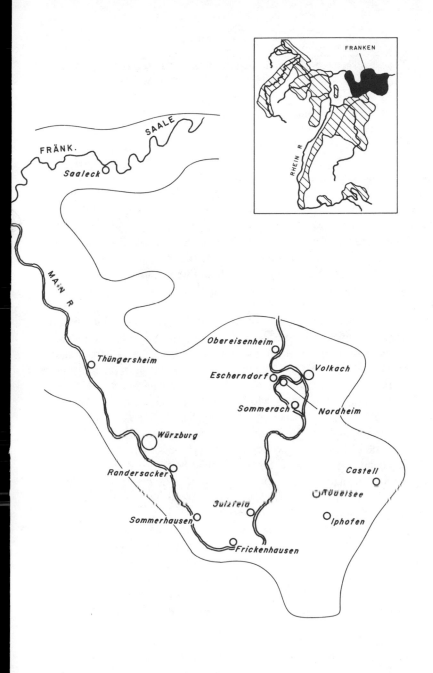

Since we seem to be embarked on the perilous seas of nomenclature, there are a few other points which can perhaps be cleared as well. First is the matter of grape varieties.

It has long been not only fashionable but legal to call the Silvaner the "Franken Riesling" in California, and of late it has become permissible to call it simply "Riesling," so that the true, the one, the only Riesling cannot be found except under the name "Johannisberg Riesling" or White Riesling. Now the truth is that Sylvaner is sometimes spelled Silvaner and sometimes called the *"Franken Traube"* (or Franconian grape) in Franconia, but, except as a joke, or by the ignoramus, it is never called the "Franken Riesling."

In the special climate of the Main Valley, where early autumn frosts are the rule rather than the exception, the Silvaner yields on the whole at least as good as, and possibly better wine than the Riesling itself, which succeeds only in rare, great years of warm autumn weather.

Here, as in other regions of Germany, the Müller-Thurgau is dramatically supplanting the Silvaner. In 1960 the Silvaner dominated the land with 60% of all plantings. Sixteen years later its percentage had shrunk to 31.4% and the Müller-Thurgau had become the indisputable variety with 46.4%. All the others are insignificant: Riesling 3.2%, Perle (a crossing of Müller-Thurgau and Gewürztraminer) 2.9%, Scheurebe 2.4%, Bacchus 2.6% and Kerner 2.1%. It is safe to say that the soil and climate seem to be a more important factor in the ultimate taste of Franconian wines than the grape variety.

A second point concerns the Franconian bottle, or flagon. This is roughly in the shape of an army canteen with a rather long neck, which is perhaps an unfortunate way to describe it, for it is both attractive and picturesque. It is called a *Bocksbeutel* (Bock means goat) on account of its fancied resembalnce to a goat's scrotum, and it has been so called since time immemorial. The spelling Boxbeutel is acceptable only to the etymologically ignorant and the very prudish.

The *Bocksbeutel* is widely used for the wines of Franconia, and in other countries, notably Chile, for supposedly similar wines. However it is no less traditional in one other district of Southern Germany, in Mauerwein near Baden-Baden.

Though Franconia's total plantings cover a mere 8,132 acres, they are so dispersed that they must have four Bereiche, 17 Grosslagen and 155 Lagen scattered over 125 communities for their classification. The majority of the 5,936 vineyard owners belong to modern well-run cooperatives who make and market half the crop each year. The remaining half is bottled by a thousand farmers and by small and large Estates.

Franconian wines have become extremely popular in their native Bavaria which makes their marketing easy and profitable. In spite of this they are rather expensive when compared to other German wines and were never successfully exported.

More than a dozen town names and perhaps twice that many vineyard names are worth remembering. The major ones are listed below, with asterisks giving at least an idea of average quality.

It should be kept in mind that because of its rather different climate Franconia does not always follow the ratings of vintage charts that are accurate for the Rhine and Mosel. For the same reason, *Spätlesen, Auslesen,* and *Beerenauslesen* are even less common here than they are elsewhere, and it has been my experience that they are usually not worth the very high price which, as great rarities, they generally command.

The few really important Franconian producers include, as usual, the State, but two venerable charitable institutions, the *Juliusspital* and the *Bürgerspital zum Heiligen Geist,* are even more celebrated, and there are several estates still belonging to old titled families. Here is a list:

Major producers of great reputation:

Juliusspital	Würzburg
Bürgerspital zum Heiligen Geist	Würzburg
Staatliche Hofkellerei	Würzburg
Fürstlich Castell'sches Domänenamt	Castell
Fürstlich Löwenstein-Wertheim-Rosenberg'sches Weingut,	Kreuzwertheim

Other dependable producers:

Weingut Johann Ruck,	Ipfhofen
Weingut Hans Wirsching	Iphofen
Weingut Ernst Popp	Iphofen
Weingut W. Leininger	Eibelstadt
Weingut Peter Otto Meintzinger	Frickenhausen
Weingut Ernst Gebhardt	Sommerhausen
Weingut Gebr. Geiger Jun.	Thüngersheim

In addition there is a central cooperative covering the entire region in Kitzingen called *Gebietswinzergenossenschaft Franken,* and dependable *Winzergenossenschaften* in Sommerach, Thüngersheim, Randersacker and Nordheim.

Here are the eighteen best wine producing towns in order of quality, with their best vineyards. The Gebiet or region of a particular community is given in parenthesis.

*** Würzburg, 750 acres (Maindreieck) Stein, Innere Leiste

*** Thüngersheim, 625 acres (Maindreieck) Johannisberg, Scharlachberg

*** Iphofen, 600 acres (Steigerwald) Julius-Echter-Berg, Kronsberg, Kalb

*** Randersacker, 675 acres (Maindreieck) Pfulben, Teufelskeller

*** Rodelsee, 238 acres (Steigerwald) Küchenmeister, Schwanleite

*** Sommerach, 478 acres (Maindreieck) Katzenkopf, Rosenberg

*** Sommerhausen, 200 acres (Maindreieck) Steinbach

*** Escherndorf, 1100 acres (together with Volkach) (Maindreieck) Geibach, Rimbach, Fahr, Lump

** Volkach (Maindreieck) Ratsherr

** Castell, 225 acres (Steigerwald) Bausch, Hohnart

** Frickenhausen, 163 acres (Maindreieck) Kapellenberg, Markgraf, Babenberg

** Homburg, 113 acres (Maindreieck) Kallmuth

** Hörstein, 100 acres (Mainviereck) Reuschberg

** Klingenberg, 63 acres (Mainviereck) Schlossberg, Hochberg

** Nordheim, 1000 acres (Maindreieck) Vögelein, Kreuzberg

** Saaleck, 50 acres (Maindreieck) Schlossberg

** Sulzfeld, 375 acres (Maindreieck) Maustal, Cyriakusberg

** Obereisenheim, 225 acres (Maindreieck) Höll

9

BADEN

IN the Middle Ages Baden was the largest wine producing region of Germany. In spite of the ravages of the Thirty Year's War, in 1800 it was still the largest with 66,600 acres of vineyards. By 1900 this number was reduced to 44,000 acres, at a time when Alsace-Lorraine with 77,000 acres was Germany's largest wine producing province. The production of Baden decreased steadily after that and reached its lowest point in 1950 when the whole region had only 15,000 acres of vineyards left.

There has been a steady rise from this low point and today once more Baden is an important area, the third largest in Germany directly after the Rheinpfalz and Rheinhessen, with 33,500 acres of vineyards.

It is by far the most diverse of all the wine growing regions in Germany. Whereas all the others have some consistency of taste and type, are geographically contiguous and traditionally homogenous, Baden is an accident of politics, comprising the regions that grew wine in the former Grand Duchy of Baden.

First is the northeastern subregion which borders on Franconia and is appropriately called Bereich Badisches Frankenland. The wines that are grown there are so similar to the wines of Franconia that one wonders why the region was divided into two. The answer is obviously politics and the inability of the Bavarians and Badeners to come to a logical agreement.

Next is a small region encompassing really just the area immediately bordering Heidelberg, which is called the Bereich Badische Bergstrasse, again an illogical partition of the Bergstrasse, that fertile piece of land stretching from just south of Darmstadt to Heidelberg, where the orchards are spottily interspersed by vineyards. Here again the political borders of Hessen and Baden created two regions, where one would have been more logical.

Then going further south comes the Kraichgau, an area that goes up the Neckar to Heilbronn in the southeast and extends to the foothills of the Black Forest in Pforzheim to the southwest. The center or heartland of Baden, the portion that produces 78% of all the wine of the region, is one contiguous area that extends from Baden Baden to Basel. Bordered by the mountainous range of the Black Forest on the east, the Vosges mountains on the west and the broad valley of the Rhine in between it is blessed by the sun, with sufficient rainfall to make it rich agriculturally, with vineyards on the hillsides, truck gardens, orchards, wheat and sugar beet growing in the plain, and where only the Rhine separates the Alsatian wine country on the eastern slopes of the Vosges mountains from the Baden wine country on the western side of the Black Forest.

The region here is subdivided into four subregions or Bereiche, which going from north to south are: Bereich Ortenau, Bereich Kaiserstuhl-Tuniberg, Bereich Breisgau, and finally Bereich Markgräflerland.

There is but one other very small region, the Bereich Bodensee which is an area of only 760 acres on the Lake of Konstanz or the Bodensee as the Germans call their largest lake.

Baden is today politically part of the German Federal State of Baden-Württemberg. They are both unique in one respect. Whereas in all the other wine producing areas of Germany individualism reigns supreme, with farmers jealously guarding their privacy and insisting on making and marketing their wines themselves either in bottle or in bulk or both, in Baden Würrtemberg almost all the wine is made and marketed by the strongest cooperative movement in Germany and possibly in the Western World.

Almost 90% of the total crop is controlled by the cooperatives; to be exact, 110 Local and one large Central Cooperative in Breisach. The latter is the largest and most modern in Europe, a marvel of tech-

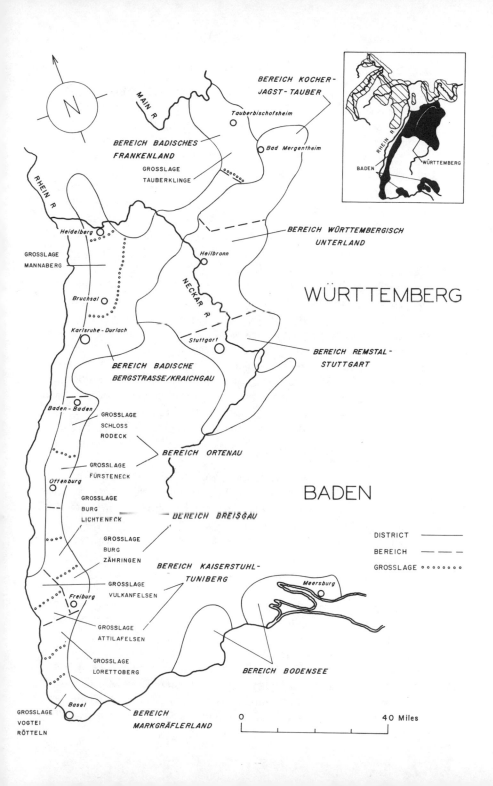

nology and size, with a storage capacity of 150,000,000 liters, enough to store one vintage in its entirety, and since the rest of the local cooperatives probably have an equal capacity among them, we can safely assume that Baden cooperatives can store two whole vintages. They can therefore market and distribute their wines with considerable sophistication since there is no pressure of inventory to influence marketing stability. Furthermore, the cooperatives sell their entire production in bottle, controlling their production, bottling and marketing. They have within their own State, Baden-Württemberg, the largest wine market in Germany. The local consumption is 53 bottles per capita per year, against a national average of only 32. There are many more singular aspects to the region of Baden.

Having replanted virtually their entire vineyard land since 1950 the wine industry was almost in the same position as all German industry after the war, able to start afresh with the latest knowledge in viticulture and technology. Nowhere else in Germany has the land been more "rearranged" by large earth moving equipment, have more roads been built through the vineyards to make them accessible to tractors and trucks, has more study gone into the exact location most suitable for vineyards, the exact grape variety most suitable to climate and soil, or have farmers more obediently followed a central scientific planning staff in every detail. If the Russian five year plan had been executed with Baden farmers, the Russians would be the most successful farmers in the world.

Only 18% of the wine farmers are full time wine growers, the others are part time growers who besides vineyards also own truck farms, sugar beet, wheat fields, possibly orchards, or are even employed in industry or the crafts.

The grape varieties vary immensely from Bereich to Bereich as the scientific selection has made it a most diverse Region. The total area of Baden has 78.8% white and 21.2% red grapes. Red grapes are important here since Baden is a major producer of Weissherbst (a rosé made entirely from red grapes, Pinot Noir) and Rotgold (a rosé which is made by fermenting together white and red grapes, Pinot Noir and Pinot Gris). Of the white grapes the Müller Thurgau dominates the area here as elsewhere in Germany with 35.1% total plantings, followed by Ruländer (Pinot Gris) 14.1%, Gutedel (Fendant or Chasselas) 9.8%, Riesling 7.3%, and small plantings of Silvaner, Pinot Blanc, (before the first World War Baden supplied grapes to the French Champagne industry) Gewürztraminer and Nobling (crossing of Silvaner and Gutedel). The red variety is almost exclusively Pinot Noir, called Spätburgunder here, it accounts for 18.6% of total plantings and is therefore the most prevalent grape variety grown in Baden next to the Müller Thurgau.

This is the only wine region in Germany within the viticultural zone "B" of the Common Market (European Economic Community). All other German regions are in zone "A." What this means is that Baden wines must have a higher degree of grape sugar in order to qualify for the different grades of quality under the German Wine Law.

Zone "B," incidentally, includes such wine regions as Alsace, Champagne and the Loire Valley. Obviously this Zone is warmer than the rest of Germany, the grapes are riper and therefore, the wines have more alcohol and less acidity than most other German wines.

About half of the 110 Cooperatives press their own grapes and make their own wine and sell it in their own immediate area. What they cannot sell, together with the grapes from the other half of the co-operatives goes to the Central cooperative in Breisach for pressing, fermentation, stabilization, blending, bottling and marketing both in Germany and abroad.

With so much concentration of production in the region few individual properties remain that are worth mentioning. The main ones are:

Weingut Freiherr von Gemmingen, Burg Hornberg, Neckarzimmern

Freiherr von Gocler'sche Rentamt, Sulzfeld

Baron Röder, Diersburg

Gutsverwaltung Freiherr von Neveu, Durbach

Gräflich Wolff Metternisch'sches Weingut, Durbach

Markgräflich Badisches Weingut Schloss Staufenberg

Versuchs-und Lehrgut für Weinbau Blankenhornsberg, Ihringen

Freiherr von Gleichenstein, Oberrotweil

Weingut St. Andreas, Ortenberg-Käftersberg

Staatliches Schloss Ortenberg, Ortenberg

Weingüter Max Markgraf von Baden, Salem

Staatliche Weingüter, Meersburg

Staatliches Weinbauinstitut, Freiburg

H. Germann, Müllheim

Fritz Blankenhorn, Schliengen

and two Estates by the name of Schlumberger, Friedhelm and Hartmut, in Sulzburg-Laufen.

And here are some details on the Bereiche and their wines. Before we start it is as well to point out that the Bereiche and Grosslagen play a much greater role in the marketing of Baden wines than in any other region. With the enormous concentration of the Cooperatives, and particularly the Central one, which goes under the initials Z.B.W., the marketing has logically concentrated on Bereiche and Grosslagen.

Bereich Badisches Frankenland

In this subregion, as in Franconia, the main grape variety is Müller-Thurgau, accounting for four fifths of the total plantings. The rest is largely Silvaner, Pinot Blanc, Kerner and some Gutedel (Fendant or Chasselas). The wines are bottled as in Franconia in the Bocksbeutel, and are similar to the Franconian ones.

The area is small with only 1,290 acres and has one *Grosslage:* Tauberklinge. The communities where the best wines grow are Königheim, Beckstein and Königshofen. The center of the wine trade is in Tauberbischofsheim.

Bereich Badische Bergstrasse/Kraichgau

This subregion actually encompasses two entirely different areas. In the north, the Badische Bergstrasse, with the villages north and south of Heidelberg and further south the Kraichgau, a subregion which is sparsely covered with vineyards, and really encompasses a rather large geographical area.

The entire area has 4,358 acres in vines of which 42% is in Müller-Thurgau, 20% in Riesling, 13% in Ruländer (Pinot Gris) and the rest is spread over a large assortment of Silvaner, Pinot Blanc, Auxerrois, Pinot Noir, and other red varieties; the red varieties account for almost 12% of total plantings.

The vineyard towns north of Heidelberg are in the Grosslage Rittersberg and the important ones are Schriesheim, Weinheim, Leutershausen and Lutzelsachsen. The main village south of Heidelberg that still belongs to the Bergstrasse is Wiesloch, in the Grosslage Mannaberg, which also includes the Kraichgau villages.

This area is planted in fruity Ruländer (Pinot Gris) and Riesling, as well as a whole collection of all the grape varieties mentioned above. The Kraichgau has two more Grosslagen, Stiftsberg and Hohenberg.

Bereich Ortenau

The northern section of that area of continuous vineyards which starts in Baden-Baden, the most typical and famous of all the European Spas, and ends four Bereiche later just north of Basel is the Ortenau. From Baden-Baden to Offenburg, it is a magnificent region where the pine trees of the Black Forest are constant companions of the Rhine valley.

The predominant grape variety in the Ortenau is the Pinot Noir, with 32% of the total vineyard area of 4,258 acres. It is largely used to make two Rosé wines: Weissherbst, usually made from the Pinot Noir and Rotgold made from Pinot Noir and Pinot Gris which are fermented together. Both are so highly popular in Baden and the whole domestic market that the supply can never keep up with the demand.

The other plantings are 30% in Riesling, 20% in Müller-Thurgau, 12% in Pinot Gris and 6% in Gewürztraminer.

The region makes a red wine called Affentaler which comes from the town of Affental and is made largely from Pinot Noir and shipped in a special bottle with a monkey on one side.

There are two *Grosslagen* in the Ortenau: Schloss Rodeck and Fürsteneck.

In Schloss Rodeck the main producing wine villages are: Steinbach, famous for its Stich den Buben vineyard; Neuweier with its Mauerberg vineyard; Eisenthal; Sasbachwalden with its Alter Gott vineyard; Kappelrodeck with its Hex von Dasenstein vineyard; and Waldulm. The Grosslage Fürsteneck has the following communities: Oberkirch, Durbach with its Plauelrain and Schlossberg vineyards and Ortenberg with its Andreasberg and Schlossberg vineyards.

Bereich Breisgau

The Bereich Breisgau is really just northeast of the extraordinary Bereich Kaiserstuhl-Tuniberg. What is surprising is that Breisgau, the old city on the Rhine and the center of the streamlined Cooperative mechanism in Baden, is not in the Bereich Breisgau, but in the Bereich Kaiserstuhl-Tuniberg.

Of the 3,378 acres of vines, almost 50% are in Muller-Thurgau, 22% in Pinot Gris, and 17% in Pinot Noir. The Muller-Thurgau produces a fruity wine here, somewhat heavier than in the Rheinhessen and Rheinpfalz and if anything, with even less acidity. It is usually fairly dry, if not completely so, and it is the main wine drunk with meals in this area.

The Pinot Gris makes a wine of more varietal character and the Pinot Noir, particularly from the Glottertal, is mainly used for Weissherbst, the famous Rose of this entier region.

The area has three Grosslagen, going from north to south: Schutterlindenberg, Burg Lichteneck and Burg Zähringen. In the Grosslage Burg Lichteneck is the viticultural experimental station at Hecklingen, the Grosslage Burg Zähringen has the well known Glottertal, famous for its Pinot Noir, which is made both into red wine and into Weissherbst. The best vineyard in Glottertal is Roter Bur.

Bereich Kaiserstuhl Tuniberg

The largest and most amazing part of the whole Baden region is the Bereich Kaiserstuhl Tuniberg. The region is dominated by an extinct Volcano, the Kaiserstuhl, a legendary mountain where fable has a German Emperor holding court in the innermost reaches of the mountain. He has been holding court for so long that his white beard has grown through a marble table.

The soil of this extinct volcano imparts an iron, fiery taste to the wines. The district has 10,083 acres, of which 35% are planted in Müller-Thurgau, 25% in Pinot Noir, 23% in Rülander (pinot gris), 10% in Silvaner and 3% in Pinot Blanc, called Weissburgunder here. The area furthermore is the best example of this reorganization of nature which has taken place over the last twenty years.

The Kaiserstuhl and the Tuniberg are the only sizable elevations in the Rhine valley between the Black Forest and the Vosges mountains. The Kaiserstuhl large and monumental, the Tuniberg a forerunner of the more substantial main monument of this region. Over the last fifteen years man has criss-crossed both with terraces and roads that have made it possible to grow grapes with a maximum of mechanization. There are even supply centers interspersed everywhere that

The Kaiserstuhl Tuniberg vineyards.

provide the right spray to the farmers for whatever might be ailing the vines during their ripening season.

This area produces the most successful wine of the three regions, one that is sold in large quantity by the Central Cooperative; it is simply called by the name of the Bereich and the grape variety: Bereich Kaiserstuhl-Tuniberg Müller-Thurgau. The second most popular wine from the area is the Weissherbst but what makes the reputation of the area is its Pinot Gris which here on the volcanic soil acquires an iron concentration and character that it does not have anywhere else in Germany.

The wines of this region are largely sold under their *Grosslagen* names, of which there are two: Vulkanfelsen, which includes the Kaiserstuhl, and Attilafelsen, which includes the Tuniberg. The three best wine producing villages (all in the Grosslage Vulkanfelsen) are Ihringen, Achkarren and Oberrotweil. Ihringen is the warmest locality in Germany. The best vineyards in Ihringen are: Fohrenberg and Winklerberg; in Achkarren: Schlossberg; and in Oberrotweil: Eichberg and Henkenberg.

Bereich Markgräflerland

The second largest subregion of Baden is the Markgräflerland which stretches from Freiburg to just north of Basel. It is a fertile stretch of land, most of it quite flat, with only a small section that is gently rolling.

Unlike the rest of Baden the main grape variety here is the Gutedel (Fendant or Chasselas) which accounts for 38% of total plantings in an area of 7,775 acres. The Müller-Thurgau accounts for 26% of plantings, the Pinot Noir for 13% and the rest is largely Ruländer, Silvaner, Pinot Blanc, Gewürztraminer and Nobling which is a crossing of Silvaner and Gutedel and produces wines with body and fruit and a fine bouquet.

The predominant Gutedel makes a neutral, light wine which is often spritzig. It is usually vinified quite dry and if consumed young it is a pleasant wine to drink with meals. The Müller-Thurgau here makes wines of a little more charm and character than the Gutedel, and somewhat lighter than in the Kaiserstuhl Tuniberg Bereich.

There are three Grosslagen, going from north to south: Lorettoberg, Burg Neuenfels and Vogtei Rötteln. The best wine growing communities with their best vineyards are:
Grosslage Lorettoberg:
(A lot of wine in this Grosslage is marketed under the Grosslage name).
Wolfenweiler, Scherzingen, Pfaffenweiler, Kirchhofen and Norsingen all sharing a vineyard called Batzenberg. Wettelbrunn, Eschbach, Heitersheim and Seefelden again sharing a vineyard called Maltesergarten. Laufen: Altenberg; Britzingen: Sonnhohle; Mullheim: Reggenhag; Badenweiler: Romerberg, and Auggen: Schaf. Mauschen, Schliengen, Niedereggenen, Liel and Bad Bellingen share yet another vineyard called Sonnenstück.

Grosslage Rötteln

This is again a Grosslage under which a lot of wines of the area are marketed. The two best wine growing communities in this area are: Efringen-Kirchen with its Oelberg vineyard and Weil with its Schlipf vineyard.

Bereich Bodensee

This is a small area of only 760 acres. The main grape varieties are Müller-Thurgau with 53% of the total plantings, Pinot Noir with

41%, and 6% Rülander. The Bodensee is Germany's largest lake, creating a microclimate which permits the grapes to ripen in spite of the 1,600 feet elevation.

The main wine producing communities are Meersburg and Hagnau. The Pinot Noir is both made into red wine and into Weissherbst (rosé) and finally the Müller-Thurgau develops rather fruity wines with some spritz.

THE LESSER
DISTRICTS

THIS must be a catchall chapter, giving scant information on four diverse growing areas: Württemberg, Mittelrhein, Ahr and Hessische Bergstrasse.

Only Württemberg, being Germany's fifth largest growing region, is important enough to justify its own chapter. Alas, the local population of Württemberg drinks all but a small trickle of the wines from the region, so that little is found anywhere else in Germany, let alone in the export market. The other three are the smallest of the growing regions, the Mittelrhein has 2,178 acres in vines, the Ahr 1,270, and finally the Bergstrasse only 895. The chapter also deals with German sparkling wines.

WÜRTTEMBERG:

Like Baden, on which it borders and with which it forms a political entity today, the old princeling state of Württemberg was one of Germany's large wine producing areas in the middle ages with 112,500 acres in vines. Today there are just under 20,000 acres, in a state that regards wine as its daily beverage and with neighboring Baden has a consumption of 53 bottles per capita per year.

Like Baden, its wine industry is dominated by the cooperative movement, with 80% of its production in the hands of 31 local, four regional and one central cooperative as the main marketing arm of the 16,500 members. The remaining 1,653 growers produce 10% of the crop which is then bottled and sold by wine shippers. The last 10% is sold as Estate bottled wine by small and very few larger growers, of which the largest has 100 acres in vines.

A large portion of the grape growers are part time growers, which explains the high percentage of cooperative members. The vineyards are planted largely along the Neckar and its tributaries, the microclimates being the only ones favorable to the cultivation of the grape. The selection of grape varieties and types is strongly influenced by the quality factor. The area has one of the finest Oenological Schools and experimental stations in Weinsberg, which has greatly contributed to the high standard of viticulture and viniculture in the State.

Württemberg with 47% of total plantings in red is the largest area for red wine grapes in Germany. The most prominent red grape variety is the Trollinger, which originally came from Northern Italy, but has been greatly improved by clonal selection. It produces a light red and fruity wine, a sort of local Beaujolais. Trollinger plantings account for 20% of the total, the other red varieties being the Schwarzriesling (the Pinot Meunier), accounting for 9.4% and followed by the Portugieser and the Pinot Noir.

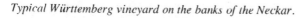

Typical Württemberg vineyard on the banks of the Neckar.

The white varieties are led by the Riesling which accounts for 22% of total plantings, covering an acreage almost as large as the Riesling plantings in the Rheingau. The wines made from Riesling here are wines of elegance and breed. The Müller Thurgau accounts for 15% of plantings and the Silvaner for 7.5 followed by Kerner, Pinot Gris and Pinot Blanc.

There is a great deal of Rosé made and consumed in Württemberg, which goes under the name of Schillerwein. This has nothing to do with the German national poet Schiller; the name derives from *schillern,* the German word for shimmer. The wine is made from the must of both red and white grapes, unlike the *Weissherbst* which is made entirely from red grapes.

The region has three Bereiche, 16 Grosslagen and 205 individual vineyards spread over 230 communities. The vineyards are located around the towns of Heilbronn, Weinsberg, Lauffen, Vaihingen, Stuttgart, Weinstadt and Esslingen.

The main growers are the *Hofkammerkellerei* of the Grand Dukes of Württemberg in Stuttgart, *Graf Adelmann* at Steinheim, *Graf Neipperg* at Schwaigern (who is the sole owner of the Neipperger Schlossberg vineyard as well as of a well-known restaurant "Zum Alten Rentamt"), the provincial Oenological Station mentioned above, the *Lehr- und Versuchsanstalt für Wein und Obstbau* in Weinsberg, *Gräflich von Bentzet-Sturmfeder' sches Weingut* in Schozach, *Fürst zu Hohenlohe-Ohringen' sche Schlosskellerei* in Ohringen and the *Fürstlich Hohenlohe- Langenburg' sche Weingüter* in Weikersheim.

MITTELRHEIN

The Mittelrhein region stretches for some 60 miles along the left bank of the Rhine from Trachtingshausen to Koblenz, on the right bank of the Rhine from Kaub to Niederdollendorf and encompasses the twenty or so miles along the Lahn before it joins the Rhine. Nature could not have provided a more dramatic and romantic setting for this region.

Until the ice age the Rhine stopped at what is now the gorge at Bingen, and formed an immense inland sea covering most of what is now the Rheingau and the northern part of Rheinhessen and the Nahe. There are still remains of this age, sandy stretches of seascape near Mainz covered by straggly pines more reminiscent of the Atlantic coast than the Rhine river.

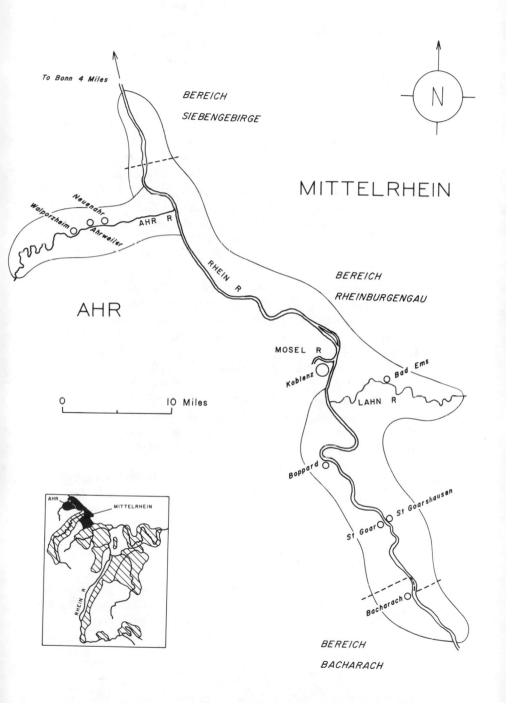

When the river broke through this gorge, it cut a tortuous way through steep hills, until it finally reached the north German plain near Bonn. It is this part of the Rhine, the newest part, that forms the small region of the Mittelrhein.

2,178 acres produce on an average the equivalent of 800,000 cases of wine in the world's steepest and most inaccessible vineyards. 75.7% of the vines are Riesling, the largest percentage of Riesling in any region. The other grape varieties are Müller-Thurgau 11.3%, Kerner 4% and Silvaner 3.6%; there is also a movement for newer varieties with a fair amount of Faber, Huxel and Ortega.

It is a difficult area for growing wine, the steep hillsides need water and sun to produce a ripe crop, and fortunately the microclimate makes this one of Germany's rainiest regions in the summer. 75% of the crop is sold directly by the growers, usually to the many tourists that visit this beautiful area, and climb up to the many castles that dot the hillsides along the Rhine. The castles were built in the middle ages by robber-barons who collected tribute from the weary merchant taking his goods to the North. Now many of them have been rebuilt into hotels and inns serving the rather austere wine of the region.

Whatever is not drunk locally is largely bought by the Sekt houses for sparkling wine, where the acidity is a desired characteristic of the end product rather than a fault.

The *Lahn,* a dreamy tributary of the Rhine is dotted with vineyards which are just as inaccessible and somehow seem more important for enhancing the beautiful landscape than for their small wine production. The area's largely part-time wine growers are increasingly attracted to the industries in the neighboring large towns and vineyards are increasingly being abandoned.

Bacharach, the area's principal "wine town", was important in the sixteenth and seventeenth century as shipping center for wines from every part of the Rhine. Shipping was dangerous through the gorge of Bingen, therefore the wine was assembled downriver in Bacharach, which became an important shipping center of wine; rather like what Bordeaux was at the same period for the wines of the southeast of France.

The leading shipper, Wilhelm Wasum, is still in Bacharach, the only shipper that does honor to the better wines of the region. The best vineyards are around Bacharach, Oberwesel and Boppard.

In the summer the area is overrun by tourists who buy wines from

The Pfalz at Kaub with Mittelrhein vineyards.

approximately 75 growers, most of which have tasting rooms and about half of which offer lodging and food as well.

AHR

The Ahr is Germany's most northern wine region. Its 1,270 acres of predominantly red grapes produce a bare 500,000 cases of wine a year. The small river Ahr winds its way through steep hillsides for some 55 miles and just before it joins the Rhine there is a stretch of a little over 10 miles of contiguous vineyard area.

The area is of singular beauty, a center of tourism as much for the healing waters of its main town of Bad Neuenahr-Ahrweiler, as for its many walks and inns. It is a favorite excursion spot for the politicians of Bonn and many a weighty political matter has been solved in its pretty inns over a glass of its red wine and a dish of its game.

Most of the vineyards are on steep hillsides planted 31% with pinot noir, 24% with Portugieser with recent additions of a new grape variety called Domina, which gives the red wine color, as well as Rotberger which is largely used for Rosé wine. 21% of the vineyard area is planted in Riesling and 19% in Müller-Thurgau. Two thirds of the vineyard area is worked by part time vintners who largely belong to Cooperatives. The remainder is grown by individual growers and Estates, the largest of which is the Experimental Station at Bad Neuenahr-Ahrweiler which also runs the State Domaine at Kloster Marienthal. There is but one *Grosslage:* Klosterberg.

The Pinot Noir was formerly vinified with a residual sweetness which did not endear it to wine drinkers accustomed to the wines of France and Italy. There is a greater trend for drier vinification now which brings out the light charm and elegance of these wines. They are almost entirely consumed locally, and locally they offer a welcome change from all the white wines one usually drinks in Germany. As their production involves an enormous amount of hand labor, their cost is comparatively high when compared with similar wines of more southern climes.

The Rieslings in good years are elegant and stylish; together with the local Müller-Thurgaus they are almost entirely consumed in the area or taken home by the many tourists that visit the valley.

HESSISCHE BERGSTRASSE

This is Germany's smallest wine region. Not quite 900 acres produce some 340,000 cases of wine a year. The largely part time vintners are organized into two cooperatives.

There are two wine producing areas, one small, with barely 120 acres, east of Darmstadt called Bereich Umstadt and one more important main area, the Bereich Starkenburg with its main towns of Bensheim and Heppenheim.

This stretch of land just north of Heidelberg is one of Germany's best fruit growing areas so it is not surprising that the western hillsides of the Bergstrasse facing the Rhine valley are planted in vines. Whereas Bereich Umstadt is mainly planted in Müller-Thurgau, in this warmer area the Riesling is king. There are also plantings of Müller-Thurgau, Ruländer (Pinot Gris) and Silvaner, though the Riesling is experiencing a renaissance, being a more dependable producer from year to year.

The wines are full-bodied and richer than those of the Rheingau, with a little less acidity. Climate and soil gave them a richer and less elegant style. They are all drunk locally except for a small percentage that comes from the State Domain in Bensheim, where they are auctioned once a year and bought as a curiosity and rarity mainly by better restaurants in Germany.

The vineyards at Altenahr in the Ahr valley.

SEKT

Germany produced 229 million bottles of sparkling wine in 1976 and imported an additional 54.1 million making up an annual consumption of 4.5 bottles of sparkling wine per capita. The word *"Sekt"* is a derivative of the Spanish *vino seco* (dry wine), which came to Germany by way of England during the Thirty Year War.

German Sekt is partially made from German wine, an approximate 20%, and principally from French and Italian. With the enormous difference in the style of the wine produced in Germany each year, it is natural that only a fraction of it can be used for Sekt. White

Bordeaux, white and red wine from the Loire and more recently wines specially produced by the large German Sekt houses in Northern Italy form the bulk of the base wines that go into Sekt.

Most of it is sold as branded Sekt, under the name of the company, the largest of which is *Henkell* followed by *Söhnlein, Deinhard, Carstens, Faber, Kupferberg, Matheus Müller, Rüttgers, Kessler* and *Burgeff.*

The wines sold by these houses are consistent in quality and taste and are remarkably good on an average. Somewhat softer and less alcoholic than French champagne, they have become a national drink in Germany, where the sparkling wine tax is not as onerous as it is in America.

With time the different houses have added to their large popular cuvées special ones, some of which almost exclusively made of Riesling. *Fürst von Metternich*, which is one of the leading brands, uses a large amount of Riesling from the Rheingau. Most of the others have sparkling wines from specific areas: i.e., Mosel-Saar-Ruwer, Rheingau or Mittelrhein.

In cases where the Sekt specifies region of origin, grape variety or vintage year it must be made by 75% from grapes of the region, by 75% of the grape variety, and by 75% from grapes harvested in the specified year.

Many of the better known Estates in the Rheingau and on the Mosel-Saar-Ruwer produce their own Sekt, usually from the grapes that are less ripe and less suitable for Prädikatswein.

Most German Sekt is made by the Cuvée close method (tank fermentation) which is a good deal less expensive than bottle fermentation. Extensive experimentation, furthermore, has shown that there is no marked difference in the end product between the two methods. Bottle fermentation, however, is a strong sales argument in the marketing of some sparkling wines, particularly French Champagne.

HOW TO BUY, STORE, SERVE AND TASTE GERMAN WINES

SINCE virtually the entire purpose of this little book is to guide the consumer through the complexities of German wines and their labels, it seems almost pointless to append a chapter such as this, and attempt to accomplish, in two or three pages, what I have possibly failed to achieve in well over a hundred. On the other hand, a brief summary or round-up can do no harm and may even prove useful, and a word or two of counsel about buying German wines in the United States may help to keep the occasional and inevitable disappointments to a minimum.

German wines are America's most popular imported white wines and can be found in any liquor store or supermarket in this country.

The selection is usually limited to the better known regional *Qualitätsweine* such as *Zeller Schwarze Katz, Piesporter Michelsberg, Bereich Bernkastel* from the Mosel-Saar-Ruwer, *Bereich Johannisberg* from the Rheingau, *Bereich Nierstein* from Rheinhessen and various brands of *Liebfraumilch*—the heavily advertised premium brands such as Blue Nun, and various price brands.

In addition, every major town in this country will have at least one or two stores that specialize in fine wines and will stock a selection from individual vineyards of the Mosel-Saar-Ruwer and the different Rhine districts, mostly estate bottled (*Erzeugerabfüllung*), with a good sprinkling of Estates mentioned in this book. These wines will be of various vintages, possibly going back to 1975 and 1976, with an odd bottle here and there of an older vintage such as 1971. Such stores will have knowledgeable personnel to help the shopper to find his way.

German wines are never cheap, they not only come from the world's most northern vineyards but also from a country with the highest farm wages and one of the hardest currencies.

Though one can frequently find a German wine on the shelf of a wine store for under $2.00, it is likely that a California wine at this price would be a better buy. It is hard in today's world to buy a decent German wine much under $3.50, and even at that price it is likely to be only a *Qualitätswein* from one of the larger *Grosslagen* or *Bereiche*. A *Kabinett* wine would run anywhere from $4.00 to $7.00 or $8.00 depending on the area and the grower. *Spätlesen* would fall into about the same price categories and *Auslesen*, depending on their provenance and year would run anywhere from $7.00 to over $10.00.

I think this book has described in enough detail the complexities of the vineyards, and the considerable difference in quality of the wine produced by the different Estates. An Estate bottled wine is not necessarily better than a shipper's bottling, though the prestigious Estates have certainly earned their reputation through their ability to produce finer wines than their neighbors.

As the supply of fine wines never catches up with the demand, it is not surprising that these fine Estates will often sell their wine at double the price of their less competent neighbors. This does not mean to say that you will never find an excellent *Prädikatswein* bargain at your liquor store, it is just that it is unlikely and rare.

If you buy a wine of a famous vintage and vineyard you would be better advised to pay a little more for a well established grower's or shipper's label than save pennies and be disappointed.

German wines, particularly *Qualitätswein, Kabinett* and most *Spätlese* are, with certain exceptions, ready to drink when they appear on the shelf, and it is safer to buy a recent vintage than risk an older bottle, unless that bottle has been well stored and is a *Spätlese* or preferably *Auslese* from an outstanding vintage, or better still a *Beeren* or *Trockenbeerenauslese*. The two latter designations are obviously rare and very expensive indeed, though I have seen bottles from first class growers in fine wine stores in every town and city I visited the last three years.

German wines have come of age in America and it is no coincidence that when the U.S. Government made the .75 liter bottle mandatory, every major grower in Germany changed his entire production to .75 liter bottles though .70 is still the accepted size in Germany and England. With the large percentage of fine German wines coming to America it was more logical to adopt the "American bottle."

There are certain rules of thumb as to the "safe" age of a German bottle. The most delicate German wines are the Mosel-Saar-Ruwer. They are usually bottled before the summer following the vintage and often retain a little carbon dioxide, what the Germans call *spritz*, left over from the fermentation, which gives them a wonderful freshness and liveliness.

If they are of the *Qualitätswein, Kabinett* or *Spätlese* quality they should be consumed within three years of the harvest, which really means four years from the date on the bottle. Not that they will not be still good for another two years, but they will have lost some of that sparkling charm of youth. The higher grades, *Auslese* and better, usually reach their peak five years after the harvest, six years from the date on the bottle and might well keep their top form for three or four more years after that. This always presupposes good storage.

The Rhine wines are more complicated, as some and particularly the Rieslings will take time to develop their full balance and style in the bottle. The Rieslings from the Rheingau in the *Qualitätswein, Kabinett* and *Spätlese* qualities will take three or four years to develop their style, so that bottles of the 1976 vintage will be starting to show to their best advantage in 1980 and will certainly keep under good storage condition for three or four more years. Not that these wines are not good before that; they just lack that last bit of perfection and it is a pity to drink them before they have fully developed.

The *Auslese* and higher grades from the Rheingau take longer, often eight to ten years and more, their youthful sweetness hiding for many years the fruity acidity that is so important for their preservation and balance. Since they are usually unavailable by the time they have reached their peak, they must be bought earlier and stored.

The wines from the other regions of the Rhine: Rheinhessen, Rheinpfalz, Nahe mature faster than the Rheingau, the *Qualitätswein* and *Kabinett* are usually ready a year after the harvest, which is when they first appear on the shelves in America. They might improve marginally for another two or three years and should certainly keep for five. The *Auslese* and higher grades might take five years to show their full style and potential, and will easily keep their top form for five years longer.

An increasing number of German wines are bottled without indication of the grape variety, which usually means that they are made from more than one and will therefore mature faster than the Rieslings. The same is true of the Silvaner, Müller Thurgau, Morio Muskat and some of the more recent grape crossings. It is really the Riesling, Gewürztraminer and Ruländer (Pinot Gris) that take longest to mature in the bottle and the old axiom that the greater the wine the longer it will take to develop is true here as it is with all wines everywhere.

Though most German wines fall under the category of wines one can buy and consume the same evening, the above remarks clearly show that many improve greatly with storage so that a real lover of German wines should be willing to age them, just as he is willing to age his red Bordeaux.

It is wise to first buy one bottle of any wine intended for aging, taste it, and only if found up to expectation buy the remaining 11 in the case in order to obtain the customary 10% reduction which most wine stores will give with a case. Storing should not pose any major problems since white wines develop a great deal faster than the red.

Few American homes have wine-cellars, and most apartment dwellers can devote at best a closet to the bottles they wish to keep for special occasions and for their discriminating friends. Such a closet is as good as a cellar for all practical purposes, especially for German wines (which do not require long aging), providing the temperature is not over 70° as an average and never, except for very brief periods, over 75°. The wines will mature a little more rapidly than they would, under ideal conditions, underground, but they will not spoil within their normal span of life if stored so that the wine is in contact with the cork. All sorts of convenient and eminently satisfactory wine racks have been designed for such limited storage space, and providing the wines are kept horizontal and reasonably cool, only the purist or the perfectionist will take exception to them. German wines are almost all better when they are relatively young, and most of the talk of cob-webbed bottles and the like is sheer nonsense.

It is as well to summarize a few points one must remember when buying German wines:

1. The better German wines carry the name of a specific town (with very few exceptions) plus that of a vineyard.
2. The better German wines are *Prädikat* wines, bearing the legend *"Qualitätswein mit Prädikat"* and such designations as *Kabinett, Spätlese, Auslese,* etc.
3. Most of the better German wines are Estate bottled; (*"Erzeugerabfullung"* or *"Aus eigenem Lesegut"*).

This book includes an appendix with up-to-date information on the quality of the last ten vintages. It should, together with all the other information enable the serious wine drinker to buy the proper wine with the proper vintage year, for either immediate or later drinking.

It is an odd fact that until recently the Germans drank most of their wine between meals and only had beer or mineral water with meals. Part of the custom was undoubtedly based on the fact that few Germans entertain for dinner at home, since the main meal is at lunch. Most Germans will have cold cuts or cheese and bread with salad for their evening meal, and that quite early.

After dinner, however, is the favorite time to entertain friends, and that was when most of the wine was drunk. Many slim bottles of German wine, usually at least one per person, were slowly drunk, accompanied by lively conversation and a few crackers and nuts.

German wines, being light in alcohol and usually with some residual sweetness are ideal to drink by themselves. There is no unbalanced acidity to tire the drinker, no high alcoholic content to dull the senses. Only in Baden and Württemberg was wine always consumed with the meal.

Those customs have changed, as have a lot of other things. The Germans now take as lively an interest in *haute cuisine* as the Americans and wine has become the accompaniment of the meal in most middle class households, with lively discussions as to which wine is appropriate with what dish.

Obviously the ideal wines for food are the *Qualitätsweine,* the *Kabinett* and the *Spätlese,* the other *"Prädikat wines"* being too sweet and fruity to really complement any dish except dessert, and even there a *Beerenauslese* or *Trockenbeerenauslese* is still better by itself.

Most *Qualitätsweine, Kabinett* and *Spätlese* go well with meals, their slight sweetness often enhancing the food. There is a tendency in Germany today for drier and drier wines, such as *Trocken* and *Halb-*

trocken but I find it more a fetish than a gustatory success as the dry wines often lack the body and the charm of their sweeter counterparts.

There is such an enormous variety of wines made that its marriage with food can easily complement each other rather than clash or dominate.

Mosel-Saar-Ruwer wines seem to go ideally with cold meats, paté, poached fish, boiled beef, crayfish, cold lobster or crabmeat, whilst Rhine wines are really all-purpose wines. They are almost ideal with any dish except those with vinegar such as Sauerkraut or Sauerbraten, where the only wine I have found suitable is a *Gewürztraminer*, and preferably a *Spätlese* at that.

I personally like Rhine wines with most cheeses, preferably *Qualitätswein* or *Kabinett* with all hard cheeses and such soft cheeses as Brie and Camembert, whereas blue cheeses such as Roquefort or Stilton go well with a *Spätlese* or *Auslese*.

I can hardly give total advice on food and wine combinations since tastes differ so that what is pleasant to one may not be to another. By and large, however, these indications should help anyone to find their way to the right thing.

As far as temperature is concerned, Germans generally serve their wines less cold than what is considered standard practice in France or England or the United States. If the wine comes from a cool cellar, they often do not use an ice-bucket at all, and drink it cheerfully and appreciatively at about 60° Fahrenheit. This is anything but damaging, possibly even helpful, to a great wine, less so to a good or fair one; but American dining rooms, in winter as in summer, are considerably warmer than German ones by and large, and most of us will prefer German wines chilled to about 52° to 55°. Unfortunately, most of our manufacturers of wine-buckets follow the French tradition, and as a result the wine in the neck of a German bottle is above the ice and is not chilled in a bucket at all. In such cases, it is perfectly good practice to put the bottle neckdown in the bucket for ten minutes or so before it is brought to the table; there being no sediment, the wine is not injured in the least. Of course it is even better and much simpler to put the bottle in a refrigerator for approximately an hour before serving. It goes wihout saying that the top of the lead capsule should be cut off, and the rim of the bottle wiped clean before the cork is drawn.

Like all other good wines, Mosels and Rhines should be served preferably in clear, thin-stemmed glasses. They look prettier and they taste better. The traditional form is a sort of flat cup, with straight or in-curving sides, mounted on a tall stem, but a tulip shape is certainly as good, and in any case the glasses should not be filled much over half full. The so-called *Pokal* or *Römer* (a goblet mounted on a cone-shaped stem) is only used in Germany for the most ordinary wine; it generally holds either ¼ or ½ liter, and is filled to the brim. Fine wines are never so served.

Since there is no real reason for buying or serving or drinking a fine wine, whether German or French or American, except the pleasure that it gives, it seems wholly nonsensical not to take the small additional trouble to taste it carefully and get a maximum of enjoyment out of something so carefully made to provide precisely that.

Far too much has been said and written about "tasting" wine, as if the matter involved some exceedingly complex procedure or technique. This is all very well for professionals, who are often asked to grade and price a hundred or more wines in a morning, who perforce must spit out what they taste, at the risk of misgrading half of the samples, who are highly paid for the job and regard it as very hard work indeed. This is not the way to enjoy wine, nor to taste it when one is drinking it. Basically, the one real essential, whether one has had a cocktail before, or two, or none, whether one smokes or not, whether the menu has been planned to "bring out" the wine, or not— the one real essential is to devote at least a moment or two of undivided attention to the wine one drinks. It is no more possible to judge and appreciate and fully enjoy a wine while carrying on a lively conversation on some other subject than to judge a pianist's performance, or appreciate a good play, or even watch and enjoy a football game under similar conditions. The concentration required to judge and enjoy a wine involves perhaps a minute, certainly less than three—a brief space to inhale and weigh the bouquet or aroma, a few seconds to take a sip or two and hold the wine in one's mouth while inhaling and then exhaling, then just the time to judge and enjoy the aftertaste.

An expert can tell a great deal about a wine by its color, but this is not easy for the amateur since such judgments have to be based on a great deal of experience and a very accurate memory for fine shades. It is possible to say that all German wines, except the very great and sweet ones, should be pale gold, with a certain amount of green in their make-up, as transparent as water, and so brilliant that they shine in their glass either in lamplight or in sunlight. The greater and sweeter wines are gold, not green, and when they begin to show a coppery tinge, they are reaching the end of their career. The Mosels, of course, are the palest of all.

In German wines the question of bouquet is primary and all-important. But the special, recognizable and characteristic bouquet which certain wines possess, cannot be described; it is as subtle and evanescent as the scent of a flower. Nevertheless, it is not difficult to distinguish, on the basis of bouquet alone, between a great and a fairly good and a poor German wine, nor does one have to be any sort of expert to tell a Mosel from a Rhine wine, providing one can sniff them comparatively at a single testing. The faculty which permits a professional taster to give a wine's class, and often name the township and precise vineyard which produced it, is much less a matter of talent and aptitude than of long practice and taste memory. It requires, of course, a high degree of concentration.

A wine's bouquet is most apparent and can be best appreciated when it is not too cold, when it is served in large glasses filled to no more than a third of their capacity, and when the wine has been swirled or shaken in the glass before it is brought to the nose. This swirling and shaking, which looks rather ridiculous to the uninitiated, is anything but silly—the entire inner surface of the tulip-shaped glass becomes thus coated with wine and serves as a sort of chimney, concentrating the wine's aroma and channeling it upwards, and just as any carbonated liquid tends to give off its bubbles when it is shaken, so a wine gives off its bouquet when it is moved.

Even to a complete beginner, the bouquet of a fine wine is immediately more agreeable than that of a small, common, or poor one. Of course there are pitfalls and one can make mistakes. It is possible to mistake the first, early traces of maderization, or oxidation, or old age, for something much better—the bouquet of a great wine, still sound; all wines, especially white wines, tend to develop a special bloom before they die, and acquire a sort of false funereal beauty which is immensely attractive on first acquaintance; let them stand half an hour in their glass, and you will readily recognize them for what they are. The elements to look for in the bouquet of a fine German wine are, principally, fruit and breed. Neither is easy to describe. The wine should have a scent as definite as that of a very ripe peach or plum or quince or strawberry, though very different from these, and a good deal more complex, so that you find yourself baffled when you try to define it in terms of anything else. It should be even more interesting and even more baffling when you sniff it for the tenth time, with nothing in its make-up which you could describe as heavy or fatiguing or flat. But these are only words.

Taste and aftertaste can only be judged and appreciated in the same way, and only described in equally vague terms. Both should be wholly agreeable if the wine is good, and any trace of anything else should render a wine immediately suspect. Both should be in keeping with the wine's bouquet (the aftertaste of a too-old wine is generally not) and both, basically, should be appetizing, so that you are left sorry that there is not more in the bottle, and reluctant to drink the last drops in your glass. This, essentially, is the proof of a fine wine.

I find it important to express in words what I taste. The verbalization of the many taste sensations enable me to formulate with some clarity my own opinion of a wine and by writing it down to almost recall its taste exactly.

In order to facilitate this process the appendix has a reprint of an Adjective Selector for Describing Wines and a List of Words Used to Describe Wines which Judy Ley Allen and I developed for *Which Wine*.

A record of tasting notes will help the wine education and will ultimately refine the taste perception. The two appendixes should be helpful for keeping useful tasting notes.

APPENDICES

VINTAGE YEARS SINCE 1970

Information on German vintage years falls into two categories. The first identifies great vintage years and enables German wine lovers to put away great bottles of Auslese, Beerenauslese and Trockenbeerenauslese for aging and future drinking. The second discusses the quality of the vintage in order to enable the German wine drinker to choose the correct vintage for his drinking.

The problem can be complex; Qualitätswein and Qualitätswein mit Prädikat Kabinett from the Mosel-Saar-Ruwer are best when consumed young. The same wines from the Rheingau, Rheinhessen and Rheinpfalz profit from some aging while wines of great years need more time to age, regardless of the Prädikat.

In view of the plethora of qualities and vintages one can at best only give some basic guidelines. One of the problems lies in the fact that some wines are consumed too early and others too late.

The German custom of selective picking, however, makes certain broad general rules applicable:

1. All Qualitätsweine from the Mosel-Saar-Ruwer and from Baden should be consumed within three years of their making. Since the harvest is usually in October or November, this means four years from the vintage date on the bottle. The same applies to Kabinett wines from these regions in average and good years. Spätlese and Auslese wines which are not made from the Riesling of the above regions fall under the same rule.

204

On the other hand Spätlese and Auslese wines made from Riesling usually reach their peak in seven years, though some live a great deal longer, particularly if they come from a great vineyard, a great year and a great grower. Beerenauslese and Trockenbeerenauslese from the Mosel-Saar-Ruwer and Baden live longer; however, one should try a bottle after seven years to see the effects of time.

2. Qualitätswein and Kabinett from Rheinhessen, Rheingau, Rheinpfalz, Nahe, Franken, Württemberg and Mittelrhein in an average year should be consumed within four years of the harvest, which means five years from the vintage date on the bottle. The exception is the Riesling of these regions which will take longer to reach maturity. Spätlese and Auslese need seven years and greater wines ten to twenty depending on the greatness of the vintage.

A great vintage year in Germany is one that produces a large quantity of Qualitätswein mit Prädikat with a lot of Edelfäule (noble rot) and with enough acidity to balance the sweetness and give the wine long life. The great German vintage years of this century were 1911, 1921, 1934, 1937, 1945, 1953 and more recently 1971 and 1976.

Here is my assessment of the last ten years, broken down by main regions. The numerical ratings are based on the principle that 20/20 is perfection, 12/20 hardly passing and 10/20 and below, something that most of us would just as soon forget. The ratings are based on the present quality of the wines in question, not on their original worth during, what was for many of them, their brief days of glory:

1979:

Mosel-Saar-Ruwer: Small vintage, 60% of average crop. Wines with fine fruit; 70% of crop Prädikat wines, mainly Kabinett and Spätlese. 16/20

Rheingau: Above average both in quantity and quality. Wines with good fruit and balance, most of crop Q.b.A. and Kabinett. 16/20

Rheinhessen: Small vintage with excellent quality wines, 75% Prädikat, mostly Kabinett and Spätlese. 17/20

Rheinpfalz: Large crop of ripe, well balanced wines, with good fruit and elegance. 40% Prädikat, mainly Kabinett. 16/20

1978:

Mosel-Saar-Ruwer: Small vintage, useful Q.b.A. wines, very few Kabinett, good fruit. 13/20

Rheingau: Small vintage, useful Q.b.A. wines, very few Kabinett, good fruit, need time to develop. 13/20

Rheinhessen: Small quantity, useful Q.b.A. wines, good quantity of Kabinett, fruit, good acidity. 13/20

Rheinpfalz: Good quantity, light fruity wines with goodly percentage of Kabinett. 14/20

1977:

Mosel-Saar-Ruwer: Average size vintage. Wines with high acidity making average Q.b.A. wines with very few Prädikat. 12/20

Rheingau: Small vintage, largely Q.b.A. wines, high acidity, need long time to mature. 13/20

Rheinhessen: Average size vintage, wine with high acidity, useful Q.b.A. 13/20

Rheinpfalz: Good quantity, useful wines on the light side, mostly Q.b.A. with some Prädikat. 13/20

1976:

Mosel-Saar-Ruwer: Small vintage of outstanding quality. Lots of noble rot. Next to 49 and '21 considered one of the greatest vintages of this century. Better vineyards made practically only Auslese and higher designations. 20/20

Rheingau: Less than average quantity. Very great year, needs time to develop fully. Lots of noble rot, the better wineyards made mostly Auslese and higher designations. 20/20

Rheinhessen: Good quantity, exceptional vintage, lots of noble rot, great wines up to Trockenbeerenauslese. 19/20

Rheinpfalz: Good quantity, very good year, lots of noble rot, wines comparable to the greatest of this century. 20/20

1975:

Mosel-Saar-Ruwer: Average size vintage. Excellent wines with good fruity acidity and ripeness, practically no noble rot, excellent long-lived Kabinett, Spätlese and Auslese wines. 18/20

Rheingau: Above average quantity. Very elegant, fruity, well-balanced wines, largely Kabinett and Spätlese. 17/20

Rheinhessen: Good quantity, good wines, will need time to mature. 16/20

Rheinpfalz: Average quantity, average good year, with some great wines made, but on an average not as good as Rheingau and Mosel-Saar-Ruwer. 16/20

1974:

Was a rather small and unripe vintage in all major areas, with the exception of Rheinhessen, where the wines had more fruit than in other areas. The entire crop was Q.b.A. and rated 11/20.

1973:

Mosel-Saar-Ruwer: Very large crop of good fruity wines with good balance. Large quantity of Kabinett wines. 16/20

Rheingau: Very large crop, good fruity wines, lacking somewhat in body, but gaining elegance with time. 15/20

Rheinhessen: Very large vintage, good average fruity wines. 15/20

Rheinpfalz: Very large vintage, good fruity wines, with lasting qualities. 15/20

1972:

Small quantity of green, acid wines, all Q.b.A.; no longer around. 10/20

1971:

Mosel-Saar-Ruwer: Average size crop, full ripe wines with little noble rot, good acidity. Great year, particularly in Saar-Ruwer, where Trocken-beerenauslese were made. 19/20 for Mosel, 20/20 for Saar and Ruwer.

Rheingau: Average size crop, full ripe wines, good acidity, and noble rot. Great year which is developing well. 19/20

Rheinhessen: Average quantity crop, ripe, great wines with lots of noble rot, fair quantity of T.b.A. made. 19/20

Rheinpfalz: Good quantity, outstanding vintage. Great wines with good noble rot and sufficient acidity. 19/20

1970:

Mosel-Saar-Ruwer: Very large vintage. Good fruity wines with enough acidity. Average quality though a little neutral. 14/20

Rheingau: Very large crop, light elegant wines without much character. 14/20

Rheinhessen: Very large vintage; wines with good acidity. 13/20

Rheinpfalz: Enormous quantity, average quality. Somewhat acid wines needing time. 13/20

WORDS USED TO DESCRIBE WINE

From pages 193, 203–206 in *WHICH WINE?* by Peter M. F. Sichel and Judy Ley. Copyright © 1975 by Peter M. F. Sichel and Judy A. Ley. Reprinted by permission of Harper & Row, Publishers, Inc.

Acetic Describes a sour, vinegary odor referred to as volatile acidity, too much of which will make the wine undrinkable.

Acid The sharp, tart effect of the green fruit of young wine on both the nose and tongue.

Aroma The perfume of fresh fruit. It diminishes with fermentation and disappears with age to be replaced by the "bouquet."

Astringent The rough, puckery taste sensation caused by an excess of tannin in especially young red wines. It diminishes with age in the bottle.

Baked Qaulity of red wine made in a very hot climate from very ripe grapes.

Balanced Having all natural elements in good harmony.

Beery The odor of stale beer from a white wine that is over the hill—usually in old Moselles.

Big Full of body and flavor; high degree of alcohol, color, and acidity.

Bitter Self-descriptive. Sign of ill-health caused by inferior treatment such as excessive stalks during crushing or even metal contamination.

Black currants The slight smell and taste of black currants often found in Bordeaux wines.

Body The weight and substance of the wine in the mouth; actually a degree of viscosity largely dependent on the percentage of alcoholic and sugar content.

Bouquet The fragrance a mature wine gives off once it is opened. It develops further after the wine is in the glass. "Nose" is the term that encompasses the two aspects of the olfactory sensations—aroma and bouquet.

Breed Having the character, type, and qualities of its origin.

Brilliant Bright and sparkling in appearance so that one can see the light through the wine. Opposite of dull and cloudy.

Broad Full-bodied but lacking in acidity and therefore also lacking in finesse.

Character Positive and distinctive taste characteristics giving definition to a wine.

Clean   A well-constituted wine with no offensive smells or tastes. *See* Sound.

Clear   Transparent and luminous appearance. Any sediment rests on the bottom of the bottle.

Closed   Not showing any character yet, usually because it has been recently bottled.

Cloudy   Unsound condition of a hazy, dull-looking wine. Not to be confused with the condition of a recently shaken old red wine whose deposit hasn't settled yet.

Cloying   Too much sweetness and too little acidity.

Coarse   Rough texture; little breed or elegance.

Common   Adequate but quite ordinary.

Corky   Disagreeable odor and flat taste of rotten cork due to a defective cork in the bottle.

Corsé   Body and consistency, having generous and powerful proportions.

Depth   Rich, lasting flavor.

Dry   Completely lacking sweetness. Should not be confused with bitterness or sourness.

Dull   *See* Cloudy.

Earthy   What the French call *goût de terroir*. The peculiar taste that the soil of certain vineyards gives to their wines; disagreeable when too noticeable.

Elegant   Well balanced, with finesse and breed.

Fat   Full-bodied but flabby, which in white wines is often due to too much residual sugar. When applied to red wines, it means softness and maturity.

Finesse   The breed and class that distinguish a great wine.

Finish   The taste that the wine leaves at the end, either pleasant or unpleasant.

Flabby   Too soft, almost limp, without structure.

Flat   Dull, unattractive, low in acidity. Applied to a sparkling wine, it means that the wine has lost its sparkle.

Flinty   What the French call *Goût de pierre à fusil*. Steely, dry wine, such as a Chablis, with an odor and flavor recalling gunflint.

Flowery   The flowerlike bouquet that is as appealing to the nose as the fragrance of blossoms, as, for example, in a fine Moselle.

Foxy   A pronounced flavor found in wines made from native American grapes; the same smell as in grape jelly.

Fruity   The aroma and flavor of fresh grapes found in fine young wines. It diminishes with age.

Full   Having body and color; often applied to wines that are high in alcohol, sugar, and extracts.

Geraniums   Smelling of geraniums, an indication that the wine is faulty.

Grapy   The strong flavor that certain grape varieties, such as the Muscat, impart to certain wines.

Green   Harsh and unripe with an unbalanced acidity that causes disagreeable odor and a raw taste.

Hard   Tannic without softness or charm. It can mellow with age.

Harsh   Excessively hard and astringent. It can become softer with age.

Insipid   Lacking in character and acidity; dull.

Light   Lacking in body, color, or alcohol, but pleasant and agreeable.

Lively   Uusually young with fruity acidity and a little carbon dioxide.

Long   Leaving a persistent flavor that lingers in the mouth. Sign of quality. Opposite of short.

Luscious   Juicy and soft, filling the mouth without a trace of dry aftertaste. Usually attributed to sweet wines well balanced with acidity.

Maderized   Flat, oxidized smell and taste reminiscent of Madeira. Term is applied to wines that have passed their prime and have acquired a brown tinge.

Mellow   Softened with proper age.

Metallic   The unpleasantly bitter taste a white wine can acquire from improper treatment that did not eliminate traces of the copper that was used to spray the vines.

Musty   Disagreeable odor and stale flavor caused by storage in dirty casks or cellars; moldy.

Nerveaux   Having a lively impact on the palate; well balanced with a flavor that is neither too alcoholic nor too acid.

Noble   Superior and distinguished; not only possessing the right credentials but also having an impressive stature of its own.

Oxidized   Having lost its freshness from contact with air; *see* Maderized.

Peppery   The Aromatic smell of certain young red wines from hot climates.

Pétillant   Effervescent with a natural light sparkle.

Piquant   Dry and crispy acid, prickling the palate with its tartness.

Powerful   Usually applied to robust red wines of great substance, such as a Châteauneuf-du-Pape, or to white wines with a full, assertive bouquet, such as a big white Burgundy.

Ripe   Full; tasting of ripe fruit, without a trace of greenness.

Rounded   Well balanced and complete.

Sève   The sap of a great wine; the concentrated aromatic savor of a luscious and ripe sweet white wine of inherent quality.

Sharp   Excessive acidity, a defect usually found in white wines.

Short   Leaving no flavor in the mouth after the initial impact; *see* Long.

Smoky   Self-descriptive for the particular bouquet of certain Loire wines, such as Pouilly-Fumé, made from the Sauvignon grape.

Smooth   Of a silky texture that leaves no gritty, rough sensation on the palate.

Soft   Suggests a mellow wine, usually low in acidity, and tannin.

Sound   Healthy, well balanced, clean-tasting.

Sour   Like vinegar; wine that is spoiled and unfit to drink.

Spicy   Definite aroma and flavor of spice arising from certain grape varieties (Gewürztraminer). The aroma is richer and more pronounced than what we call "fruity."

Spritzig   A pleasant, lively acidity and effervescence noticeable only to the tongue and not to the eye and mostly found in young wines.

Sulphury   Disagreeable odor reminiscent of rotten eggs. If the smell does not disappear after the wine is poured, it is an indication that the wine is faulty.

Sweet   Having a high content of residual sugar either from the grape itself or as the product of arrested fermentation.

Tannic   The mouth-puckering taste of young red wines particularly from Bordeaux. Too much tannin makes the wine hard and unyielding but also preseves it longer. Aging in the bottle diminishes the tannin and softens the wine.

Tart   Sharp, with excessive acidity and tannin. In the case of a young red wine, this may be an element necessary for its development.

Thin   Lacking body and alcohol. It is too watery to be called light, and will not improve with age.

Velvety   A mellow red wine with a smooth, silky texture that will leave no acidity on the palate.

Vigorous   Healthy, lively, firm, and youthful. Opposite of insipid and flabby.

Watery   Thin and small without body or character.

Woody   Odor and flavor of oak due to long storage in the cask. Often found in Spanish wines.

Yeasty   Smelling of yeast in fresh bread. Sign that the wine is undergoing a second fermentation, possibly because it was bottled too early, and is therefore faulty.

Adjective Selector for Describing Wines

Appearance	Color		Bouquet		Taste
Brilliant	WHITE WINES		Acetic	Astringent	Insipid
Clear			Acid	Austere	Light
Cloudy	Pale green	Young	Beery	Baked	Lively
Dull	Straw yellow		Black	Balanced	Long
Watery	Gold		currants	Big	Luscious
	Yellow-brown ↓		Clean	Bitter	Maderized
	Brown	Old	Corky	Body	Mellow
			Flinty	Breed	Metallic
	ROSÉ WINES		Flowery	Broad	*Nerveux*
	Onion skin	Young	Foxy	Character	Noble
	Pink	↓	Fruity	Clean	Oxidized
	Orange	Old	Geraniums	Closed	Peppery
			Green	Cloying	*Petillant*
	RED WINES		Maderized	Coarse	*Piquant*
	Deep purple	Young	Musty	Common	Ripe
	Ruby red		Peppery	Corky	Rounded
	Red		Powerful	*Corsé*	*Sève*
	Red-brown		Smoky	Depth	Sharp
	Deep brown ↓		Spicy	Dry	Smooth
	Amber	Old	Sulphury	Earthy	Soft
			Woody	Elegant	Sound
			Yeasty	Fat	Sour
				Finesse	Spicy
				Finish	*Spritzig*
				Flabby	Sulphury
				Flat	Sweet
				Flinty	Tannic
				Foxy	Tart
				Fruity	Thin
				Full	Velvety
				Grapy	Vigorous
				Green	Woody
				Harsh	Yeasty
				Heady	

BIBLIOGRAPHY

Ambrosi, Hans: *German Wine Atlas and Dictionary,* Ceres Verlag Rudof-August Oetker KG, Bielefeld. 1976

Ambrosi, Hans; Becker, Helmut. *Der Deutsche Wein,* Gräfe und Unzer Verlag, München. 1978

Ambrosi, Hans; Breuer, Bernhard: *Der Rheingau,* Seewald Verlag, Stuttgart. 1978

Ambrosi, Hans: *Where the Great German Wines Grow,* 1976 Hastings House, N.Y.

Ambrosi, Hans: *Vom Weinfreund zum Weinkenner,* Gräfe und Unzer, München.

Becker, Werner; Hicke, Eugen; Jargen, Heinz; Sebastian, Richard: *Wegweiser durch das Weinrecht,* GEWA Druck Bingen. 1977

Claus, Prof Dr. P.: *Sonderausgabe: Die Weinwissenschaft* Müller Thurgau-Rebe und Wein, Zeitschriften-verlag Dr. Bilz & Dr. Fraund KG, Wiesbaden. 1976.

Deutsche Landwirtschafts-Gesellschaft: DLG Bundesweinprämierung 1977 & 1978, Preisträger Verzeichnis. DLG Frankfurt am Main.

Deutsches Weininstitut, Mainz: *The Wine Industry in the Federal Republic of Germany.* Evaluation and Information Service for Food, Agriculture and Forestry (AID), Bonn 1979.

Galet, Pierre: *A Practical Ampelography,* Translated and Adapted by Luci T. Morton, Cornell University Press, Ithaca and London 1979.

Götz, Prof. Dr. Bruno; Madel, Prof Dr. Waldemar: *Deutsches Weinbau Jahrbuch 1977 & 1979* Waldkirscher Verlagsgesellschaft, Waldkirch im Breisgau.

Hallgarten, S. F.: *German Wines,* Faber and Faber, London 1976.

Heinen, Winfrid: *Mosel Saar Ruwer,* Verlag Heinen, Essen. 1979

Hillebrand, Walter: *Taschenbuch der Rebsorten,* Zeitschriften-Verlag Dr. Bilz & Fraund, KG, Wiesbaden.

Hoffmann, Kurt M.: *Weinkunde in Stichworten.* Verlag Ferdinand Hirt, 1977.

Hynitzsch, Dr. Wolfgang: *Weinfach Kalender 1979, Das Jahrbuch des Deutschen Weinfaches.* Deutscher Weinwirtschaftsverlag Meininger GMBH Co. K. G. Neustadt an der Weinstrasse.

Jakob, Dr. Ludwig: *Lexikon der Önologie,* Verlag D. Meininger GMBH Neustadt/Weinstrasse 1979.

Johnson, Hugh: *The World Atlas of Wine,* Completely Revised and Updated, Mitchell Beazley, London 1977.

Koch, Hans-Jörg: *Weinland Rheinhessen,* Südwestdeutsche Verlagsanstalt, Mannheim 1977.

Meinhard, Heinrich: *The Wines of Germany,* The Intl. Wine and Food Society's Publishing Company, Stein & Day New York 1976.

Sauerwald, Peter; Wenzel, Edgar: *Könige des Riesling an Mosel, Saar, Ruwer.* Seewald Verlag, Stuttgart, 1978.

Schmoll, J. A. gen. Eisenwerth: *Die Mosel,* Deutscher Kunstverlag München Berlin 1963.

Stabilisierungsfonds fur Wein: *German Wine Atlas and Vineyard Register,* Georg Westermann, Braunschweig 1979.

Witte, Hedwig; Ambrosi, Hans: *Wo's Sträuss' che hängt, werd ausgeschenkt, Weintrinken im Rheingau,* Verlag: Wiesbadener Kurier, Wiesbaden.

Schoonmaker, Frank; Wile, Julius: *Encyclopedia of Wine,* Revised & Expanded by Julius Wile, Hastings House, N.Y. 1978.

Schoonmaker, Frank: *The Frank Schoonmaker Report from the Wine Country, Almanac of European Wines.* Published by Chateau & Estate Wines Company. N.Y. 1977.

Die Weinwirtschaft: Authoritative magazine of the German Wine Industry—at least twenty articles over the last three years were basis of some of the statistical information in this book. Published by Deutscher Weinwirtschaftsverlag Meininger GMBH & Co. KG Neustadt an der Weinstrasse.

INDEX

215